LIE IN THE DARK AND LISTEN

LIE IN THE DARK AND LISTEN

The Remarkable Exploits of a
WWII Bomber Pilot and Great Escaper

WING COMMANDER KEN REES

WITH KAREN ARRANDALE

GRUB STREET · LONDON

Published by
Grub Street
4 Rainham Close
London
SW11 6SS

British Library Cataloguing in Publication Data
Rees, H.K.
   Lie in the dark and listen
   1. Rees, H. K. 2. Bomber pilots – Great Britain
   3. World War, 1939-1945 – Personal narratives, British
   4. World War, 1939-1945 – Aerial operations, British
   5. World War, 1939-1945 – Prisoners and prisons, German
   6. Prisoner-of-war escapes – Germany
   I. Title II. Arrandale, K.A.
   940.5'44941'092

ISBN 1 904010 77 6

Typeset by Pearl Graphics, Hemel Hempstead

Printed and bound in Great Britain by
Biddles Ltd, King's Lynn

Contents

Acknowledgements

My sincere appreciation to Karen Arrandale whose hard work and expertise enabled this book to be published. Rob Davis for the use of his research. The late Ley Kenyon for his sketches. The RAF Museum, Hendon. Bill Fordyce for his cartoons.

To my wife for her support over the years it took me to complete this book. And in memory of Gwyn Martin, my navigator and life-long friend.

Lie in the Dark and Listen

Lie in the dark and listen,
It's clear tonight so they're flying high,
Hundreds of them, thousands perhaps,
Riding the icy, moonlight sky.
Men, material, bombs and maps,
Altimeters and guns and charts,
Coffee, sandwiches, fleece-lined boots
Bones and muscles and minds and hearts
English saplings with English roots
Deep in the earth they've left below,
Lie in the dark and let them go
Lie in the dark and listen.

Lie in the dark and listen
They're going over in waves and waves
High above villages, hills and streams
Country churches and little graves
And little citizen's worried dreams.
Very soon they'll have reached the sea
And far below them will lie the bays
And coves and sands where they used to be
Taken for summer holidays.
Lie in the dark and let them go
Lie in the dark and listen.

Lie in the dark and listen.
City magnates and steel contractors,
Factory workers and politicians
Soft hysterical little actors
Ballet dancers, 'Reserved' musicians,
Safe in your warm civilian beds.

Count your profits and count your sheep
Life is flying above your heads
Just turn over and and try to sleep.
Lie in the dark and let them go
Theirs a debt you'll forever owe
Lie in the dark and listen.
                              Noël Coward

Introduction

'Today in an age when the mere fact of being in a theatre of hostility (not necessarily hostilities) generates the media's definition of "hero", I can still only think of the Great Escape as an event in which men did their duty. That, I think, is sufficient, and if others will think of all of us, those who were murdered and those who survived, in such a manner, I believe we would all be content.'

Tony Bethell

Life is pretty dull these days.

When I was twenty-one I had already flown fifty-six missions, got married, been shot down into a remote Norwegian lake, questioned by the Gestapo and sent to Stalag Luft III, where I took part in what became known as The Great Escape.

If the war hadn't intervened, instead of the stuff of films I suppose my life could have been the stuff of television. *Are You Being Served* say, rather than *The Great Escape*. My father had me down for a nice, steady career at Gorringe's, then one of the smartest stores in London and the ultimate in stuffy respectability, where the most exciting event on offer was a deadpan discussion (by one's superiors, of course) of the woven texture to be found in ladies' foundation garments. Well, I escaped Gorringe's, lied about my age and joined the RAF instead. At seventeen I craved danger and excitement; I liked fast planes and cars, rugby, speed and women, not necessarily in that order, and like many of my generation I thought myself lucky to get caught up in a wartime which provided both.

It is difficult to convey to a generation not brought up to it the intensity of life back then and the extremes we lived through. On the one hand we were moving away from the rigid social systems of our parents and grandparents, but there were still more rules around to break and bend. Any schoolboy can tell you how much fun it is and how satisfying it can be breaking rules which are primarily designed to keep you in your place. Having said that, I must also draw attention to the fact that this same naughty schoolboy climbing up the drainpipe of a night to some girl's bedroom window, might the next day be in charge of an aircrew, with responsibility for a large and expensive aircraft, six men on board, and going three hundred miles behind enemy lines where he was expected to avoid the enemy flak and fighter aircraft, drop his bombs accurately and then get his crew safely back home. He might have to do this and watch other planes being shot down, and watch men who were his friends being incinerated alive but still stick to his orders. All this, when most of us were barely out of our teens. Rules, we all knew, were different from orders. Rules you could break and have a good laugh about it; orders you had to obey, no question.

I want to tell my own story, my own part in these large events which are rapidly passing into legend as we former kriegies gradually move out of this world. It's difficult to recapture, much less convey to non-kriegies what it meant to us. Prince Philip, though, summed it up pretty well at a recent dinner for ex-POWs:

'I do not believe that anyone who has not experienced it can understand what life as a Kriegie must have been like. It is really a secret society or, rather, a society which shares a secret which very few others can hope to penetrate. The common bond which draws these men together is composed of many strands. The death casualties in Bomber Command far outstretched those of any other arm of the services. So that the main strand of the bond is gratitude for continuing life. The others are the sharing of the formidable dangers, and the realization of the gifts of freedom and liberty. These are among the secrets which are shared by men who, in some cases for many years, existed in the closest proximity under unique conditions.'

Part One

'the most delightful flying club in the world'

Max Hastings

CHAPTER ONE

The Most Delightful Flying Club in the World

Ignorance, someone once said, is one of the most effective survival modes. But there's nearly always a turning-point, when some ferocious rite of passage into knowledge changes you forever.

It was 1940 and life seemed pretty damned good. I was young and fit, driving my own car – a decrepit Baby Austin, true, but mine, affectionately called 'Clattering Clara Clutterbuck' – as fast as I liked along deserted wartime roads in North Wales, on my way home to be fussed over and fed by my loving mother and admired by my sisters. I had a weekend pass in my pocket and was totally full of myself. At that moment it didn't matter that there was a vicious war going on or that the grim struggle called the Battle of Britain was being fought elsewhere while I enjoyed the relative safety, security and good food of the family farm near Ruabon. When I pulled up at a garage and flashed my official voucher for supplementary petrol I was sure I could detect in the proprietor's face how impressed he was by the 'Royal Air Force Station, Meir' and 'U/T Pilot' after my name. Well, so he should be impressed. I was Aircrew now.

Aircrew had special petrol allowance for leave. Aircrew had special food rations, flying gear and medical care. There were changing rooms, dining rooms, briefing rooms, all with 'Aircrew Only' on their doors. In 1940 Aircrew were hot stuff, at the cutting edge, and now I was one of them. I'd gone solo; I didn't quite have those actual wings on my breast pocket yet, but I knew it wouldn't be long.

I'd had to wait a year since enlisting on 5 September 1939, a year full of frustration. I knew what I wanted to do, had known for a long time now: I was aching to be a fighter pilot and I wanted to be in on the action. Having to sit and listen to the wireless report of the fall of France, hearing of the air battles near London and the south coast as Fighter Command clawed the Luftwaffe out of the sky, and not being able to do anything about it had been the hardest thing to bear. But now driving up to Ruabon in the growing darkness I was happy. Soon, very soon, I would be up there in the skies with them.

Then came a faint, far-off sound of sirens. Off in the distance, beyond the mountains were searchlights, spits of flames and bursts of anti-aircraft guns: the mountains outlined in glowing fire. Must be Liverpool, I remember thinking, funny that it feels so close. It *was* close, as it turned out: the German radio-navigational beams had bent so they were dumping their bombs on the mountains. I would remember this later. So instead of the usual peace of a North Wales night, I arrived home in the middle of mayhem, with the cacophony of many aircraft above, and the whistle of dropping bombs and explosions, bashes and bangs. Knocking at our door, surrounded by the noises of war, I didn't mind; I remember finding it all exhilarating and wishing I could be out in the middle of it. I banged at the front door some more; at last it opened. The look on my mother's face pulled up short me and all my youth and cockiness. 'Harold has been shot down and killed,' she said in careful tones. 'Betty is with the others in the cellar.' The war had come home.

Even now I can still see their tear-streaked faces peering up at me from the dim light in the cellar: my young brother, sisters, mother and father hiding from the bombs being dropped on them in this remote, rural part of Wales, but really, much more in shock from the news of my sister Betty's young husband, Harold. Harold, whilst commanding his squadron in the Battle of Britain, had baled out of his blazing Hurricane. His parachute had opened and he was uninjured, drifting down safely, until two Junkers 88s had circled him and machine-gunned him to death. No husband for Betty, no father for their unborn child, no brother for me.

When I went back after that weekend to complete my flying training, war had become something else. I now knew what burned inside the Poles, the Free French and the Czechs I had met. I knew because I had it too now. One death can touch you in a way a thousand have not. In wartime you have to learn to walk alongside death – the friends you'd had a jar with the night before now disappeared into the ether, blown to bits into the air you were still breathing. But Harold's death was clear and cold before me, a part of me. Years later I was to feel something similar upon learning of the cold-blooded murders of the fifty men in The Great Escape. Now war had become more than a great adventure: I didn't just want to fly planes, I wanted to kill Germans because of what they had done to my brother-in-law. I wanted revenge.

So how did I get this far? Me and the thousands of young men like me. School was all right, but what I really liked about Ruabon Grammar was the rugby. I won the Victor Ludorum cup at junior, middle and senior levels. I was fifteen when my father presented me with a choice of future: either stay on at school or go off as an apprentice to the draper's trade at Gorringe's. A nice, steady future for a nice, well-brought-up young man like me. But your nature will out, and that's what mine did. I've always been, as they say, resistant to authority (the usual phrases involve the words 'bloody-minded' and 'Welsh').

The decider came at school camp that summer of 1936, when a chemistry master, who also happened to be my cousin, stuck his nose into our tent and told us to get out and get on with some of the cleaning duties. We politely (as well-brought-up young men do) informed him that not only were we as seniors above such menial stuff, but that we were already engaged in cleaning our rugby boots. He demurred, and to show he had no favourites (especially me), gave me a flat-handed clout on the side of my head. But it was his yell that rang out, as he stepped back, with red indentations of cleaned boot studs forming nicely on his forehead. While he ran off to the Head and the rest of the occupants of the tent evaporated I sat there alone, knowing what would be asked of me, and knowing further, that I would never, ever apologise. Later that same day, as I was packing my bags to leave, I spotted two things: my cousin just getting into his car, windows rolled down, and a full bucket of water just outside the tent. Who could resist? You might as well do the thing thoroughly. Shame he rumbled me just in time and got the window up.

'You will realise I am sure, Mr Rees,' the managing director of Gorringe's said to my father, 'that this is a great Opportunity and Privilege we are conferring on your son. The slightest deviation from our high standards of conduct and courtesy will not be tolerated, and might, in fact, lead to dismissal.' Why is it that such people always seem to be speaking in capital letters?

For my projected three-year apprenticeship I was to be paid nothing in the first year – bar an allowance of ten shillings (about fifty pence) per week from my father, then two shillings and ninepence the second year, rising to four shillings and ninepence the final year. Gorringe's was in the heart of smart London, on Buckingham Palace Road, and behind the store were the sparsely furnished, strictly segregated hostels for its young male and female apprentices, presided over by male and female sergeant-major types in a way the goons at Stalag Luft III could have taken lessons from.

In spite of all this built-in lack of promise I learned a lot: how to drink beer, how to get in and out of hostels without using a door, how to lie about my age to play rugby for the Polytechnic's first team and how to chat up nice young ladies who had probably been warned about all the unreliable Welshmen they would meet in the draper's trade in London. I set my sights on one of these, a very pretty vicar's daughter from North Wales, and spent a lot of time and effort trying to get her friend Mary to put in a good word for me. It didn't take me too long to realise that I actually preferred the friend. We got married just before I was shot down in 1942. Still are.

I lasted in the draper's trade about two years, from September 1936 to September 1938, before the overwhelming dullness of the dreary dogsbody work got to me, of doing endless petty tasks for petty-minded customers and shop assistants alike. I was seventeen, and my father patiently suggested I try farming, so I did six months at Llysfasi Agricultural Centre, passing out to father's surprise and delight, 'with distinction'. We could smell war coming; most of my friends in the Wrexham Rugby Club were joining the TA. My brother-in-law Harold was already a flight lieutenant in the RAF, and my elder brother had taken a short service commission and was doing his flying training. My parents didn't know about it until long after the deed was done, but that August I caved in and sent off for application papers to join the RAF. It was already a well-worn maxim that you'd tell your mum you'd decided on a career playing a piano in a brothel before you'd confess to having signed up for the RAF. By the time I'd filled them in war was declared.

I spent the next two days ferrying refugee children from the cities to their safe new rural homes while at the same time trying to get myself recruited. I needed a selection committee, any selection committee would do. I tried Liverpool, but since they were not recruiting any more aircrew, I went to Chester. They wanted pilots, and I filled in the forms, only to see them being torn up when they read my stated occupation, 'farmer'. Farmers were 'reserved occupation'; in wartime they seemed to want the farmers kept alive even more than they needed the pilots. Anyway, I recovered from that bitter disappointment enough to have yet another go the very next day: I went down to Shrewsbury, where just to be safe I lied about my age and put down my occupation as 'draper'. Persistence – aka bloody-mindedness – has always been one of my personal strengths. This time it paid off. About three weeks later I got a letter with a railway warrant, instructing me to report to RAF Cardington, near Bedford, to appear before a selection board.

Years later, when I was president of a selection board myself at Biggin Hill, I would look back on how we were chosen for active service in wartime and shudder. It was terrifying in its outdated simplicity. Cardington itself was a kind of historical monument, dominated by vast airship hangars left over from the days of the R100 and R101, and Florence Nightingale would have recognised the conditions we lived in there: the bell tent with its primitive radial sleeping arrangements, the long trough where we all washed and shaved, with only icy-cold water coming from its taps. She might personally have designed the latrine seats on buckets, each tiny cubicle open to the sky above, your feet visible below the fore-shortened door.

The selection board, like most senior officers in the services then, had had twenty years of virtual atrophy since the last war to work out how this one would be fought and sort out who would be most suitable to fight it. However, there were no objective intelligence tests or initiative tests, and no assessments of aptitude to help the board begin to measure essential qualities like leadership potential, resourcefulness under stress and so on. Apart from the routine business of form-filling, detailing medical history (TB, VD, bedwetting, et al.), next of kin, education (I had a surprisingly good reference from my former Headmaster which did not mention my thumping his chemistry master), they had nothing objective at all to go on really. Our ability to fly was settled in a ten-minute exchange which did not even include the obvious question, 'Why do you want to fly?'

They asked me instead why I had not stayed on at school (awkward), how was my maths and did I have any relatives in the RAF. I told them, yes, my brother was a pilot with the rank of flying officer (I thought it would help). But then I was asked if I had considered the idea that one member of the family likely to be killed wasn't enough. 'Oh, no,' I said, 'with six of us, two probably won't be missed.' I thought I'd had it after that, but then the president asked me what turned out to be the clincher. An elderly squadron leader, with inches of First War medals below his pilot's wings, he leaned forward and said earnestly, 'Can you ride?'

The mental reflexes came to my rescue again. He was being perfectly serious. 'Of course,' I said, as if this was just what I had been waiting for them to ask me all along, and went on to elaborate in some detail about the previous season's hunting in our area, including some nice touches of gossip about the local master. I preferred cars and girls, but I had grown up on a farm and sometimes it does you unforeseen good to pay attention to your horsey sisters. The squadron leader, without so much as a word with his colleagues, declared me suitable for pilot training. Good thing there wasn't a horse parked outside.

It wasn't until December 1939 though, that I was at last summoned from the farm, given a railway warrant, and directed to the Initial Training Wing, with an address at one of the halls of residence in Cambridge, Clare College, later moving to Emmanuel. How was I going to learn to fly in the middle of Cambridge? The RAF had the idea that before they could be allowed near an aircraft cadets needed to be given regulation haircuts, be taught how to salute smartly, march in step, put their hats on straight, take in lectures on Maths, Theory of Flight, Meteorology, and much more of the same. It didn't seem to matter that most of the lecturers were themselves only Volunteer Reserve Officers and barely knew any more than we did; they just kept one page ahead of us in the text books. The non-academic side was far more rigorous. Tough senior NCOs and warrant officers of the old school were specially selected to lick into shape the eclectic collection of cadets who only had in common a mad desire to get flying and operational. They had their work cut out for them.

In the teeming mass of would-be pilots were hundreds of Canadians, New Zealanders and Australians, young men from all the farthest reaches of the Empire, even one or two Americans. Some had taken even more devious routes than I had to get there, such as signing on as ship's crew then jumping ship once in Britain, coupled with a few dubious changes of nationality. Many were here out of a spirit of adventure rather than a sense of duty; we would need both. At this early stage in the war a lot of the British were pre-war Volunteer Reserves, while some had flying training but were only waiting for vacancies at flying training schools. These were expanding rapidly, but I suppose it called for the nicest judgement to maintain the right balance between keeping operational units up to strength and sending off some of the trained pilots to do further training as instructors. My future brother-in-law Harold, for example, was then instructing at Andover, but would return to operations later. All in all we were a wild bunch and made the disciplinarians work for their money. It still astonishes me that at the outbreak of war, and for the five years that followed, the Royal Air Force was in a position to be able to select its aircrew exclusively from volunteers, and these came forward in such numbers that only a small percentage were accepted. I was glad I had volunteered so early.

They wouldn't give me leave to go to Harold and Betty's wedding, but still they kept me kicking my heels in Cambridge for months, waiting for a place at a flying school to fall vacant and doing very little that was constructive. By March 1940, only a few, mostly pre-war VRs, had been posted, and they hadn't really thought through what to do with all the rest of us. I got volunteered to learn how to box from Joe Mullins, a former heavyweight who'd done most of his fighting just after the First World War. Boxing got me out of PT and drills, and it had a few other advantages, too. Having trained us all day at his gymnasium, Joe would untrain us each evening at his popular pub, aptly named The Volunteer, then in Green Street. He thought we deserved it. What he didn't know was the kind of training we got up to most afternoons. After an early lunch Joe would send us all off on a run to Grantchester, about a mile up the river from Cambridge. We'd run until out of sight, then catch a bus out to Grantchester, where we'd settle in for a few pints at the Blue Ball or the Red Lion before catching the bus back, sprinting the final hundred yards most convincingly. When eventually after all this training we had our match against the ITW team from Hastings, I only managed a draw. Joe reckoned I'd run out of steam. He couldn't understand how, considering.

The people of Cambridge were wonderful to us. They had a lot to put up with, containing hundreds of young men who were waiting to go off to war, but this they did with patience and accommodation, inviting us to parties when they could have been fed up with our outrageously silly behaviour. We used to congregate for the tea-dances at the Dorothy Tea Rooms (now a Marks & Spencer) where for the price of a cup of tea and a cream-cake, you could sort out a partner for the evening. There was considerable rivalry between the undergraduates and us, even though we shared the same college accommodation and dining, but uniform won out every time when a girl was offered the choice of fox-trot partner.

It was after one of these, and well after midnight when the college gates closed, that Harold Pawson and I were climbing illicitly back into Emmanuel when we noticed that everyone was on parade in the darkness and roll-call had obviously been taken. In the confusion someone hissed to Pawson that we were all being posted at last, and that we two had been marked absent. This was serious. But Pawson was equal to it. 'We'll soon sort this out,' he said, and grabbing my arm, he marched us off to the CO's office and barged straight in without so much as a knock. I watched with awe as he struck an immediate moral high ground, ranted on at the CO, and acting all outraged that everyone should been posted without so much as informing us. The poor CO, inexperienced and obviously not yet a party to the RAF maxim that 'Bullshit Baffles Brains', didn't have a chance against Harold. He rang for his NCO, and apologising profusely to us, told him to make sure we were on the draft.

But that was not by any means that. The posting simply meant that until more places became vacant in the flying schools, we were to be shunted around the operational stations in East Anglia on 'ground defence' duties, i.e. fooling around with World War I rejects: rusty, leaking, water-cooled Lewis guns. Some defence. At Bircham Newton, after months of this 'ground defence', we all decided if the paratroops did drop here we would simply get the hell out. It was May 1940, and the first of many, many times over the following years when I was to be fed up with such waiting around.

This time, completely brassed off, I got in touch with my brother-in-law Harold, who had just been posted onto operations and was doing an OTU (Operational Training Unit) course at nearby Sutton Bridge, up in the Fens, before taking over as commanding officer of a Hurricane squadron. If anyone would know how to get the system moving he would. A terrible plane crash before the war had left him with a limp and recurring pain, but still he had managed, with great patience, persistence and a medical officer friend, to retrieve his flying category and get himself onto operations. After listening patiently to my misery, both on the phone and in the pub, of how I had to sit each day at my useless Lewis gun watching the Hudsons take off on strikes, he did something about it. He phoned a friend in the Air Ministry, and what exactly he said I'll never know, but within a week the posting came through for Leading Aircraftman Rees, Pilot U/T. I was to report to No. 5 Elementary Flying Training School at Meir, near Stoke-on-Trent. It was July 1940. At last, at long last I was to learn how to fly.

CHAPTER TWO

Getting off the Ground

Meir, Staffordshire, was a small civilian flying school converted soon after
the outbreak of war into the No. 5 Elementary Flying School for the RAF.
There was no accommodation so about forty of us trainee pilots were
housed two miles up the road in Longton, in the town hall. We slept in
what must have been the civic ballroom, a vast upstairs room with pilasters
and a good floor and not much else, the only nod to privacy being some
clothes lockers used as space dividers. As you might expect in a civic
ballroom, there wasn't much in the way of washing facilities and the food
provided was terrible – overcooked cabbage, mushy potatoes, and mystery
meat in uniform brown gravy – but nobody minded in the least. We were
young, and we were being let loose to find out first-hand about danger. We
lived off our fantasies of outwitting Messerschmitts, not mouldy cabbage.

When I found myself on that morning of 7 August 1940, togged up in
a flight jacket, helmet and goggles out of Biggles, I could have wept for
joy. When you're in love you never forget your first experience. Flight
Lieutenant Purdy, introducing himself as my instructor, would have been
horrified and deeply embarrassed to realise how much superior to God I
thought he was. Perhaps he was used to it. He moved away to talk with the
ground crew and I had the chance to take in fully my first aircraft. I stared
at it with love and fear.

It was a Miles Magister, with a fixed undercarriage, an open cockpit
(hence the WWI helmet and goggles; even in August you would freeze)
and a tiny propeller tacked onto its front like the nose of a dachshund. I
didn't see how that flimsy piece of machinery could possibly get both me
and Purdy off the ground. But these tiny trainers, together with the even
more popular Tiger Moth, were responsible for the initial training of
thousands of pilots who learnt to fly in the UK during the war. And long
after. They were sturdy and reliable, easy to service, and a much safer bet,
as I would learn, than some of the rusty hulks used later on in our training.

I watched Purdy climb into the front cockpit while a cheerful airman
strapped me into my parachute. 'That, matey,' the airman held up the
ripcord, 'is the handle you pull when the wing drops off.' He grinned,
watched while I gingerly squeezed myself into the rear cockpit, then began

strapping me securely in, parachute and all, with the Sutton harness which
stopped you falling out of the open cockpit to the earth below.

'How can I use my parachute in this?' How could I move at all?

He grinned again, the bastard. He'd done it all before, many times.
'Oh, there's a pin in the front that will release the harness.'

'When the wing drops off.'

He nodded, still grinning, and jumped down.

I sat there, all strapped in, and watched over Purdy's shoulder as he
prepared for take-off. I was surprised to see how long it took him. It had
never occurred to me that one had to do more than simply start the engine
and go, just like they did in the films. It was of course a dual-control, and
I tried to follow Purdy's movements, his eyes and hands, as he
methodically checked that the ailerons and the rudder moved correctly,
checked the throttle lever, the trim control and petrol taps. A speaking-tube
was supposed to keep us in contact, and I could hear him faintly through
it, whistling cheerfully to himself as he went through his drills. I stared at
the apparatus in front of me. For such a small aircraft there was a
bewildering mass of instruments, taps and levers, covering every inch
inside the tiny cockpit. The compass I could recognise; a comfortingly big
N for North on its rim. The airspeed indicator went up to an astonishing
250 mph. (A bit hopeful, I would realise later, but still faster than anything
I'd ever been in.) I could feel myself going breathless, taking in the
distinctive smell of oil and fabric dope, then as Purdy primed the engine,
alarmingly strong fumes of petrol. That couldn't be right, I thought in a
sudden certain panic, something must be wrong. A petrol leak, and with it,
fire – I was nearly clawing at my Sutton harness to get out of the damned
thing when I caught sight of the calm, confident signals being exchanged
between Purdy and the ground crew, slowing everything down. My panic
dissolved, and once more I lost myself in the complete enjoyment of the
thing I was doing. I wanted to know *everything*.

One of the airmen held his thumb up. Purdy said, 'Switches on.
Contact.' And the engine burst into snarling, rumbling life. As the engine
warmed up his voice came at me from the speaking-tube like an old wax
recording, but through the din I could only hear fragments of what he was
saying: 'Take off . . . climb to . . . get you used to i . . . are you okay?'

Am I okay? Well, here I was, doing what I'd joined up for, and besides,
I now knew in theory at least how to bale out. 'Okay,' I muttered into the
speaking-tube, 'sir,' and we bounced and clunked our way into take-off
position. I watched him do more checks, then, turning into the wind, he
opened up. Instantly we gathered speed; I felt myself being pressed hard
back into the seat with the sudden acceleration, the tail lifted and we were
airborne.

It was the first of many take-offs and I was not even at the controls, but still I can remember it vividly as my first experience of how a smelly, complex bit of machinery can suddenly be transformed into a light creature of the air. It was overwhelming. On the ground an aeroplane is static and awkward; it bumps and judders its clumsy way over uneven ground to take-off, but once in the air, as the slipstream flows over the aerofoil shapes of the wings and gives them lift, it – and you – become freed of the ground altogether, the aeroplane released into its proper element. In the air it is an eager thing, quick to respond to the slightest movement of the pilot's hand. Perhaps, I remember thinking with a heady laugh, this was what that elderly squadron leader on the board back in Cardington had in the back of his mind when he'd asked me if I could ride a horse.

I have always been grateful to Flight Lieutenant Purdy. Rather older than the other instructors, gentle and quietly-spoken, he gave me the perfect introduction to flying, with little actual praise but much encouragement as I strove to coordinate hands, feet and eyes. It would become a time-honoured path we travelled together then, for the flying training techniques developed by the Royal Air Force during the war have been refined over the years to produce a teaching method unsurpassed in the world. Foreign air forces sent, and still send, their men to be trained by the RAF, and many training schools set up overseas would be modelled on our teaching methods. The main aim was to teach the basics, but to teach them so well that they became second nature. In the air survival often depended on your quick, almost instinctive responses.

Exercise One: Air Experience. Usually, your first experience of being in an aircraft; all you were allowed to do was simply take a short trip around the local area.

Exercise Two: Taxying, and Handling the Engine. This was to accustom you to the movement of the aircraft, weaving from left to right. The sense of motion was important to know, since you could not see straight ahead of you when on the ground, as the nose of the aircraft blocked your view.

Exercise Three: Effects of Controls. You very quickly picked these up! To turn to the left, you ease the control column to the left (I say 'ease', because all too suddenly the wing will tilt dangerously and green fields appear below the wing tip), and as you do so the nose will tend to drop so you apply a little top rudder to hold it up. Then you have to ease the control column gently back out of the turn. Not bad. Now try it the other way. Even now I can hear Purdy's careful voice talking me through it all: 'Ease the stick back, not yank it, that only makes the turn get tighter, probably making the aircraft stall and maybe spin. Okay, try again.' So much of this is touch and experience, the 'feel' of your aeroplane. The one thing I could never understand though, was why a machine so expressly masculine as an aeroplane, control-stick and all, was referred to as 'she'.

Exercise Four: Straight and Level Flight. At first I thought, easy, but Purdy quickly disabused me. Straight and level meant absolutely straight and dead level. I grumbled mentally at this; birds don't fly arrow straight and dead level for any length of time, but Purdy made me realise that birds can't spin, or fly in clouds or land in a lake at night on fire, and I was going to have to be able to do any or all of these things, should the need arise. Such knowledge had to be almost automatic, and Purdy was making sure it was. Conscious thought is too slow for what we had to do, pedestrian slow. Although, when Purdy first told me to turn left, I had to think it through consciously: move the stick to the left, oh, yes, and look to see if it's all clear, remember a little top rudder, now ease the column back. It took a lot of repetition before the reflexes began to act instantaneously, coordinating all these separate movements before I was aware I had done it. It was a major lesson, that when learning to fly your reflexes have to be conditioned to react automatically to every manoeuvre of which the aircraft is capable. You never switch off until you're back with both feet on the ground.

On we went, through the exercises for stalling, spinning, climbing, gliding, turns, etc, etc. When I had more or less mastered these, we started to pound the circuit with powered approaches and glide approaches. At last, when I had about ten hours in my log book, appeared 'Exercise Eleven: First Solo'. It was 26 August, 1940. It all happened very casually. Flight Lieutenant Anderson, the flight commander, came up with me and gave me a check. We did stalls and spins and two landings. After the second landing, we taxied again to the take-off position and a voice in my earphones said, 'I value my life so much I'm getting out. You can go solo. Just one circuit.'

It was of course absurd that I should feel anything but complete confidence after ten hours of dual instruction. It really should not have been necessary for the adrenaline to pump itself in that disturbing way around my system, but my heart felt like it was trying to bang its way out of my chest, my suddenly sweaty hands clutched at the control column and everything which should have been familiar by now dissolved in a strange haze. No Purdy reassuringly there in the front should I cock things up. In that first intimation of what war was to be like, I was on my own and my head had somehow been emptied of everything put in it over the past weeks. But there was my flight commander, grinning cheerfully and waving me off. The sight made me feel better, and I began the familiar cockpit drill to get my mind back on track, then, checking I was cleared, turned the aeroplane into the wind and gently opened the throttle. Keep her straight with rudder, watch you don't overcorrect, and before you realise it you are airborne. The sudden ache in my hand made me realise how tightly

I had been grasping the control stick and my equally sudden expulsion of breath showed how I had been holding my breath throughout take-off. Deep breath, I said to my nervy, exhilarated self. Relax – everything is fine.

Although we (first 'she', now 'we': I felt then that the aircraft was a part of myself and we were in it together) had left the ground, I realised that we were climbing faster than usual. This was of course because the instructor was absent and we were so much lighter. By now I was at 500 feet and must make a gentle turn left through 90 degrees. I climbed to 1,000 feet and kept my eyes on the airfield. (There is always a haze in the Black Country, and it would have been extremely embarrassing to get lost on one's first solo.) Turn downwind, and as the wing-tip passes the end of the airfield, turn across wind and throttle back to start losing height. My confidence was growing. Keep a lookout for other aircraft, I told myself, check your landing area is clear and at 500 feet turn into the wind for the final approach. But I was too high; I was not losing height fast enough. I kept forgetting how much lighter we were without the instructor. Adjust throttle, check speed; I was aiming too low if anything, as I did not want to be too high and have to go around again on my first solo. I wanted it all to be perfect. So, full flap and a bit more throttle, speed okay. I crossed the airfield boundary too high, so had to make a frantic forward movement of the stick, too much so and thump! We bounced; and airborne again momentarily, I caught it on the throttle and eased it down . . . Thump! We landed. This time, thank heaven, we stayed down.

I taxied in. What I felt then I was to feel again and again in each new, intense flying experience. Reluctantly, I can only say that it was like having had good sex. Orgasmic. The euphoric feelings of complete physical and mental engagement and accomplishment. This may be clichéd, but like many clichés it is over-used only because it is so true. It shows a kind of love affair with flying, and the residual feeling after the excitement is over has much in it of sexual satiety. After each flight, whether a peaceful training flight or a bombing mission over enemy territory, the sequel was always the same: first a sense of complete physical and mental release, then storing away the whole thing and forgetting about it until the next time.

With my solo flight behind me I was given a new instructor. Flying Officer Desmond Plunkett was young, well-built, cheerful and ginger-haired, and an extrovert, with a reputation for a cavalier approach to flying I found very much to my taste. He lived for his flying, especially aerobatics, and every time we flew, regardless of the exercise we were supposed to be doing, we always managed to include a few. Although an enthusiastic instructor, he was very keen to get on operations. He would have made a brilliant fighter pilot, but such were the incomprehensible ways of the powers that be, he eventually got posted to a bomber squadron. When two years later I entered the gates of Stalag Luft III, one of the first people I saw was Desmond. Such was his dedication to flying that when I met him in 1989 at a POW reunion in Canada, he told me he was still flying, doing aerial surveys over Africa.

Flying with Plunkett made life altogether much more interesting. Once, when we were practising forced landings in some farmer's field, he spotted mushrooms growing off at the side. Briefing me to carry on and do some more landings he got out and wandered around, filling his helmet with mushrooms while I flew in and out. By the time I picked him up the mushrooms were all gone.

Another time, Plunkett called me into his office and announced that he was getting up a team to box against the Army. He had seen from my records that I had boxed while at Cambridge and so I had been 'selected'. Detailed, more like. I was furious. I didn't want to bloody box, I wanted to fly. With my flying commitment, I tried to argue, I would have no time to train. However, it did no good to argue with Plunkett; I was in the team. I didn't feel any better about it when a few nights later in the pub in Longton a notice about a boxing match caught my eye. The main bout being advertised was between some lance corporal – billed in large print as 'Northern Area Champion' – and, in much smaller print, 'LAC Rees'. Fear filled my bones. During the war professional sportsmen were allowed to fight as amateurs; I would be facing serious injury if not death by heart failure. First thing the next morning I tried to explain this to Plunkett. I really should have known better. He sat back in his chair and considered deeply. 'You'll really have to get yourself fit,' he said at last. Then, smiling: 'Tell you what, I'll spar with you.'

Silently we changed into PT kit and went into the hangar, where there was space enough to spar. To do him justice, I think he was actually surprised by the raw ferocity in the first few blows, and even more surprised when I actually cracked one of his ribs. So much for any training. For days I brooded, went off my food. Miserably, the only thing I could think of was to go down at the first decent blow and hope it didn't take my face off. But I was let off in the end. The Battle of Britain was under way, and a big invasion scare had the Northern Army Champion and his unit sent off to the east coast. I think that was the only thing I ever had to thank Hitler for.

We were now reaching the end of our elementary training, about fifty hours for most of us, which included cross-country trips using instruments under a hood. Some of us also did a bit of illegal formation flying. I flew over my parents' home in formation with Pete Gee, a drinking friend. My brother was home on leave at the time, and when I smugly asked him if he had seen us, he replied, 'Well, I saw two aircraft going the same way on the same day.' I realised we were not as good as we thought we were.

Still, the euphoric mood held. We had, we felt, crossed the first hurdle – or near enough. At any rate it was decided to let down our hair and have an end-of-course party. Five or so piled into Clara, my Austin Seven, and off we went to the fleshpots of Stoke. I have very little recollection of what exactly we did apart from consume a great deal of ale in quite a number of different hostelries, but what is fixed in my mind is what followed after we were turned out of the last pub and I was trying to keep the Austin in a straightish line back to Longton. I had not reckoned on Hitler's part in this.

The journey was fairly uneventful, until just outside Longton we hit a snag in the shape of an anti-invasion roadblock. I took an officer-type decision to divert and got the car up onto the pavement. Unfortunately, I hadn't spotted on the other side a rather portly policeman manning the ramparts. I didn't really take any notice until I heard his outraged yell. But this I shrugged off. After all, I hadn't exactly run him down – he was still standing when I looked in the mirror. But he yelled again, and launched himself into a hot pursuit. I put my foot down, and when we screeched up outside the town hall and parked the car, he was nearly on us. He was much faster than I'd thought. We ran up the town hall steps, he ran after us. It was like something out of the Keystone Cops. As we pelted into the civic ballroom, leaping the beds, he was only about two beds behind. We might yet have got away from him, but the noise was beginning to wake up the occupants. One of them sat up abruptly and our lead runner fell into him, then the rest of us all followed suit, collapsing in a giggling, heaving, drunken heap.

We'd had it. Out came the notebook, names were taken down. We were accused of mounting the pavement (more giggles) and taking the buttons off his uniform. When I ventured to point out that it was lucky his stomach stuck out or his toes might have been run over, it was not appreciated. By now the whole ballroom was up and joining in the debate, and Plod was looking a bit sheepish, if not actually nervous. I think it might have occurred to him that the best line of defence against invasion was not so much his roadblock but the fit young men around him about to go off and fight. But it was all good-natured. He decided at length not to arrest us but to report us to the station commander. In the end we were marched before Plunkett, who couldn't think what to do with us except confine us to camp. We didn't live in camp, so honour was satisfied and we were free.

For my final test in September, I flew the Magister for the last time, the Chief Instructor in the front cockpit. He tested my ability to recover from a spin, to roll, loop and roll off at the top of a loop. He cut my engine at about 3,000 feet and set me the task of selecting a suitable field and getting down into it, which after a few anxious moments, I managed to do.

'All went pretty well,' he said to me back down on the ground. 'I could tell you're one of Plunkett's pupils.' I got an above-average assessment and a recommendation for fighters.

This was it. This was what I wanted. Soon, I thought, soon I'll be up there flying Spitfires. Not everyone made it, though. One had crashed and was injured, while two others failed to go solo.

With two others who had got similar assessments I was posted to the Royal Air Force Depot at Uxbridge, where, together with fifty more from flying schools around the country we were to go on to be trained as fighter pilots. Moreover, we were to be the first group designated to go on the newly set-up Empire Training Scheme, strange as it might sound today, the idea being that aircrew could be better trained in the relative peace and less congested skies to be had overseas. And better equipped: the trainer aircraft was the American-built Harvard, the intermediate craft before going on to the more responsive Hurricanes and Spitfires. In spite of the fact that most of the trainer bases were in the frozen north of Canada, with names like Moose Jaw, the RAF had not yet adapted to the idea that an overseas posting was not in a hot climate; they insisted on issuing us with tropical kit. When we tried to point out that Canada was not best known for the heat of its winters, the equipment sergeant growled: 'We only have one overseas kit in the RAF and even if you are going to the bleeding Arctic you bleeding well take it.'

Uxbridge was a peacetime depot well-known, in the parlance, for its bullshit. None of us were ready, though, for such complete pettiness when it was revealed on our first parade. Some of us had dressed just as we had at Meir, which was in shoes instead of boots and wearing the much better-quality Van Heusen shirts that officers wore. I was standing next to Bill Edrich, of Middlesex cricketing fame, when the warrant officer stopped in front of him and barked, 'You're wearing an officer's shirt.'

'No, sir,' said Bill. 'It's mine.' He was off to the Guard Room.

My turn next. When the bark about my shirt came I was able to say quite truthfully that it belonged to my brother.

Both of us spent the next two nights in the cold guarding the boundaries of Uxbridge. Fortunately, we were only there for a few weeks in all.

In September 1940, after embarkation leave we were on' our way to the local train station when we were abruptly recalled. The initial version of this was that Canada 'was not ready' for us, so we were to be trained instead in England. Fine, I thought, but a bit disappointing. Half of us were sent to Cranwell, while the other half were sent to No. 11 Flying Training School at Shawbury, in Shropshire. Shawbury was equipped with Airspeed Oxford twin-engined trainers; this meant bombers, not fighters. I was devastated.

CHAPTER THREE

Flying to the Limits

It had simply never occurred to me that I might become a bomber pilot. My older brother Brian was a flying officer on fighters; my brother-in-law had been shot down flying a Hurricane; Flight Lieutenant Plunkett had trained me to be a fighter pilot, with that recommendation. Every roll, loop and dive under his aegis had been executed with an imaginary German in my imaginary gunsight. In the RAF, in wartime, you do as you're told, but it was not going to be easy to change my whole view of who I was and what I was for. At first I considered protesting, but the more I thought about it, the more I found myself coming around to the new position.

At this juncture I think I ought to try to explain more, not just about my own personal disappointment, but about the different roles at that point in the war being played by Fighter Command and Bomber Command. I wasn't the only one suddenly being shifted like this, and there were reasons behind it we didn't understand at the time.

Of course it is far easier to view this with hindsight, but in September 1940 Britain stood alone against Germany. The Battle of Britain had still to be won, and the invasion barges, upwards of three thousand of them, were gathering in the French ports. After Dunkirk the army was re-equipping as fast as factories and lend-lease from America could supply it, so shipping lanes had to be kept free. At the same time in every village and town the Home Guard was mustering for a possible last-ditch defence. The threat felt dire, yet Churchill wanted to go on the offensive and take the war back to Germany: 'The bombers alone provide the means of victory.' For this Britain needed more bombers and more trained crew.

Despite this state of national uncertainty and insecurity it felt to us trainee pilots as though the Royal Air Force Flying Training Command was never for one moment diverted from the calm, deliberate process of creating pilots from the raw materials of civilian life. There was a syllabus and a timetable. There were Oxford trainers with specific hours of flying available between regular inspections in the maintenance hangar, and not even the threat of invasion was going to disturb this systematic routine. Those first few weeks at Shawbury were spent in ground school, with exams to be passed before we would be allowed to move on to the flying stage. I hated ground school; at this stage the idea of exams seemed to me pointless, but as the problems of flying aircraft long distances began to emerge, the purpose behind all this meticulous theoretical training became clear.

A fighter pilot has comparatively fewer problems than a bomber pilot. He's up there basically alone in his aeroplane, responsible only for himself. He must be able to handle his aeroplane under every possible attitude of flight and be able to fly it to its limits. He must shoot with the correct deflection, that is, if an enemy aircraft is flying at an angle across you, you need to be able to judge the distance and speed to shoot ahead, anticipating the time it takes for the bullets to get to the target, not unlike shooting pheasant. If the table of conflict turns and he finds the enemy on his tail, he must be able to keep calm. But he has got the means to fight back, and the outcome depends mostly on his own skill and his quick reflexes; he is in charge of a finely-tuned machine designed to respond to his slightest touch. I have always thought that a fighter pilot was like a boxer. It is single-combat, and any decisions are more reflex than conscious; they have to be quicker than instantaneous if you are not to find yourself knocked out.

A bomber pilot, on the other hand, is responsible not only for himself but his crew, and if he is to inspire any confidence in them he must know and appreciate their jobs, and understand their problems as well as his own. He has to carry explosives to distant targets in the face of anything – the weather, the enemy or the numberless idiosyncracies the aircraft itself may throw in the way. The cool determination that serves a fighter pilot for minutes has to be maintained by a bomber pilot for hours. If it was freezing bloody cold (and in those early days of the war the freezing conditions on bombers were legendary; after four hours at –40°C rear-gunners would often find their hands useless, frozen to their guns), it would be cold for hours, until you got home, if you got home. In daylight missions you could be a sitting target for German fighters and German anti-aircraft guns, but still you had to do your job, dropping your bombs as accurately as possible, through flak and cloud. Courage in such circumstances is more a kind of fortitude, and it needs to be reinforced by confidence, both in oneself and in the crew. They needed to know that I was capable of getting them through while they did their jobs and then getting us all safely home.

Such confidence can only be built up with a complete understanding of all the factors involved, human and mechanical, and those few weeks of ground school helped equip me with the knowledge I was going to need, basic information, but essential. We had drummed into us fundamental information about engines, about meteorology – the theory of frontal systems and recognition of clouds, and about airmanship – the pilot's highway code, navigation, and theory of flight. As I said, I detested ground school, and the grind of having to learn theory did not come naturally to me, but at the same time I knew that if I was to fly I had to pass these exams. I was determined to fly, and it would be too humiliating to fail ground school. I gritted my teeth, gave up drinking for a few nights' cramming and passed.

I'm glad I did put in the effort, as it soon became clear how important it was to have all this knowledge filed away inside one's head, and I've always found the practical applications more appealing than theory. What I learned was of course not isolated theory. I quickly came to appreciate how if an engine fails one needs to have in one's head a picture of the fuel system, the correct position of all the fuel cocks, of the ignition system, the possibility of oil loss and overheating – all these would need to be sorted out possibly over enemy territory, while maintaining the confidence of the crew in my knowledge and decision-making. The same was true of factors like reading weather signs and understanding the flying controls – in fact, every aspect of my aircraft while it was being flown by me.

The next phase of my training came as something of a shock. After the small Magister the twin-engined Oxford seemed vast and complicated. I remember my first view of what appeared to be innumerable, incomprehensible knobs and dials. After Plunkett's exuberant, engaging style, my new instructor's dour reserve was a let-down. Pupil and instructor sat side by side, so that while the instruments and flying controls were duplicated, we shared the throttles, mixture controls and flaps. For him, flying was strictly a duty and a discipline, while I felt the exhilaration and pleasure of it, the sense of adventure. After Plunkett he was a miserable creature. In any event I could never please him. We exchanged no confidences, and I never knew what had made him so sullen and joyless. But he was a wonderful pilot; the Oxford in his hands was a precise flying machine, and I tried hard to follow his example.

Taxying with two engines, I quickly realised, required a completely different technique. There was a good view ahead, so there was no need to zig-zag to see in front as with the Magister. Turns were made by simply opening up the engine on the opposite side to the direction one wanted to turn. During take-off the aircraft tended to veer to starboard, which was a side-effect of the torque produced by both the propellers revolving clockwise at high speed. This had to be corrected, first with the throttles, and then with the rudder. Once in the air the Oxford was a joy to fly: light on the controls and without any vice. Rather like a good horse really, I should think.

It was soon clear to me, not least partly from each pre-flight briefing session, that the main principle behind flying training was to learn to fly the aircraft to its limits, to the limits of speed, both in the dive and in the climb before the stall, and to the maximum possible endurance. This aim suited me completely even if my instructor did not. Although actual aerobatics were not allowed on the Oxford we were encouraged to 'fly to the limits' in steep turn, peel-overs as one would do in dive-bombing, stalling, and so on – all the drastic manoeuvres. These were all exercises geared specifically to get the pilot used to unusual and extreme positions, and to the sensation of G-force when the body is pressed hard into the seat and the blood drains from the brain (or in my case, as my instructor tartly said, from the head). It was also a deliberate foretaste of just what could happen in extreme circumstances; we were being equipped to deal with emergencies.

The greatest hazard met by the pilot of a twin-engined aircraft is to have one engine fail, especially if this happens during take-off. Then, with full fuel tanks and, during operations, a full bomb load as well, both the engines are at full throttle and airspeed is increasing only slowly. If at this most critical moment one engine fails, you lose with it any chance of building up enough speed to gain lift-off and height: no speed, no height. Great flying skill is required if a pilot is to recover from situations like this. A glance at the grim statistics for flying accidents shows how common it was.

With my instructor I now went through all the normal flying manoeuvres with two engines and with one. I thought I wasn't doing too badly, until I made a poor approach during one single-engine landing, nearly brushing the top branches of a tree. At this my glum instructor was suddenly, furiously, astonishingly angry. Grabbing the controls, he said between clenched teeth, 'That's it. Bowler hat for you, then.'

I don't remember the landing; I was too distressed. This was more than a slap in the face: 'Bowler hat' is RAF jargon for civilian life or any category of aircrew that doesn't fly. I staggered back to the crewroom and flopped miserably onto a chair, close to tears, all my hopes in shreds. As I sat there swallowing back the tears the flight commander came into the room. It must have been pretty clear from my face that all was not exactly well, because he came over and asked me what my troubles were. But as I blurted it all out I was surprised to see that he was laughing. 'It sounds to me like a straightforward case of clashing personalities,' he said. 'Come on, I'll pass you on to another instructor.'

Perhaps it was not a bad thing that I should have had a check of that kind. I could be a bit too full of myself, and returning to flying with a more sympathetic instructor turned out to be like discovering all over again the pure joy and delight I'd had from the start. Sergeant North was a younger man, a fighter pilot with a first tour of operations already behind him. I was his first pupil and he was determined that I should do well. My complete enthusiasm returned. Every flight was now something entirely to be looked forward to.

But Shawbury was not all flying. We were young, and when we had time off or the weather was too bad for flying, we would find our way the seventeen miles down the road into Shrewsbury and let off steam in the usual ways, involving beer and women and a lot of what passed for singing.

The training quickly moved on to formation flying, low-flying and a great many cross-country navigation exercises. It is strange now to recall that our Oxfords were not then equipped with radio, and in order to prove our accurate arrival at prescribed turning-points, we had to make a quick sketch of the ground below us for our instructors to check on our return to base. The extremely bad weather of that 1940/41 winter had put our course behind schedule, and some of our flying had to be curtailed. I finished the course with only thirty-five minutes solo night-flying, when the norm was around ten hours, and even that flight involved landing in a snowstorm. Not a lot of night-flying, considering that I was supposed to be going on to night bombers.

Suddenly, on 25 January, we had officially 'completed' the course, but no ceremony marked it. Instead, about thirty-five (I think two had failed) of us were simply dispatched to the Orderly Room to collect our wings, those long-desired symbols of our piloting skill, only to be peremptorily handed them by a busy NCO clerk, whose sole comment was: 'Make sure you sew the bloody things on level.'

It was during the brief period of leave that followed, in early February, when Mary and I decided to get engaged. We were only nineteen, but had known each other for three years, and neither set of parents expressed any real objections, whatever their private reservations. How could they? This compulsion to get married in wartime is difficult to explain in any practical or logical terms; certainly as yet there were no practical advantages – no widows' pensions or benefits – but the churches and registry offices had never been so busy. I think in such uncertain times the constant threat of death is more than matched by the need to cling to the symbols of survival. We all felt the realistic possibility that we might not survive the war. Mary and I had talked about it and decided hands down to snatch what happiness we could at the time. So, having borrowed the money from my sisters, we went into Chester for a ring and got a massive discount from an old friend who was a jeweller there.

When my posting to an operational unit finally came through I was horrified to see that it was for Whitleys, those slow, clumsy-looking, first-generation heavy bombers. Although I had by now long since come round to the idea of being a bomber pilot, it was not the Whitley I had in mind. Anyone who actually enjoyed flying didn't in a Whitley. At any rate I told them flatly that with my short legs I wouldn't be able to use the rudders or see out during take-offs. It worked. Bullshit Baffles Brains.

I was swiftly posted onto Wellingtons at No. 11 Operational Training Unit, Bassingbourn, Cambridgeshire.

In those early days the Wellington carried a crew of six: two pilots, front and rear gunners, wireless operator and navigator, and in the course of training I had to experience for myself the duties of every crew member. I spent hours stripping the Browning guns and learning to recognise every possible stoppage, and firing the guns into the air. I learned to operate the radio and practise navigation. I needed to practise navigation. Once, when I'd swapped and my navigator Gwyn Martin was piloting and I was navigating, we got lost. We were even – here was a real leftover from the Great War – given quite a few hours tuition in the techniques of laying down gas. But it never, thank God, came to that.

Quite a lot of time was spent flying as a crew on cross-country exercises. On one such flight, to win a bet I took us on a slight detour and flew the Wellington under the central span of the Menai Straits Bridge. My home is now on Anglesey, and whenever I see that bridge I have to shudder at my earlier foolhardy self and that stupid exploit. I suppose it is ignorance which gives you the illusion that you're up to such a stunt. I went on with it, even though the rest of the crew were not keen and you could smell the rotten eggs of their less-than-confident view of things. The day's excitement did not stop there though.

We were supposed to go on to drop practice bombs from 2,000 feet onto a small island just off the Llyn Peninsula, but just as we were approaching the area our intercom failed, and a terrible noise, a wild screeching as if something inside was being murdered, was coming from it. As a crew we unanimously decided to carry on in spite of this and briskly disconnected the intercom by pulling out its plugs. Almost immediately, the plane sank from 2,500 feet to 2,000 feet, and I found I couldn't ease back the control stick to level it out. It was stuck and we were plunging fast. My co-pilot, Beardshaw, grabbed at the stick and tried to haul it back with me, but it was no good. I yelled at him to look and see what the trouble was. He must have spotted it more or less instantly, because he yelled at me to push the stick forward. Forward? Forward would help us get down even faster, but now at 500 feet I didn't have a lot of choice. Sighing what I thought might be my last breath before hitting the drink, I pushed the stick forward. Beardshaw appeared with the bell-shaped end of my helmet intercom cord in his hand, which he found had slipped down behind the control column when I'd first started to descend. More rotten eggs in the cockpit, but at least today we weren't going to feature in those grim statistics labelled 'flying accidents'. We had got away with it and learnt a valuable lesson: *don't* leave loose bits and pieces around the cockpit. We'd completed our detail but, needless to say, the official version left out the more exciting bits.

Bassingbourn was only a small village, so most off-duty evenings were spent in Royston, a few miles to the south, in the Banyers Hotel. On a Saturday night we would slip up to the town hall, book a last waltz, then get back to the pub, returning to the dance in time to claim our partners for that critical last slow number. It didn't always work out, but if it did and you missed the last bus, no-one seemed to mind the walk back to camp.

By early March 1941 we were working well as a crew, almost at the end of the course, with just night-flying left. I had completed two details of dual instruction, and then went off solo in the Wellington. This solo trip was cut short rather abruptly, when I received instructions to land immediately. I was on the downwind leg and just turning in for my final approach, so I was on the ground in no time at all, with another aircraft coming in behind. Good thing I was, too. As I cleared the runway, tracer bullets started flying all around, and the aircraft following me disappeared. I quickly pulled onto the nearest hard-standing and closed down. When I got back to the flight office there was great excitement. A German night-fighter, one of those lethal Junkers 88s, had joined the circuit and shot down the aircraft following me in. My neck prickled. My lucky night. Very, very glad not to have been shot down before even joining a squadron. It was one thing to choose to risk my neck flying under a bridge, but quite another to feel death popping up so unexpectedly behind one. As it happened, the shot-up aircraft was not too badly damaged and had managed to crash-land just short of the airfield. I now know that it was shot down and claimed by Oblt. Schulz of 4 Staffel. After this episode, though, all aircraft doing night-circuits had to carry a rear gunner, which was not at all popular with the rear gunners. Night-flying was cancelled for the next few nights, which meant no more practice for me before I was posted with my crew to 40 Squadron at RAF Wyton, near Huntingdon. This was in March 1941.

It is a bit unnerving. I had by then amassed a total of 166 hours flying, of which only eleven were night-flying. Looking back on it I can hardly believe that I reached a night bomber squadron with only eleven hours night-flying experience, of which only three hours were solo! I never knew what the crew felt about this. You don't ask. And of course ignorance is a wonderful state; I thought I was a highly-trained bomber pilot. All that mattered now was that at last I was on a squadron.

I had learnt one thing, though, one very important thing, which probably saved my life more than once, and that was to keep up a healthy respect for and knowledge of my aircraft. Throughout my training I had seen many who started with me at Cambridge fall by the wayside, some at the Initial Training Wing stage because they could not pass the ground school exams. Several others failed to go solo on Magisters, while others had been taken off flying because they could not cope with the twin-engined Oxford. Sadly, more than one had been killed in flying accidents. In fact only two of our FTS course survived the war. I wanted to fly well, to have a complete understanding of my aircraft, a pedantic, almost obsessive insistence upon everything being mechanically right, and always to listen to and learn from the more experienced crews.

CHAPTER FOUR

Flying in the Dark

Before reporting to 40 Squadron at Wyton I went home to Ruabon for two weeks' leave. Because I had thought I would – if I was lucky enough to survive – return to farming after the war, Mary had herself decided to join the Women's Land Army to get some useful experience on a farm. This seemed a good idea, since having been raised in Birmingham, she had only recently realised that United Dairies didn't actually make the milk but had to get it from cows. After her initial training and a spell on a farm in Lincolnshire where she managed to overturn the milk van while trying to learn to drive it, she was now nearby, on a farm in Farndon, near Wrexham. Perfect for me, since I could spend time with my family during the day and meet her each evening. As usual, I was full of myself, excited about the war and keen to join my new squadron. It must have been very difficult for my parents and Mary to share in my cheerfulness about it all. I couldn't really explain to them that whatever the casualty reports in the newspapers indicated I intended to survive. I was sure of it. I would be the poacher the gamekeeper could not catch. It was arrogant and maybe self-delusive, but it was the only way to play it.

There was certainly not much precedent around for this optimistic view. Of the men who had inspired me, my late brother-in-law Harold and his friends I had met while he was training at Sealand in 1934, four had already been killed while serving with Bomber Command. In those early days the leaders directing operations from the Air Ministry believed that our bombers (mostly Hampdens, Blenheims, Wellingtons and Whitleys, all two-engine) flying in formation were more than a match for the Luftwaffe. They couldn't entertain the notion that a fabric-clad Wellington armed only with its limited Browning .303 short-range machine guns might not be a real match for the 350 mph armoured fighters firing at them with cannons.

On 18 December 1939, twenty-four Wellingtons took off at midday for Wilhelmshaven. Of these twenty-four, two returned with engine trouble, twelve were shot down during the battle, two ditched on the way home and three crash-landed at base. It took the disaster of Wilhelmshaven to convince the Ministry at last that our bombers were no match for the modern fighter, and night-bombing became the policy from then on. But what a waste of highly-trained, experienced pilots. I would have more of a chance of survival.

When I arrived at Wyton I discovered to my delight that on an operational station my sergeant's stripes and flying brevet actually meant something. I was operational now. The NCO at the Guard Room took me along to the sergeant's mess and showed me where I was to sleep in the aircrew barrack block, introduced me to several of the other sergeants and wished me good luck. He meant it, too. I would need all I could get. I quickly picked up the sense of urgency about Wyton. We were part of 3 Group, that section of Bomber Command stationed in East Anglia, and now Britain stood alone against Germany, Bomber Command was the only force taking offensive action. The cutting-edge was here. Within a couple of hours I had been kitted out with lockers and a parachute, interviewed by my flight commander, Squadron Leader Woods, and my squadron commander, Wing Commander E.J.P. Davey, a New Zealander. I soon met up with the crew I had brought with me from Bassingbourn. They were to be taken over by an experienced pilot getting his first crew as captain, while I was to be second pilot to another pilot who had just been made a captain. You were supposed to fly for about ten operations to get experience before being given your own crew, unless heavy casualties decreed otherwise.

Meantime, I had yet to be 'blooded' myself. The captain, Dick Broadbent, a Royal New Zealand Air Force pilot, had the characteristic quiet reserve I found in most of his compatriots I met during the war. Like myself a sergeant, Dick eased me very gently into his crew: first, with an air test the day after I'd arrived and a two-hour cross-country flight, the main aim of which, as far as I could see, was to introduce me to a lot of dogsbody work, finding out the things I'd need to know about the aircraft. Part of this was logical, part pragmatic. It seems that when the Wellington first arrived from the factory, the second pilot's seat was removed by most crews, because 'it got in the way' of the gangway between the front turret and bomb-aimer's panel, back to the 'office' where the navigator and radio operator worked. I couldn't help wondering what my mother would think of this complete waste of the precious saucepans she had given to help build aircraft, when we had dozens of second pilot's seats piled up in a dump. In any event, the gangway was clearer for me to do my running around the aircraft on the many jobs I was now given to do: managing the petrol cocks, pumping oil when required, watching for night-fighters, map-reading and handing out the tea (without spilling it) in its flask and sandwiches to the crew. Electric torches were not used in flight unless it was an emergency, so everything in the aircraft had to be known and recognised by touch and memory. I had a lot to learn. This became my mantra.

The Wellington – or 'Wimpy', from Popeye the Sailor's friend J. Wellington Wimpy – was a lovely aircraft to fly, with no bad habits, very responsive. The earlier versions, both the Mark Is I had in 40 Squadron and in Malta, had Pegasus engines which could not maintain height on one engine. By the time I got back on 150 Squadron in 1942, the newer Wellington III would have the far more powerful Hercules engines which could get you home on one engine. You develop a certain fondness for your aircraft, which becomes for long hours your place of work and your home. Directly behind the pilot, in his little 'office', was the wireless operator, while behind him was the navigator's 'office'. As I said, on operations the navigator had a lot of moving about to do, and the second pilot's seat was removed to make it easier for him to come forward to map-read or to get down to the bomb panel in the nose. Behind the navigator, a main spar ran across the aircraft; on its other side was the main fuselage. Halfway down the fuselage, on the port side, was a canvas bed, of no use at all unless you happened to be taking a WAAF for a joy ride. We stood on the bed to look out of the astrodome. And at the end of it all was the poor, isolated rear gunner.

One of the things which most impressed me was the relationship between Dick and his crew. He had operated with them for some time; they were friends. Moreover, they were very efficient at their jobs. As we flew along on that first cross-country jaunt, they all chatted cheerfully together, calling Dick 'Skipper', but not with any crass familiarity. There was a great deal of respect for him as captain, even though he held the same rank they did, and for the first time it was impressed upon me how well this worked with wartime crews. There was no regimentation. Selected from a host of volunteers and trained with infinite care to face any emergency, these men soon welded themselves into a closely-knit unit, each with its individual identity. There were no rules and no specific training for captains. It was assumed that young men capable of flying a multi-engined bomber in wartime must possess powers of leadership, and in most cases, this proved right. In the occasional crew where it didn't work, the chances of survival were minimal. Doubtless it was this same spirit which helped us all later in Stalag Luft III.

My 'blooding' was to come the day after that cross-country flight. We arrived at 'Flights' on the morning of 15 April to find that our crew was detailed for an operation that night. The news was greeted with great relief; at last the real thing. While the rest of the squadron was being sent off to Brest, we were detailed to a short flight across the Channel to bomb the docks at Boulogne. We were to take off after the main stream, so I stood on the grass after our dispersal, watching the rest of the squadron leave. I cannot begin to convey the intensity of the feelings I had at that moment, of being a part of all this, of belonging. When it was our turn, I was ready for it: the pre-flight checks, the taxi down to the end of the runway. A steady green from the flight-control caravan and we were off, me standing beside Dick, who was juggling the throttles to keep the Wimpy straight until enough speed built up and the rudders took over.

Airborne: and as soon as the wheels retracted and we circled over the airfield to set course, I made way for the front gunner to enter his turret. (Although one would always take off with the rear gunner snug in his turret, in case of engine failure the front gunner did not enter his turret until the aircraft was safely airborne.) All unnecessary lights were now extinguished, and the others dimmed as we set the controls for a steady climb eastward. I went down to the bomb aimer's panel with my map to try to give the navigator an accurate reading of the coast so that he could check wind speed and direction. Map reading, especially on dark, moonless nights over a blacked-out Britain, was not easy. The only other navigational aid was from the flashing recognition beacons situated between the many airfields dotted around East Anglia. The navigator would have been given a codebook, changed every day, giving the code letters in Morse and position of each beacon. Unfortunately, since most pilots, including me, hadn't bothered to learn Morse properly the usual and safest method was to read it out to the navigator: 'Dit, dit, daa, dit daa', etc. When you reach the coast, you can normally get a good fix, simply because you can see it more clearly.

As soon as we crossed the coast and were now out into the Channel, I went back to the cockpit to check the fuel for Dick. If it was not flowing evenly you could cross-feed the tanks. All was well though, so I was dispatched to stand on the canvas bed halfway down the fuselage with my head in the astrodome at the side to look out for night-fighters. Here I had a good view as we climbed through broken cloud and into a beautiful night sky, clear and starry. Enchanted, I reported this to the captain, who was unmoved: 'I don't want a met report, just keep a sharp lookout for fighters!'

Silence, apart from the constant, reassuring hum of the engines, then: 'Ten thousand feet, oxygen on.' We answered in turn to confirm oxygen on and flowing. Constant staring into darkness makes you drowsy, so to keep alert I kept changing focus from cloud to stars to wingtip and back. Cruising altitude of 14,000 feet was reached. We levelled off, and from then on Dick's voice could be heard over the intercom at regular intervals checking each crew member to see that all was well, and to keep us on our toes too, I think. For myself, I found the sound of his voice cool and reassuring. He checked again our ETA at the coast, and since it was very near, I was recalled to the cockpit: three pairs of eyes scanning the broken cloud for a glimpse of the enemy coast ahead were better than two. The front gunner saw it first, while to our right, at the same time, I found myself staring at my first ever burst of flak. It was not being fired at us.

'Someone's got there before us,' Dick called out as we crossed the French coast north of Boulogne. I went back to the astrodome, watching the searchlights which had begun to probe the skies around us. The steady drone of the engines now became broken, with different revs on each engine: Dick had de-synchronised the engines to make detection more difficult for searchlight and flak crews, who were listening for the constant sound of two engines. It was an uncomfortable sound to have to listen to up there at 14,000 feet, almost as if the engines were breaking up, but we all knew it was necessary.

Dick had begun the now-standard procedure of weaving the aircraft from left to right instead of following a straight course, making it more of a problem to aim at us from below, while making for the eastern part of town, since our orders were to bomb from east to west, then continue out to sea. As we approached the target area, flak and searchlights suddenly became much more intense, a mid-air maelstrom of exploding sound and light – they were now aiming for us.

The navigator had left his office and taken up his position at the bomb aimer's panel. Waiting for him to get everything lined up is one of the worst, most agonising times on an operation, when although it is only a few minutes really, the time seems to go on forever while you're expecting to be blown out of the sky. Part of you wants him just to dump the damned things so you can all go home, but you know you can't do that. You have to wait and get it right, stay calm and do your job properly. At last he called out: 'Bombs fused', then Dick said: 'Right. Turning on the target.' Then: 'Bomb doors open . . . running up on target.'

Although my mouth was dry and I could feel myself shaking, I have to say that what I felt then was sheer excitement. All around us the dark was filled with bright deadly flak flowers and odd black blobs I thought might be barrage-balloons, whose steel cables could take a wing off. The searchlights, huge fingers of light, twice swept across us but failed to fix us. I could hear Dick's voice giving the navigator his course, height and speed for the bombing run to feed into his bombsight. It all had to be quickly if not instantaneously done, all the while the plane weaving violently, until at last: 'Target in sight.'

Now really was the worst time, the dangerous time, as we had to fly straight and level, just what the guns wanted. You are a sitting duck. Another check of height and airspeed, and the navigator took over: 'Look left . . . steady . . . right . . . steady, left a little, steady . . . steady, bombs gone.'

'Bomb doors closed.' Having closed the bomb doors, Dick gave a sudden, vicious turn of direction, just as the flak and searchlights seemed to zero in on us. Not tonight though. Nose down, throttles open and we were soon out to sea, homeward bound. It was only then that I realised how hard I had been gripping the astrodome; my hands ached but my underpants, to my intense relief, were dry. I remember hearing the wireless operator calling out that he had sent the 'Q' signal which means a successful operation.[1]

'Did you enjoy that, Ken?' Dick called.

'I think he's baled out, Skipper.' The rear gunner. Laughter. I grinned.

'Tea and sandwiches, I think. Can you get them, Ken? Okay, now everyone, keep a good lookout. We're not clear of night-fighters yet.'

I had stopped shaking enough to pass around the tea and sandwiches without spilling anything, amazed at how they all seemed so easy and collected after all that had happened only a few minutes before. Later I would more fully appreciate just how good they were at their jobs, and how good a captain Dick was. With typical tact he asked if I could take over while he went for a pee. Still under the happy spell of it all I flew back to base, where he took over again for the landing.

On arrival at dispersal we chatted with the ground crew, who were pleased to see that we had sustained no damage and that everything aboard was still serviceable. Ours was one of twenty-three 'freshman' crews sent out that night to bomb the docks, a kind of training op. One Whitley didn't come back. Transport arrived in the form of a truck, and a cheerful WAAF drove us to the operations block at Wyton for de-briefing by the intelligence officers.

As I walked in I was surprised to be greeted by the station commander, Group Captain Foster, who said: 'How did you enjoy your first trip, Rees?' and offered me a cup of tea. It was typical of him to take the trouble to single out a new young sergeant-pilot and have a word with him: an early lesson in leadership. The de-briefings would always be like this first one. The crew, exhausted through lack of sleep and nervous reaction, stumbling over again what they had just been through; the intelligence officer duty-bound to drag from us details of the operation – bombing height, flak, searchlights, any night-fighters. Did we see where the bombs landed? How many on target? The questions repeated over and again for accuracy; accurate de-briefings meant more accurate briefings. This over, we would finally be allowed to eat our post-operational meal of precious bacon and eggs and get off to bed.

---

[1] The 'Q' or 'QDM' signal sent back together with your aircraft call sign officially meant: 'Target located and successfully attacked.' Of course many RAF squadron weddings would be graced with the telegram: 'Remember to send your QDM.'

Three days later, on 17 April, we were off again: ten Wellingtons going to Cologne, in the heavily-defended, much-bombed Ruhr. It was known as 'Death Valley', or later 'Happy Valley'. This was the real thing, not just a hop across the Channel. The build-up was much the same, an air test as soon as we knew we were on for that night, and briefing three hours before take-off. In those early days of the war each aircraft was given a take-off time, but it was up to the captain to decide what route to take to get to the target, as well as height and direction of the bombing-run. Later on in the war all that would become much more closely coordinated, with a much larger force attacking each target, and crews being given specific routes, height, time on target, and so on. But in early 1941 the attack force could be anything from a dozen to a hundred bombers of various types. Tonight, as well as five other minor operations going on, a main force of 118 Wellingtons, Hampdens, Whitleys and one Stirling was to attack Berlin. Every night for years until the war ended this would be the same.

After briefing, the usual pre-flight meal, again bacon and eggs, we'd collect our in-flight rations, sandwiches, an orange and a couple of bars of precious chocolate, which most people stowed away for leave. (It never failed to amaze me that the medics thought such goodies essential for fitness. We certainly kept fit enough without them, possibly because in those days of rationing a few bars of spare chocolate helped your sex life no end, i.e. they helped you to get one.) Then we were driven to the aircraft by the same cheerful WAAF, who always said: 'I'll be here to pick you up when you get back.' It helped.

At dusk we took off in turn with the rest of the squadron and headed east. Once over the North Sea, the gunners were given permission to test their guns by firing a quick burst, and we all got our first sharp, dusty smell of cordite for the night. The enemy coast, as all that coastline was called, was crossed between towns in relative peace, with only the odd burst of flak off in the darkness as some aircraft flew over defended areas. With a good landmark, some obvious or well-defined part of the coast, the navigator could get a strong fix and now gave a new course to fly for Cologne. Dick's calm voice asked if everyone had their oxygen on, and that the IFF (Identification Friend or Foe, the device our own radar would use to identify us when we returned – you don't want to be shot down by your own people) was switched off.

Most of this route was tricky, practically a major highway for the more or less constant bombing of the Ruhr factories, and so had to be flown with utmost caution at all times. Our engines were already de-synchronised, causing some vibration and discomfort, and all idle chat was stopped. This went on right up to the target, the silence punctuated by the odd engine noises and 'Keep those turrets moving, gunners', from Dick. 'Time to pump some oil, co-pilot, then stay in the astrodome and keep a good lookout.' I went up, but wasn't to stay long.

'The first aircraft have reached the target,' came from the wireless operator. The first 'Q' code had come through, which meant we would soon see action. In those early days each aircraft arrived at the target in its own time. I was moved out of the astrodome so the navigator could get his fix, and returned to the cockpit to keep a lookout there so Dick could concentrate on keeping a steady course for the navigator to fix on. All at once, it seemed, ahead of us was a wide belt of searchlights, practically across the horizon, weaving and crossing every inch of sky. I didn't see how we could possibly get through them without being coned. It was magnificent and utterly terrifying, one of many vivid views you get of death just waiting for you to come along. The navigator quickly finished his astro shot, so we were weaving again, left to right, to avoid any lethal hold from the ground below. It was like space invaders, only it was real. Now the mass of searchlights froze and formed its deadly cone of solid light. My heart stopped. 'Now they've caught some poor bastard.' The front gunner in a grim voice.

'Hard luck on him.' Dick had no time to spend on sympathy. 'It'll help us sneak through.'

I watched, riveted, the drama ahead of us as the Wellington caught in the cone wove and danced like a moth or some poor fly, desperately trying to shake it off. It reminded me of one of those cellular balls you see in shooting booths at the fair, bouncing balanced on a jet of water. But in the end all his dodging efforts paid off, and the searchlights on him veered off at too much of angle – just enough time for him to slip through into the welcoming safety of darkness.

'I bet there's a nasty smell in that aircraft,' said Dick. 'Not much flak. . . they must be leaving it to the night-fighters, so keep your eyes open.' A little more weaving and we were clear of that first hurdle.

I had scrambled back into the astrodome, and just as my stomach and hands decided it might be a good thing for my circulation if they relaxed for a second, I heard the front gunner call out: 'Flak ahead, slightly to port.'

'That's Cologne all right,' said the navigator. I scrambled back down into the cockpit again. From the cockpit you had the most splendid, awesome view.

We were keeping a course south of the target, the idea again being to bomb from east to west, weaving all the time from left to right and back again. Some flak came our way, but nothing like what I could see to port, just over the target. At last, turning for the run-in, the navigator took up his position on the bomb aimer's panel and fused the bombs. Dick gave him the height, course and speed for the bombing-run, but continued prudently to weave until we got much closer to target. The visibility was good. Then all hell broke loose.

The world was suddenly all light and fire, as if a mad switch had been pulled and we were centre-stage. A blinding mass of searchlight beam hit us, with coloured balls of flak like great firecrackers shooting up so slowly you could watch yourself being blown up, and then trailing away. On the ground below I could see fires burning. 'Dummies,' Dick said tersely. 'Put there to confuse the bombers. Sometimes works if visibility's poor. Not tonight, though.'

On a 'good' night, like tonight, with high visibility and the useful proximity to the Rhine, the target (in this case the marshalling yards) could be easy to pinpoint, but there was no easy way in as they were heavily defended. Weaving, we headed straight for the yards, then: 'Target in sight, get ready for the run-up. Okay. Left . . . left, right . . . steady . . .'

This was the hardest part: flying a steady and accurate course while all around you seemed nothing but bursts of flak, yellow bursts of exploding flak pockmarked with black puffs of spent bursts, all so close you could smell the bittersharp burning cordite. Blackness and fire, blackness and fire. It felt as if every gun, every searchlight was for us alone. In 1941, attacks on targets were more spread-out over a longer period of time, and as there were seldom more than seventy aircraft on a raid, the Germans were able to concentrate better on individual aircraft. The flak here was so close the Wellington juddered; I was sure we'd had it. It could not have been much more than minutes really; time seemed to stretch itself agonisingly. But then came: 'Bombs away, bomb doors closed.' That sweet call! Dick closed the bomb doors, at the same time turning violently to port, full-throttle and nose down, and we wove our way from the target area.

'Worst part over,' Dick called. 'But don't relax, we've got a long way to go yet, and there's that searchlight belt to be crossed.'

As I left to go down the fuselage, I could hear the navigator reporting how he hadn't been able to see if any bombs hit the target. He was being honest; a lot of bombs didn't reach their target but people would still report they had done. As I sat there in the freezer-air of 15,000 feet, pumping another gallon of oil into each engine, difficult, since the oil was thick with the cold, I could feel the reassuring weaving motion of the aircraft, Dick taking us home. Still chilled, I decided tea from one of the flasks we had would be the thing, and having had a cup for myself, I took one up to Dick, stepping over the main spar, balancing the cup as we wove along. It had been a real lesson in keeping cool under fire, I thought as I watched Dick, now calmly sipping his tea over enemy territory.

Once we'd got through between defended areas – no problem, since the visibility was so good – Dick decided to stretch his legs and told me to take over. He'd been at the controls for about four hours by now. All was so peaceful, I thought, listening to the crew beginning to chatter now that we were relatively safe. 'Bloody awful sandwiches.' 'Tea's cold.' 'Where are we going for a drink tonight?' 'Hasn't that second pilot come off the bloody bog yet?'

I was desperate to join in. 'Flak was pretty bad tonight, wasn't it?'

Howls of derisive laughter. I should have known better. 'Christ, you wait until you go to Hamburg!'

'Keep a sharp lookout for night-fighters,' Dick cut in, 'we're not home yet.'

Afterwards, de-briefed, bacon-and-egged, lying between clean white sheets in the quiet morning, I could hardly believe that we had been so close to being blown out of the sky only hours before. I later found out that of our ten Wellingtons, three had been lost; while on the Berlin raid, eight of the 188 aircraft didn't come back. One of those had been from our squadron, its captain and navigator – Sergeant Jenner and Joe Noble – both good friends of mine. They'd had 'navigational difficulties', that useful euphemism for cock-ups, coming back and wound up over south-west England, out of fuel. The rear gunner baled out and was sadly killed, but the rest of them crash-landed and survived. Joe was good at survival. When I entered the gates of Stalag Luft III Joe was the first one there to greet me.

Reporting to ops after a good sleep, we found out about Noble and Jenner, and also that we'd been stood down for the day, so Dick and some of the others decided to celebrate my first operation and take the relatively good news about Jenner and Noble to what had become a second home for a lot of us, The Market pub in Huntingdon, kept by a kind and affable couple, George and Eve Ashpole, mother and father to us all. George was a major in the local Home Guard, so was keen to hear all the news. At the end of an evening's drinking we'd help him collect and wash up glasses, and he would keep us supplied with free beer. In spite of rationing Eve always managed to produce food for her starving boys, while if we were without transport, George would run us back to base.

Because of bad weather there were no operations for a few days, at least not for us, so Dick and the rest of the crew went on leave. Because I'd just come back from leave I became a spare pilot until their return, which proved to be the most useful experience I could have asked for. First I went to Hamburg with Squadron Leader Woods, my flight commander, then to Brest with Wing Commander Davey. Hamburg was an education indeed, very heavily defended.

On 4/5 May, attacking two battleships, the *Scharnhorst* and the *Gneisenau*, in Brest harbour with Wing Commander Davey, we reached the highest I ever got in a Wellington, 17,000 feet. The more height you could get the safer you were from flak, especially the lighter flak, but more height meant less accuracy. When I asked him how he managed it, he told me: 'Just be patient. Don't force it, just let it creep up.' But I never quite got there again, even though the official ceiling for a Wellington is 18,000 feet.

Because they felt so much older and more senior to us, any operation with Davey or Woods was far more serious in tone. No cute remarks over the intercom like: 'Coast ahead, navigator; I hope it's the French coast, not the Irish.' But it was also very, very professional. I kept my mouth shut, listened hard and realised all over again from watching such pilots that I still had a lot to learn. The flak over Brest was heavy, but since it was a small coastal port, very concentrated as well, thus easier to avoid. We turned on target from the land side and Davey throttled well back and made a semi-glide approach, telling the navigator we would be bombing at 14,000 feet. Although the target had been covered in smoke-screen, this was ineffectual, and in the bright moonlight, a real bomber's moon, the two battleships stood out clearly. Bright or not, we missed, the bombs landing right between the two ships[2]. As we headed for home, though, I got the fright of my life. Sometimes it does you no good being the spare tyre.

'Rees, please take over from the rear gunner and give him a break.' Davey's voice over the intercom.

What? I cannot describe the wave of sheer horror that came over me. I'd had a go at operating a turret during my training at Bassingbourn, but this nightmare was for real. As I crawled away from the warmth of the office and into the rear gunner's perspex barnacle at the back of the aircraft, it was suddenly freezing and I could feel every engine vibration in every frozen bone. The vast empty sky behind was cold and threatening. I doubted my hands would be up to any rapid and accurate shooting with the twin Browning .303s. And being such an obvious target scared me silly.

'How do you bale out of this?' I asked the rear gunner on his way up for a cup of tea.

'Oh, I wouldn't worry about that,' he said cheerfully, 'you'll be the first one to get killed.'

I have never felt so vulnerable or afraid. If any night-fighter came roaring up on us we'd be easy meat, left to me. But it was one of the best, if not the most frightening lesson I think I learnt. In future I always appreciated what a terrible, truly rotten job a gunner had, especially a rear

---

[2] In spite of all the efforts of Bomber Command to get rid of them and 3,413 tonnes of bombs dropped in their direction, these two and the *Prinz Eugen* would continue to raid the Atlantic shipping lanes until retiring badly damaged in February 1942.

gunner. It was the worst job in the crew, and to my mind, the bravest.
While the two pilots, wireless operator and navigator are close together
(and warm), the rear gunner is stuck out at the back of the aircraft in the
freezing cold on his own, a sitting duck. We could mostly move around
and chat, if need be, or go down the fuselage to the Elsan to relieve the
tension. The gunners had to use a bottle. Our rear gunner always took a
pint bottle and threw it out with the bombs over the target. I understand
that it made a whistling noise, rather like a bomb, as it fell. I often
imagined some poor German panicked at the noise only to be hit on the
head by a bottle of piss. This same gunner also used to take along a brick
as his personal contribution to the war effort, with some very rude words
chalked on it, and heave it out with the bombs and the bottle.

By the time we reached the east coast I felt more like I was sitting on
the Elsan than a rear turret. My mind drifted off onto thoughts of poor old
Beckett, a friend from Gorringe's, who had joined up when war broke out
and become a rear gunner on our squadron. He was killed on a raid on
Hamburg. I'd never before appreciated what he'd gone through.

Over the next ten days I flew two operations with a sergeant from my old
crew at Bassingbourn, on 8 and 9 May. These were major operations: 188
aircraft to Hamburg, and 146 to Mannheim. For us they were relatively
uneventful trips, with a bright moon and plenty of flak, but none coming
our way. The Hamburg operation was 'successful', a lot of the city left in
flames. The Squadron lost two aircraft, while a third, damaged by a Me
110, managed to crash-land at Marham, with several crew injured and the
rear gunner killed. The captain, Pilot Officer Smith, was awarded a DFC;
the wireless operator, Sergeant Robbins, a DFM.

As for me, after a very bumpy landing, better described as an arrival
than a landing, I decided to avoid flying with this particular pilot. More of
this later. By the time Dick got back from leave I had flown with four
different captains and I had learned a great deal about what I would be
facing when I had responsibility for my own crew. I would like to be able
to say I was in on the sinking of the *Bismarck* on 27 May, a beautiful day
for flying over the ocean, with lots of big cumulus clouds, but by the time
we reached the target area nothing was there to be seen, not even our own
Navy (not a bad thing, since the Navy had a nasty habit of shooting at
everything in the sky). After some time spent in a futile search for the sister
ship, the *Prinz Eugen,* we'd been six hours in the air and fuel was running
low, so we made for St Ives, where they told us it had all been over hours
before we'd got there. Oh, well.

CHAPTER FIVE

My Own Crew

Throughout that May of 1941, life consisted of intense bursts of experience, the life-threatening and the life-enhancing, from cool professionalism to complete loucheness, and I found I ricocheted happily from one to the other. I kept company with Dick Broadbent, who had become a good friend. After flying operations by night, and having survived the flak, the tracer fire, intense fear and cold, we'd play rugby hard, drink hard at The Market and chase after every woman who caught our eye. Years later I saw a film in which one of the female characters posed the half-serious question, 'Why do men chase women?' The answer she arrived at was: 'Because they fear death.' Not far off. I never felt I was being unfaithful, only demonstrating that I was still alive and in good working order.

For example. One lovely day in May we were invited to a party in the grounds of a Group HQ in Huntingdon by some WAAF we'd met in the pub the night before. There was always a lot of such socialising going on, especially in summer. This started off as a relatively staid tea-party, but moved smoothly on into drinking-time. Towards the end of the evening I seemed to have got paired off with the sister of one of the WAAFs, called Doreen, who was a secretary for one of the contracters building Alconbury airfield. She was extremely pretty, and got prettier as the night wore on. Through the usual idle chatup I found out that she lived in digs in Huntingdon, so I could 'walk her home'. I had no idea if we might be called up for ops tomorrow, but that mattered not a whit right now. Here and now was the lovely Doreen, and my immediate intentions were entirely evil. About midnight, I hissed to Dick that I'd make my own way back to Wyton, and we set off, Doreen, getting more beautiful by the minute, and I. It was soon pretty obvious that I could barely walk in a straight line, but the heady whiff of Doreen's scent and the feel of her warm, female body mustered my determination and sense of purpose. When we pulled up at her front door I was more than ready. At that primed perfect moment the door suddenly opened, her landlady took one hard, cold look at the two of us, especially at me, and had hauled the girl inside and slammed the door before I could say one word.

I stood there, swaying slightly and swelling with a deep resentment, when my eye was caught by the sight of the downspout climbing the front of the house, right past the window Doreen had coyly informed me was hers. I smiled to myself, one of those heroic smiles, and began my ascent. Romeo himself would have been proud. Except that I suppose the drainpipes in Italy were sturdier than this one. At about six feet up I could hear a groan, then a resounding crack as the whole thing peeled away from the wall and deposited me splat on the pavement. The noise had been tremendous, the jolt onto the pavement painful, and any ardour dissolved into the night. And so, prudently, did I.

It was miles to Wyton, my rear end hurt like hell, and I was still dizzy from all the booze I had shipped earlier, so I decided it would be a good thing to stick to the white line in the middle of the road. Before I'd got very far a whickering sound caught my attention: a big carthorse, at least seventeen hands high, poking his long nose over a fence. I went over and introduced myself. He seemed friendly enough, so I decided to muster up my farming background and cadge a lift from him. I liked the idea of riding splendidly up to barracks; it gave the evening less of a wasted feel. But this was definitely not to be my night. I couldn't even heave myself up onto his back. No girl, no horse, no way home. I went back to the road and feeling increasingly sorry for myself, followed the white line. By the time I came to some houses I was feeling pretty rough. It was about two a.m., and the inevitable hangover was beginning its creep into my system. It then occurred to me that there weren't supposed to be houses here. I knocked politely on the front door of one of them, which was answered after several of these polite knocks by an irate gentleman who appeared not to believe that I didn't know that the way to Wyton was back the way I'd just come, a long way back.

You always embraced such moments though; they might be your last. Two nights later, on 2 June, we had a rough time of it over Düsseldorf, with heavy flak and terrible cloud cover making it impossible to find the target. As our aircraft approached the target area another one could be seen off in the distance going down in flames. We assumed it was a bomber and hoped the crew had managed to bale out in time. There was also the tacit prayer that we ourselves might have better luck. Bombs gone, the smell of cordite still lingering with us, we hared through spent flak bursts for home. As we stood shivering on the tarmac in the early morning light, safe and home, chatting with the ground crew, another Wellington joined the circuit and approached to land, but came in too high and overshot the runway. As it turned for another go, I could see it was Sgt Sergeant's aircraft, with my old crew aboard. I cannot begin to describe the fearful tension you felt at such terrible moments poised between life and death, the underlying strain that did not move until everyone was safe around you.

We all stood there and watched in silence as the Wellington went downwind, and as it turned back towards the runway it climbed steeply, then just outside the boundary it stalled, dropped a wing and plunged straight into the ground. Stunned, for a long moment no-one moved, then the emergency services rushed into action, but it was no good. They managed to pull the rear gunner out with only a broken back, but the rest, all of my old Bassingbourn crew, my old friends, were all killed. They had gone through all that flak and got home only to be killed trying to land. For the first time I felt tears creeping down my cheeks; for I don't know how long I stood there and wept.

In early June Dick had spoken to the flight commander, recommending that I get my own crew. By this time, I'd flown eleven operations as second pilot, and at this point in the war you would be given your own crew after twelve to fourteen ops, depending on casualties. Several rookie crews like mine had already been lost, so I was thrilled when on 17 June, just before we were to be briefed for an operation that night to Cologne, the commanding officer called me into his office and told me I was to have the next crew arriving from Bassingbourn. Of course we had to celebrate, so off we went – Dick, Joe Noble, Ken Jenner and several others – down to The Market. But any celebrations were somewhat muted because both George and Eve were both too saddened by the loss of the young men they knew. We were like family to them. That evening Eve was so overcome she had to go upstairs. When I met George after the war he told me how badly he felt about all the young aircrew he had known who had failed to return. One night they would be there drinking with him in the cosy bar, and the next night he'd ask where they were only to be told, 'Oh, they bought it last night.' At first this careless attitude upset him, but he quickly realised it was just a façade. We hated it, too, but it happened every day, and if you let your mind dwell on dying and death you would soon crack up. Many did.

About this time, Air Marshal Sir Hugh Trenchard, himself a distinguished First World War pilot, one of the founders of the RAF and a proponent of modern theories of air warfare, came to give the squadron a pep talk. He spoke well, with a perfect combination of understanding and good comic timing, and could tell a story against himself. He told us how one day he was walking down the Strand, when he came across a barrier closing off the way for about a hundred yards. However, on approaching it, a policeman silently opened up the barrier and simply let him through. As he walked along the deserted street, it struck Sir Hugh that he was the only living soul in the entire area, so when he got to the other end, he asked the policeman at the barrier there what it was all about.

'Unexploded bomb, sir.'

'A bomb? But then, why did that other policeman let me through?'

'Oh, he must have recognised you, sir.'

Before I would be allowed to take over my own crew, Squadron Leader Stickley said I was to do an hour's night circuits and landings. It was a pleasant summer's night, and I took off without a care in the world, happy to be flying. Less happy was the rear gunner being obliged to baby-sit in case some German intruder came along and took pot-shots. He'd just finished a tour of operations and was looking forward to leave before his next posting. After a few (good) landings, I was just taking off for my final circuit when I noticed that the airspeed indicator wasn't working. We were past the point of no return and too near the end of the runway to abandon the take-off, so I just had to ease it off and climb gently away, hoping not to hit anything. I cruised round the circuit, trying to contact the control tower to tell them I had no airspeed, at the same time trying to reassure the rear gunner he had nothing to worry about. He wasn't buying it. 'Christ,' I could hear him saying over and again, 'thirty bloody operations over Germany and here I am about to crash on my own patch with a sprog captain.'

Where was that bloody control? My language into the useless R/T was by now pretty ripe. I was going to have to get down as best I could, sod them all, the bastards, etc, etc . . . Taking a deep breath, I went downwind, quickly losing height, then put wheels down and with full flap with plenty of throttle, thundered in. As we crossed the boundary, far too fast, I braked hard, and at last, just as we were running out of runway, she stopped.

Squadron Leader Stickley came up just as we were climbing down. 'Good show, Rees,' he said. 'But I must say, I didn't appreciate your opinion of us here on the ground.'

I felt my face go red. The R/T had been working after all.

In spite of this I was given my new crew, all young sergeants about twenty-years-old, and over the next couple of weeks we were well and truly blooded. My second pilot was Byrnes, the wireless operator Smith, front gunner Joe Arsenault, a French Canadian, the navigator Mason, also RCAF, an old man of twenty-three, and rear gunner Barrington, an Aussie in the RAAF. The crew had been together at the OTU and got on well. We did four raids in quick succession, including Brest and Munster, where we all watched as another Wellington got caught like a fly in the searchlights and was blown apart. You could only hope that some of the crew got out. As we headed back for the coast and comparative safety the crew were silent. I think it had been forced upon them that it could have been us and that you need more than luck; you need to stay fully alert and ready for any emergency. With both sides praying to God you could only hope at least He stayed neutral.

It didn't take long for little idiosyncracies to reveal themselves. In spite of every encouragement to get him to enlarge his vocabulary, Barry, the rear gunner, called everything from flak, searchlights, to the blonde waitress in the mess a 'bloody beaut'. More irksome was the tendency of the navigator, Mason, to get rid of his bombs at the earliest opportunity, literally jumping the gun even before we were over the target. On the first trip to a Channel port he called out: 'I've got the target in my bomb sight.'

'You can't possibly,' I told him. 'I haven't even made my final turn.'

'It's there.'

'It's not. We're going around again. I'll tell you when we're lined up. And if those bombs get released before they are well and truly running down the wires of your bomb-sight, we'll all do a third run.'

The rest of the crew were silent. No-one wanted to have to go round again. It worked, and I had no further trouble. But I knew how frightening an experience it was that first time you had to lie on the bombing-panel over the target and you could see all too clearly the flak coming your way. I thought about it all the way back to base, and when we got there, I had a quiet word with him, reiterating my threat about extra runs. The next trip Mason turned up carrying a tin helmet.

'It's for the bombing-panel,' he said when we asked him. 'To cover up my vital parts. I'm not afraid to die, but if I'm spared I want to be able to live a full life!' It wasn't his head he was worried about.

Throughout that June and July life was made up of operations, or being on stand-by all day only to be stood down in the evening, whereupon anyone who felt like an evening out hot-footed it down to The Market. We were lucky: we'd got caught in the searchlights a few times, but escaped with only a few shrapnel holes and no pursuit by night-fighters. Every crew has its little superstitions, its tokens for continued luck. Ours was against all regulations to have a quick, rather nervous pee on the aircraft before getting in. Mason was learning his craft, too, with some success: bomb-bursts near the targets and fires started. Every time we went up we learnt something new about how to act as a crew. On some trips when we encountered bad weather with complete cloud cover we'd use dead reckoning, and when heavy flak was encountered and visibility poor, we'd aim for the flak area, assuming it was the target or near enough, and bomb blind. During these operations you would sometimes see someone hit and plummetting to earth in flames, either from flak or night-fighters, and you never knew what or who it was. But there was one night in early July, when we could see not far away in the moonlight a Wellington being attacked by a night-fighter. We didn't know it at the time, but it was being flown by a rookie captain, Sergeant Evans. A tight spot for anyone, much less a novice. As we watched her, suddenly the Wimpy turned hard, and we could see lots of tracer flying, but going down in flames before us was the attacking fighter. Later, back at base we heard the whole story. The rear gunner had spotted the night-fighter tracking them and warned the pilot.

'Right,' said Evans, 'let me know when he gets within range, then I'll throttle back, drop my wheels and flaps, then really turn to port. Got that?'

It was exactly the right thing to do, clever and quick-witted: slow your aircraft right down so that the fighter following you so closely overshoots and wanders right into the rear gunner's sights, and bingo. Before it had gone down the fighter had managed a last burst, which damaged the undercarriage enough for it to collapse on return to base, but Wimpys were famous for sustaining damage and still being able to get you home. Two of the crew were slightly injured in the crash-landing, but everyone else was safe and full of their glory. In such moments you feel on top of the world. Evans' cool action earned him a DFM. But it's not a happy ending; few were in those days. A month after that he was shot down during a raid on Brest, and all the crew were killed. Any luck in war is usually brief and selective. Even that same night as the fighter went down, of two other crews from our squadron, one was shot down by a night-fighter, with everyone killed, while Squadron Leader Redgrave's Wellington was hit by flak and crashed into the Scheldt estuary. Although injured, the crew survived to become POWs.

In late May I had moved into Alconbury House, sharing a room with Dick Broadbent and a pre-war navigator, Monty Coe. We were all NCOs, and so the administration in its infinite wisdom felt that we could put up with a little spartan accommodation, even though we did the same jobs as officers. Furnishing consisted of three very basic beds, three wooden chairs and three nails in the wall. The mirror I am afraid we had lifted from a pub in Bedford. It wasn't so much the complete lack of comfort, since when not on ops we spent time either at The Market or in the mess, we found difficult, as the lack of sleep. Because we were all in different crews and therefore not always on operations together, one of us invariably returned from ops weary and still hyped-up in the middle of the night or early morning while the others were still trying to get precious sleep for that same night's operation.

This didn't last long; my life was to change. I had done twenty operations, and was beginning to notice something going on – pilots were being posted to an Operational Training Unit before they had finished their full thirty operations tour of duty. That I did not want. It had taken long enough to get onto a squadron, I wasn't ready to slow down and instruct yet. So when on 7 July the adjutant (known as 'Tom Tit' but not to his face) asked for a volunteer crew to go out to the Middle East, I put my hand up. Of course, the rest of the crew didn't have to follow suit. My second pilot, Sergeant Byrne, was close to getting his own crew so didn't want to come, and neither did Smith, the wireless operator. They were replaced by Pilot Officer Slater, a pilot new to the squadron, and another Sergeant Smith as wireless operator.

Dick came home with me for embarkation leave, so he got to meet my family and Mary. Perhaps I have him to thank for the graceful, unfussed way my family took the news of my latest departure, certainly as usual I was too selfish and excited to make it any easier for them. The leave also marked the sad demise of Clattering Clara, my Austin Seven. Of course, Dick and I decided to throw a party. Why change your habits just because you're home? Off we went into Wrexham to consult a good friend who was head brewer at Border Breweries. After a lot of sampling and decision-making, we eventually left, carting with us a four-and-a-half gallon barrel of best bitter. A stop at the Rainbow Stores for whisky and gin, then another thirst-quenching exercise at the Wynnstay Hotel. Two young pilots home on leave were good for quite a few pints, and it was an old haunt of mine. Eventually, leaving town behind us with Dick driving, poor old Clara was having a rough time of it chugging up the hills near Johnstown, when a large saloon car passed us, cutting in rather sharply. His bumper seemed to catch Clara's wheel, and the whole kit and caboodle finished upside-down off the road. The (undamaged) Austin 20 pulled up and two men got out. Well, I have to say that two inebriated young pilots, however cross at having lost their car and at having to witness the terrible sight of all their gin and whisky flowing away, were no match for a doctor and a solicitor, especially ones happy to give us and our barrel of beer a lift. The garage came and gave Clara a decent burial. There, I thought, went the last of my youth, together with her well-worn back seat.

My father, ever the decent man, came to the rescue with bottles of gin and whisky, so the party was a success. Mary came over, too, and I managed to get her back to the farm just in time for milking. I'll never know how she managed that fortnight's leave of mine on no sleep at all.

Then we departed: Dick for a successful tour at Alconbury, me to Harwell to collect a brand-new Wellington to fly out to Egypt via Gibraltar and Malta. The Wellington needed ten hours of cross-country fuel tests, so the time seemed right to do a few low-level flypasts over the houses of the crew members, then over Mary's farm, and of course, over my own home, Gardden Hall, where I got a little carried away and took off the tops of three poplar trees, nearly putting an end to my war after twenty operations over Germany. Stupid, arrogant behaviour. Fortunately, it was only the soft, leafy parts of the trees, the scratches soon repaired by a friendly flight sergeant without an embarrassing word to the engineering officer. About this time the Air Ministry clamped down on unauthorised low flying; they were losing almost as many aircraft from this as from German guns.

CHAPTER SIX

Mediterranean Views

To get to Malta in 1941 you had to fly via Gibraltar, a long haul, as it meant ten and a half hours in the air and all the extra fuel on board you could manage. The Wimpy was carrying all its fuel tanks plus nacelle tanks taking up every spare inch of space, two auxiliary tanks in the bomb bays, besides all our personal belongings and a lot of stores for Malta and the Middle East. 'Personal belongings' included the standard RAF tropical kit I had been issued with for Canada, a bit more apt this time: thick khaki shirts and shorts that came down to the knees, and a pith helmet I don't think anyone ever used. But at four o'clock that dark, chilly morning of 17 July, we were all kitted up in warm blue battle dress, and eventually, grossly overweight, the Wellington staggered off the Oxfordshire runway, bound for the Bay of Biscay before the dawn light might inspire any stray German fighters off the French coast to have us for breakfast.

After a few hours in bright, hot, increasingly southern sunshine, everyone was wishing we'd started off in our khaki drill. There was no-one there to object so the whole crew peeled off down to their skivvies. After seven hours' constant cruising for maximum range, flying at about 7,000 feet the sun gets to you: with a start my eyes blinked open. I'd fallen asleep, and saw with a surge in my innards that we were at 1,000 feet above endless blue ocean and in a gradual descent towards it. I grabbed at the controls, pulling us back up into the sky and yelling for the second pilot, Slater, who eventually wandered in from where he'd been sleeping on the bed in the fuselage. In fact, the entire crew had been caught napping. A near-miss like that focuses your mind wonderfully; I made Slater come up and sit right beside me for the rest of the trip.

At last we approached the Rock from the south. Spain was officially neutral, we had been briefed, so any approach was very tricky indeed, in order to avoid neutral air space. No circuit of the airfield to get the lie of the land, instead straight in, with a lot of water and Rock to avoid. We had to get clearance by Aldis lamp as we approached, turn slightly to port and start our let-down for landing. At about 500 feet the airfield (really the old racecourse) came into view on the starboard side, small and sandy, the landing-area beginning at the sea and finishing in what appeared to be a very short distance indeed, even in the Mediterranean. Not much room to manoeuvre, and, having used up all our fuel, we could not go round again. Quick wheels-down as I turned in, full flap, and at a dangerously low speed we literally thumped down just over the road on the west end of the runway. I braked hard, and I mean hard, and she finally came to rest amazingly quickly in the soft racetrack sand.

'I'm not looking forward to taking off tomorrow,' I said to Slater, as we all climbed out into the blast-furnace heat. 'We'll have to make it first light, while the weather's still cool.'

The ground crew were all staring at us. I realised we were still wearing only underpants.

After a jolly evening sampling the kind of cheap, plentiful wine not to be found in England, the entire crew were all a little rough rolling up for departure the next morning. Standing by was an officer looking expectantly at us, surrounded by luggage. It came as a horrible surprise to find that we were somehow being expected to take on an extra passenger: a squadron leader, with a mountain of luggage, which he cheerfully stuffed in to what must have been an obviously overloaded aircraft because it took a fair while to make any space. I'm not sure at what point in one's career one actually learns how to say 'Do you really think this is such a good idea?' to a squadron leader who is of course older, wiser and better than oneself. Whenever it was I wasn't there yet, and in that cool morning we were all sweating like pigs as I undertook to get us off the ground. To start with, I practically put my tail in the sea on the other side of the road leading to Spain, opened up on the brakes to full throttle, and with a swift and silent prayer, headed off across the sand. It seemed to take an age to pick up any speed at all and get the tail off the ground, and as we reached the end of the run and the beginning of blue water I literally heaved it up off the ground. We were technically in the air now, skimming over the waves like an overweight pelican. Thank heaven we didn't sink, but flew on for what felt like aeons of sweating uncertainty before I could finally get enough speed to climb achingly slowly, gently, to a reasonable height. The air in the cabin was purest rotten egg. No-one needed to say a word.

Even after six hours of brilliant sunshine the crew were wide awake, yesterday's lesson still with them. We were just within range of fighters coming out from Sicily so I warned them to be extra vigilant. After eight hours of such dull vigilance the front gunner called out that he could see Malta. It was tiny, alone in the vast blue, covered with what looked like a mosaic of small walled paddocks about the size of tennis-courts, broken by villages and towns, the largest being Valletta, and the three airfields, Luqa, Ta Kali and Halfar. But I didn't know which was which.

'Ah, that's it.' The squadron leader was standing beside me and pointing to a smallish airfield. You don't question authority and besides, I'd been flying for eight and a half hours and was tired. I took him at his word and landed, surprised to see on taxying in that there were only Hurricanes around, parked in the grass. When I asked him about this the squadron leader with the imperturbable rightness of his kind, said, 'Oh, you've made a mistake. This is Ta Kali, but don't worry, this is where I want to be.'

Without him and his luggage and quite a lot of fuel, we were considerably lighter, so had few real problems taking off. I later learned that ours was the first ever twin-engined aircraft to land there. Luqa was only a few miles away, and we landed there only to be torn off an undeserved strip by the wing commander flying. I never did see that squadron leader again. Never there when you really want them.

Malta was the first of several hot stages where we had to wait before being told to go on to the next stage, and in July it was very hot, and very crowded besides, mostly aircrew in transit without aircraft to take them off the island. Only sixty miles from Sicily, Malta was then under more or less constant attack. It appeared that a lot of aircraft had been lost on the ground through enemy bombing, while some had been taken over to replace aircraft lost in operations and still more taken on to Egypt by crews who had already been stuck in Malta for some time. I listened with an ever-increasing sense of gloom to the tales of woe from stranded crews, and decided I had better do something about it if we weren't to share their fate and be stuck here ourselves for weeks. So I went to the wing commander flying and pointed out to him that we were an operational crew who had been called for by the Middle East Pool. He accepted this rubbish – I'd known he had no means of confirming it – and said that we could leave in a couple of days.

The two days turned out to be three weeks, which we passed getting used to the frequent air raids, swimming in the sea in between air raids and visiting the many bars. In spite of its dire situation Malta was a great meeting-place. The second day there I went to Flights to check up on an old friend from Gorringe's days, Bradley, a wireless operator who had just finished his OTU and been posted to the Middle East, due here the day after us. They told me that the two aircraft on their way from Gibraltar were overdue and must be considered missing. I knew all too well what that meant. Poor Bradley, his war had finished almost before it had begun. I also met up with Carl Haggett, my old friend from FTS, who had just finished a tour as flying officer on Blenheims. We spent a pleasant few days in the bars and swimming off the rocks at Sliema, where he told me how lucky he felt to have survived a near suicidal tour of low-level attacks on shipping and how he hoped to get back to his wife and child he'd never seen. It was the last I ever saw of him; he was killed soon after his return to Britain, on a low-level strike.

It was 18 August before we were finally told to report to Flights. A Wellington was due in from Gibraltar, and because of the constant air raids all transit aircraft were moved off the island as quickly as possible, so as soon as it was refuelled and serviced, the Wellington carried us over the Mediterranean for our first amazed view of the Nile Delta, that sharp contrast so clear from the sky between pale desert and fertile green. After landing at Abu Sueir, a few miles outside Cairo, we had to sit around for hours in the choking heat and dust before any transport arrived, then when it did, endure hours more in an open truck before arriving at the Middle East Pool, at Kasfareet on the Sweetwater Canal, near the Suez Canal.

In true military fashion no-one had told us what exactly the Middle East Pool was. As soon as we laid eyes on it we could see why they hadn't. Water in the Sweetwater Canal was filthy and stinking; in fact it was always appearing on routine orders that if we so much as put a hand in it we were to report immediately to sick quarters. And yet the local Egyptians washed their clothes, their donkeys and themselves in its disgusting water, as well as using it for cooking. As for the camp itself, it was a vast sea of bell-tents, apparently full of discontented aircrew waiting to be posted to a squadron, or further training, or indeed, anything but being stuck in a place like this. The only facilities were the mess tent and the NAAFI tent. As someone said about the camp, 'If Shallufa up the road is the head of a cow, this is the other end.'

After spending an evening in the mess listening to endless tales of woe, I found out that there were two Wellington squadrons at Shallufa, about ten miles up the road, so first thing the next morning I hitched a lift there and made my way down to 38 Squadron headquarters, where I went straight to the adjutant's office and asked to see the CO. Although I was only a sergeant, recent experience had taught me that often the direct approach is best, and in wartime things don't always go by the book. In any event, I got away with it, and was granted an audience. I explained how we were an experienced crew who had volunteered to come out to the Middle East to join a squadron, and what a shame it was and a waste that we should be kicking our heels in the Middle East Pool. The CO was very sympathetic and appeared to be interested in getting an experienced crew. After a moment of thought he told me to go back to the pool and that he would arrange a posting. I was over the moon.

We were stuck there for three horrible, miserable weeks in that hole before the posting came through. The only good thing about it was a sneaked very long weekend trip to Cairo. Besides doing all the usual tourist things like visits to the Pyramids, the Blue Mosque, the bazaars, of course we could not resist a sortie down the infamous El Berka, full of exhibitions, brothels and a lot of Australians. I have to say that nothing I saw there caught my fancy, but the Australians were down on leave from the desert and from Crete, and I would think El Berka came first on their must-do list because they were everywhere. I watched a line of Aussies queued up outside one door, all talking or reading the newspapers, quivering with a kind of cup-tie excitement. Every five or ten minutes the door would open, and out would pop another Aussie, slightly embarrassed grin on face, tucking himself in while a slim blonde beauty (I didn't get a close look) invited in the next in line. She must have made a fortune in turnover. Perhaps, after El Alamein, when all the troops moved out, she retired to a little cottage in Cornwall or some such place, and lived happily ever after in the firm knowledge that she had done her bit for the welfare of the troops.

As we stood there and watched the age-old drama, Joe Arsenault began to express an interest in joining the queue. I felt like his father. I told him sharply that he'd likely lose a whole lot more than his virginity. Then Barrington, the rear gunner, decided to join a school of other Aussies playing 'Two-Up', where you throw three coins up in the air and bet on how they land, in the middle of the street. Wonderful. Suddenly it was all too much like keeping under control a litter of rowdy puppies with tongues hanging out, eager to rush off and get themselves into everything. Sighing with my heavy responsibilities, I gathered up my errant crew and got them to leave behind this interesting but sordid part of town.

At last in August 1941 we were posted, to 38 Squadron, Shallufa. Any initial joy was soon stifled after sitting in the mess and listening to the crews talking about their ops. Most of the trips then were against Benghazi, mainly because at that time there was not much else around to bomb. They called this 'the mail run'. You took off, bombed Benghazi, then landed at a desert landing strip where you refuelled from four-gallon drums, then returned to base. Ho-hum. The trips were generally uneventful, except for heavy flak over the target. So I was delighted to be called into the flight commander's office and told that my crew, together with a new second pilot, Pilot Officer MacPherson, were to join the 38 Squadron detachment in Malta. It was now early October. Our posting had taken months.

From Shallufa we set off in our new Wellington T2749 for Malta, stopping at LG60, a basic desert airfield on a salt lake, for refuelling from the four-gallon drums, hot and tiring work when you have to do it all yourselves and then fly for seven more hours. The take-off at dusk in the middle of the desert was a bit unusual, hazardous, really, since all we had to go by was the dying light at the far end of the salt basin. I pointed to it, opened up, and, as we got close and had flying speed, just eased off and set course. After that it should have been routine all the way to Malta, only it wasn't. We hit every flyer's nightmare.

We had just passed the point of no return when in the dark ahead I could make out a line of huge clouds, cumulo-nimbus clouds, tall cloud-formations made partly of ice-crystals, characteristic of thundery conditions. Not nice. There was no way around them; they seemed to reach from the sea upwards to a tremendous height. I was going to have to fly right through them. We were flying at around 5,000 feet, and as we entered the thick cloud I don't think I have ever experienced anything – not flak, tracer-fire, nothing – like the next ten minutes in all my years of flying. Outside the aircraft it was pitch black, and I could hear hailstones banging at the cloth fabric of our bomber, while abrupt shifts in pressure kept tossing us about as if by a large cat's paw. With the co-pilot's help I had literally to fight the controls just to try to keep the wings roughly level against this constant lurching pressure from outside. I put the nose down slightly to avoid stalling and to increase our speed so we could get through these damned clouds as quickly as possible. My arms ached as we both continued to struggle with the controls, and after what felt like hours of constant battle, really only five minutes, suddenly we appeared to have been spat out into a relatively clear blue sky. I looked at the altimeter: 10,000 feet. Incredible. Even though I had put the Wimpy's nose down, the terrific up-currents in the middle of the cu.-nim.clouds had lifted us right up about 5,000 feet, and a Wellington weighs, at rough estimate, about 30,000 pounds. These things were all too common at this time of year. We had been extremely lucky. About three hours later, a very tired, very relieved crew set foot in Luqa, the right airfield this time.

Although tiny and in an 'undefendable situation', Malta was an excellent base for a wide range of targets in Italy, Greece, Cyrenaica and North Africa, and at that time one could well perceive its significance in the overall Mediterranean war. It lay on a direct route to Tripoli, then the chief port for Italians and Germans in North Africa. But on the debit side it is less than sixty miles from Cape Passero, Sicily, and suffered almost daily from the proximity. For about 140 years it had been a British naval base, and when war broke out the entire strength of the airforce there was, I think, four Gladiators. One was wrecked, leaving the remaining three, known as 'Faith', 'Hope' and 'Charity'. By the time I reached Malta these three were history, the defence of Malta now left to Hurricanes, flown in at great expense and sacrifice from aircraft carriers. Of the three airfields only Luqa had a runway. In November 1941, the Axis air force in Sicily was reinforced by Luftflotte 2, in from the Russian Front, and soon after all air force units in the Mediterranean were placed under the command of

Feldmarschall Kesselring, whose brief it was to suppress Malta. It became of vital importance for the Axis to neutralise the island, and they set about this in no mean fashion; the constant raids on airfields and docks, known as 'The Siege of Malta', went on for years. But now that the Germans had taken over from the Italians there was a marked increase in accuracy and firepower. Luckily our air officer commanding was the redoubtable Air Vice-Marshal Hugh Pughe Lloyd, whose own brief was not just to defend the island, but also to attack targets in Italy, Sicily, North Africa and Greece (Crete).

Although we were an experienced crew, conditions in Malta were very different from those back in Britain, so we still had to do a proving flight on joining the 38 Squadron detachment. Mine was as second pilot to an Australian, Sergeant Nankiwell, attacking Naples (usually the railway sidings and docks), a target I was to come to know well. It was uneventful, but the large amount of flak over the target surprised me. Having done this I was soon in action with my crew, and on 21, 22 and 24 October, we attacked Naples and had two trips to Tripoli, where we bombed the railways and docks. The Naples operation took about five to six hours; Tripoli took only about four and a half. Although heavily defended, Tripoli was a fairly easy operation, only two hours across the sea so crews were much more alert, less tired from a long flight. The only problem was on the way back, as we missed Malta, and this was the major disadvantage of being based there. It is a tiny island, barely 117 square miles if taken together with its neighbour Gozo, and if the weather was bad, or your radio was playing up, Malta could be very difficult to find. Sometimes, although they were not too keen on doing it, they put a searchlight up, which was a great help to us, but could also serve wonderfully well as a guide to enemy bombers. Whenever, on returning to base, I could see a lot of flak and searchlights, I'd circle well away until it was all over and we could land, if the runway had not been too damaged. On Malta you got used to landing on anything as long as it was ground.

We very nearly were not allowed to get used to landing on Malta. Incredible as it may sound, after only three operations, and after all the time and trouble of getting us there and training us, we were to be sent back to Egypt, replaced by another (inexperienced) squadron coming out from the UK. I was furious, but the fury was mitigated somewhat by finding out when they arrived the next day that the new squadron was in fact my old one, 40 Squadron, from Alconbury. Two different flights were coming out: B Flight had come direct, a dangerous way, since by the time they could look around in the sea for Malta they would be at the limit of their endurance and fuel. They'd mostly been lucky over Sicily and not attracted any interest. But still one aircraft failed to arrive, Sergeant

Paine's, which had, we found out later, run out of fuel and crashed into the sea, no survivors. Some lesson was learnt from this at least: A Flight came out a few days later via the 'safer' route, Gibraltar. Even so they too had lost a crew who had crashed on take-off, killing all on board. My old flight commander, L.J. Stickley, was now CO, so I went to put my tale of woe to him, of how I had been buggered about since leaving Alconbury, and how we were now being shunted back to Egypt.

'Hm.' I think he was smiling. 'I can well do with another experienced crew, especially now that we've lost two. I'll see if I can fix it with the AOC.'

It worked. Not only did I stay with my old squadron, but kept my aircraft, too.

By this time – late October/early November 1941 – the raids by Ju88s, Me109s and Me110s were getting heavier and more frequent, especially on the harbour and airfields. I think that the Maltese were probably the most bombed population of the war. All the squadron NCOs had been living in barrack blocks on the airfield up to now, but the CO decided this was too dangerous, so we were moved to what had been the Poor House and Leper Hospital, both large, barn-like buildings with cavernous dormitory rooms, about half a mile from the airfield. Living conditions generally were pretty primitive, but there we were better off than most of the locals, many of whom had taken to living in underground caverns. Our crew finished up in a huge dormitory for six without any electricity, but Smithy, the wireless operator, said he could soon fix that. He climbed through the window, brought in a wire from the mains somewhere outside, acquired a fuse box and put a nail in it as a fuse, so at last we had light. I don't think the clerk of works would have been too pleased. More than anything else daily life in Malta prepared me for Stalag Luft III.

Despite the winter weather, mostly a mixture of rain and sunshine, and the constant bombing raids, between mid-October and late January 1942 I averaged almost four operations a week. But the bombing took its toll in many ways, one being that it made it difficult to do the usual air tests, those necessary short trips to check that everything worked when flying. Of the twenty-three operations I flew between 1 November to 28 January, I flew only one air test, and that one was very close to the airfield. So it was with relief when one got safely airborne, since there was always the worry that the aircraft had sustained shrapnel damage on the ground, unnoticed in the pre-flight checks. Night take-offs were a bit of a worry, too; with a bomb load on, not very much runway and one end of that finishing in a bomb storage area and the other in a deep, boulder-strewn ravine, the margins for any error were slim indeed.

By December the bombing was devastating: the airfields torn up and many aircraft lost on the ground. Just after Christmas part of our Poor House was hit, no casualties, luckily, but eight or nine Wellingtons destroyed. Some of the bombs dropped had been dispersed amongst the bomb dump, causing a massive explosion. Any time spent on or near an airfield was dangerous, consequently any flight-planning, briefing and take-offs had to be kept short and quick. Arriving back from ops was also a worry; you had to fly around until the all-clear, hoping that you had enough fuel, that any stray fighters didn't take a sudden fancy to you, and that the runway hadn't been too damaged for you to land in one piece. The safest place to be, as well as most congenial under the circumstances, was any bar in Strait Street, that part of Valletta known as the 'Gut'.

The shortage of aircraft after some of the heaviest raids meant that even together with 104 Squadron, on some nights we could only put up a few aircraft. We tried everything. Wellingtons in transit from Gibraltar to Egypt would be requisitioned. Once or twice when aircraft returned from operations they would be quickly serviced, refuelled and sent off again with another crew. In spite of the ceaseless intense pressure the ground crews did an amazing job repairing damaged Wellingtons and cannibalising wrecked aircraft, working all the time under the most terrible and frightening conditions, prime targets for any raid. I hope they know how much they were appreciated.

I still had the crew who had come out with me from England, except for Gordon Byrne the second pilot, who now had his own crew. After about seven ops I settled down with Sergeant Joe Brogan, a good pilot who fitted in well with the rest of the crew. I always felt that if anything did happen to me the aircraft and crew would still be in safe hands; Joe could get them back. It makes for a happy crew when you all have faith in each other's abilities. Joe stayed with us for the next twelve trips.

Our targets were varied. Naples was the most common, but we went to Brindisi and Taranto in Italy, Patras in Greece, Tripoli and Benghazi in North Africa, bombing mostly rails, docks, airfields and any transport. It was different from Germany in that there were no searchlight belts and the flak was not so ferocious, so we were able to bomb from a much lower altitude which also made for greater accuracy, making two or more runs over the target, and we didn't carry oxygen. On some of the raids – the so-called 'nuisance raids' – we would stay for up to two hours over the target, dropping our bombs one at a time, like stinging wasps that would not go away, keeping people stuck in their air-raid shelters for as long as possible.

My first three raids with 40 Squadron were on 1, 6 and 8 November, all to Naples. The first was uneventful, but the second was more in the line of flying under the Menai Straits Bridge under fire. After we had dropped our bombs I spotted, shining in the moonlight, a barrage-balloon, so I thought we'd have a go. I had her in a dive towards it when the rear gunner reported a night-fighter coming up after us. Pulling her out of the dive, I did a semi-stall turn, but while we were still in a steep dive from that we were coned by searchlights and I found myself suddenly disoriented. By the time I'd shaken my head and recovered, the Wellington was only 500 feet above the streets of Naples, with a couple of searchlights still on us.

'Get the searchlights!' I yelled at the gunners, and took her down to rooftop height. We lost the searchlights, and the night-fighter as well; searchlights didn't go down to street level, which was where we were now, and I guess the night-fighter had more sense. Heaven only knows what the local residents thought as they looked out into bright moonlight to see a Wellington screaming full tilt down their (nice, wide!) main street. There is a point after which you can't do anything except get on with it. We howled out over the harbour, the gunners silent now so that none of the warships would notice us passing by; just as I'd got us low over the water I spotted a warship hard on the starboard side. As we shot past it full throttle, I could see Joe's .303 Brownings blazing away. Silly bugger was trying to sink a battleship with a pair of .303s. On the battleship, meanwhile, all hell was breaking loose. The only reason I can think of that we survived this episode was that the Italians couldn't hit an oversize barn door with an .88 mm. Our front guns abruptly stopped, replaced by the sound of rude French words; Joe's guns had seized, much to my relief. 'Sorry, Skipper,' he sounded genuinely regretful, 'my guns jammed.'

The island of Capri, beautiful in the moonlight, beneath us, we headed out to sea for Luqa, our only damage being a few bullet holes and a bit of our port aileron missing.

Two nights later, on another beautiful, moonlit night, we were off to Naples again, this time on a nuisance raid. Approaching Naples, looking down on Capri and over to where Vesuvius was smouldering, a bright glow in the night, I couldn't help but feel sorry for the Neopolitans, being so highly visible all the time. Thanks to Vesuvius, even smokescreens gave the city pretty ineffectual cover. From Capri we simply ran up to our targets, the railway and dock area. After about twelve attacks, each from a different direction to confuse the guns (it didn't work, they were not confused), I was coming in for the final run, west to east and inland, when I spotted in the distance an airfield, with a lot of planes parked around it. It was too good to pass up. I called out to the gunners to be prepared, and told Smithy to man the single Browning (fitted specially for all Wellingtons in Malta) in the port side of the fuselage. I went off some distance from the airfield, throttled back, then turned in a shallow dive for it. We got down to a low level, running at a fair speed for a Wimpy, and, giving it full throttle, roared down the starboard side of the runway, all guns blazing. I think we must have taken them completely by surprise, because we'd nearly got clear before the shit began to fly. Fly it did, in all directions, hardly any of it our way. As we climbed away I told the gunners to stop firing so we could creep quietly out to sea.

What damage we inflicted I'll never know, but our little initiative had done the power of good for the crew's morale; we all felt a bit wild. The gunners had enjoyed really being able to fire their guns, letting loose. As I climbed away over the sea, Smithy came into the cockpit, a look of what could only be described as excitement on his face. 'I think I've been hit!' he announced, his hand on his cheek. The co-pilot peered at his face, but could only find a red mark, caused by a bullet hitting his chin-strap which then whipped against his cheek. I think Smithy was disappointed, and certainly more thrilled than frightened about his close encounter with a bullet. Listening to him in the mess later one would have thought he'd just destroyed the entire Italian air force with his single Browning.

This would be the last trip with us for Joe Arsenault. It was a few nights after our airfield raid, and we had been stood down, so were just going off to bed when a runner came in to tell Joe that one of the other front gunners had gone down sick, and he was being detailed to stand in for him. Joe pulled his flying kit on over his pyjamas, and that was the last we ever saw of him: the entire crew never came back, and Joe, dour, fearless, dependable, inarticulate Joe, was gone with them. 'I only hope he hit a few on that destroyer,' said Smithy, and we all agreed. It was all you could say. That evening we tried to drown our sorrows in Valletta, but it didn't work, everyone was too miserable.

Operations went on throughout November and December. We completed thirteen operations in November, including bombing the Italian fleet in Taranto, a couple of trips to Naples, a low-level attack on the MT (Motor Transport) yards and petrol installations in Tripoli, a long trip of seven and a half hours to Patras in Greece to attack three petrol tankers in the harbour, and another low-level attack on Berka Airfield, Benghazi. We escaped with only a few hits over Benghazi.

When I say these trips were 'uneventful', I mean in the sense of our not getting actually shot. In other respects they could be anything but. On one of the trips to Naples, just as we were over Sicily, the navigator Mason (he of the tin hat protection for his manhood) was seized up with violent stomach pains, a case of the legendary 'Malta Dog', an extremely nasty form of advanced dysentery, and he had to make a hasty run for the Elsan propped up in the fuselage. Joe Brogan, the co-pilot, was detailed to drop his bombs instead so poor Mason could stay on his throne, and all the way to Naples his moans could be heard above the engines. It wasn't that we weren't sympathetic, since Malta Dog was all too common and left one completely debilitated, but we just wished he'd come down with it before getting on board. All was going pretty well – we'd done three good runs at the target in spite of the heavy flak – when we were caught by searchlights. Instantly I took violent evasive action, including some negative 'G', which forces you out of your seat. Alas. A scream from the fuselage, then: 'I'm covered in shit!' Now, the chemical toilet was not normally used for such extreme conditions and so there were no toilet rolls. Everyone else was keeping well away from Mason and his smelly plight. Flak on the outside, Mason on the inside – I don't know which was worse.

'Can you get yourself cleaned up?' I shouted back to him. Then I had an idea. 'You could use some of those propaganda leaflets we're supposed to drop. There's masses of them.'

So I circled around for a while until in language I could never repeat Mason announced that he was as clean as he could manage. I made that final run over Naples to a chorus of: 'Get rid of ALL the leaflets!' I often wonder what those poor Italians unlucky enough to pick up one of Mason's special leaflets thought. When we got back to Luqa he was still on the bog (now stood upright). You have never seen an aircraft abandoned so smartly. They even refused point blank to let him onto our transport, so we left him, pale and dejected and stinking like a sewer, sitting alone in the moonlight, waiting for an open truck to take him to station sick quarters.

This wasn't the last of Mason. Once, just as we were about to board our plane for Catania, in Sicily, Mason discovered that he'd forgotten to put his navigation bag on the bus. 'We haven't got time to go back for it,' I told him shortly. 'I've got an ordinary map; you'll just have to map-read.'

We took off and set course for Cape Passero on the southern tip of Sicily. We'd done this so often that I knew the course well, and, with such a clear sky, one could almost see it. As we approached the coast, Mason was standing beside me with his map in his hand, ready. He then slid open the window on his side and turned to say something to me, gesturing with his hand, yes, the one with the map, right beside the window. It was gone. We had no maps. I thought Joe Brogan was going to cry. We informed Mason that he was now completely redundant and he could go off and sit on his bog if he liked for the rest of the trip. In fact it was all fairly easy: we followed the coast up to Catania, where the ferry goes across to Italy, dropped our bombs and went home the same way. Who needs navigators?

In between operations we kept away from the airfield, for obvious reasons, and spent our days in the Poor House mess. It was too cold to go swimming, so in spite of the more or less constant bombardment life was a little boring. The main diversion was when the air-raid siren sounded and we'd all go up to the roof to watch the Junkers 88s coming in and our boys, in whatever serviceable Hurricanes they could find, would engage them in combat. Evenings we headed for the bars in Valletta, especially those in the Gut, where we had a couple of favourites, mostly The Egyptian Queen. The bar girls found in The Egyptian Queen were mostly decent, ordinary girls who'd been caught up in the war with no other work available to them. As bar hostesses they would join your table and you bought them a drink – really coloured water – which cost about a shilling, then you could dance with them. They got half the drink money, and we danced the night away to the strains of a local three-piece band, mostly playing Glenn Miller. When I got back home from the Middle East, Mary wondered where I'd learnt to dance; I didn't like to tell her at the time that it was with another Mary in a dive called The Egyptian Queen. As NCOs we were paid every fortnight, and towards the end of each fortnight we were usually skint, so one economy was to change from drinking beer to drinking the local wine, which I think we called Ambeit. This was not a good idea: Ambeit was rough and red, and only cost us about one penny in present-day money for a tumbler full. It might have been made from grapes; it was certainly vicious, and it featured regularly in orders that aircrew were not to drink the stuff. Quite rightly, it was definitely not life-enhancing. At any rate, during this period of financial embarrassment our two hostess friends, Winnie and Mary, would come over to the table several times in the course of the evening, buy us drinks (not Ambeit!) and have a dance. I think the management knew pretty well what was going on, but as we were good customers turned a blind eye. The girls had good, warm hearts, but tarts they were not; none of us ever got further than a dance and a chaste goodnight kiss.

We made the most we could of life on Malta, but all the time I felt sorry for the local people. Because they'd been bombed on a daily basis by the Italian Air Force, they hated the Italians, and when the sirens sounded they all disappeared underground. Valletta is built on soft sandstone, and even before the war the city was riddled with catacombs, but now the Maltese had bored many more tunnels into the sandstone, and these, together with many natural caves, became home to hundreds of families, living in bunk-beds and existing on the most meagre rations. It was sad to see the carts collecting discarded slops from the mess, and the village people fighting to be able to buy a dip of our kitchen waste for a few pennies. The worst hunger we had to put up with was during a raid, when the mess staff disappeared and the dining room was locked. If we were off on operations, too bad; we got no food. There were grumbles, but we all knew it was nothing compared to what the Maltese were having to put up with.

Christmas 1941 arrived, and for some unfathomable reason we had been stood down for a week. The squadron officers invited a collection of us NCOs into the officers' mess for drinks. This sedate drinks party wasn't quite enough, so when it had wound down, the CO and several of the officers invited us – me, Bob Munro, a New Zealander, and a Canadian,

Pete Potter – to continue with them in an officers-only bar in Valletta. They gave us their raincoats to wear to cover up our NCO stripes. They also gave us a lot of the kind of booze we just weren't used to drinking – shorts of all sorts, all very warming and very strong. After a while you don't notice much, and as the party was getting a bit out of hand, we were all eased out into the cold Christmas night, our new officer pals declining to come down with us to the Gut. It was a wise move. Around this point my memory fades, but we must have made our way to the Gut, because Pete fell through a window (plate-glass, we later found out) into some small dive there. I'm not sure how we managed it, but we wound up after him, on our backs in the middle of a very surprised three-piece band. There were also some tables involved, and quite a bit of noise, one way and another. The service personnel there were very amused; the hostesses much less so. By the time we'd managed to stand up more or less, the place was full of Maltese police, who tried to march us down to the police station. I don't think they found it easy. In the police station everything was just beginning to quieten down when one of the officers started making crass and insulting remarks about the RAF. I took exception to this and tried to get over his desk to deal with him personally. I was pulled off him by about three police and they locked us all up in a cell.

After we had been in the cells for about an hour, just enough time for the hangover to kick in, the adjutant, 'Tom Tit', appeared, our Christmas angel. He had a long discussion with the officer in charge – unfortunately, the same one I had gone for – and we were released into his care, but there would be a number of charges brought, including one of assault (that was me). Back we went to the Poor House, sore and hungover, not looking forward to Christmas Day. But every day is a new day, especially when you're young, and you don't dwell too much on the mistakes of the previous day.

Because we had been stood down over Christmas and in spite of pounding heads and faulty memories of the cells the night before, we enjoyed a lie-in until we had to be on duty later together with the officers, serving the airmen their Christmas dinner, as is the tradition in the RAF. After that was finished we had the officers over to our mess for drinks, before sitting down to our own dinner. This was a magnificent meal, and where it all came from God only knows. I assume it had been flown in by one of the transit Wellingtons or perhaps a Sunderland from Egypt, but believe me, I wasn't about to ask. We'd be back on corned beef and tinned rice pudding soon enough, but right now we tucked into hors d'oeuvres, oxtail soup, fillet of whiting, roast turkey, pork, assorted vegetables, Christmas pudding, Scotch woodcock and coffee. (I know this, because Joe Brogan recently gave me a photocopy of the menu, signed by most of the squadron.) Later that night we were back down in Valletta, avoiding the Gut, having a few quiet jars and pondering last night's activities. 'Life in the Gut is more dangerous than over bloody Naples,' Bob said sagely, and the rest of us agreed.

The following day Bob and I were called into the CO's office, where he told us we were to go before the AOC, Air Marshal Sir Hugh Pughe Lloyd, for a commissioning interview. That night found us both desperately scrounging around the billets trying to rustle up clean shirts and collars and tamping the most egregious stains out of our uniforms. I thought we were looking spruce that morning of the interview, until I spotted a big hole in my sock. 'Never mind,' said Smithy, 'we can paint your leg with blue ink. They'll never notice.'

At last I was called into the office to face a board of three senior officers. I'd met Sir Hugh before on some of his visits to the squadron, and he had been in attendance at one of our de-briefings, but still I was surprised and flattered when he smiled at me and said, 'We've already met.' In this august presence I could feel that hole in my sock shouting out loud, so I tried to hide it by tucking in my legs and looking reliable. That apart, the interview seemed to be going well, and Sir Hugh expressed amazement that although I was only twenty I had completed forty-two operations. After fifteen minutes I saluted smartly and left.

New Year's Day the entire squadron was stood down. I was just wondering what to do with the day when I was called in to the CO, Wing Commander Stickley's office. He told me that one of the new Wellingtons, the Mark II, had landed, and before it went on to Egypt the AOC wanted someone to take a 4,000 lb bomb in it and drop it on an airfield in Sicily. I don't know where they'd got the bomb from, since the Wellington Mark I with its Pegasus engines couldn't carry it, but the Mark II with its Merlin engines certainly could. I was a little apprehensive at flying with these new engines, with only the Pilot's Notes and a 'Good luck' from the CO to help me on my way. We took off after dark, the sheer power of the aircraft taking me by surprise. I was beginning to enjoy myself; I loved the idea of dropping this huge bomb on Castel Ventrano airfield, and flying this new model Wimpy was a joy. So when, as we were approaching the target, the Wop/AG called up that he was getting a recall message on the radio, I told him to ignore it.

'We'll just tell him the radio was temporarily u/s.' I was blowed if I was going to miss a chance like this one. Besides, the airfield was right below us in the moonlight, with a lot of aircraft dotted about; it was too good to miss. We had a good run up and bombed from about 7,000 feet. By this time there was quite a lot of light flak about, so I simply turned tail and got the hell out. Meanwhile, the rear gunner called that he'd seen a big flash and thought it was the airfield. 'That'll wake them up, if nothing else,' I said. I was pleased with the whole thing.

As we headed back to Luqa the wireless operator said he'd sent a 'Bomb Gone' signal in the Q code, but so far had heard nothing back. 'It's too late now,' I said. 'They can't have it back.' And anyway, I did not fancy landing on the runway at base in a strange aircraft with a 4,000 lb bomb on board. If I was being truthful that was probably why I'd ignored the recall in the first place. The landing, even without the bomb, was more of an arrival; I hadn't appreciated how heavy those Merlin engines were, but with a few bounces we were down, and that was it. I'd had my first and only flight in a Merlin Wellington.

At de-briefing they asked us why we'd ignored their signal. They must have sent it while the operator was still struggling to get the new wireless serviceable, we blandly told them. Wing Commander Stickley gave me a funny look, but we heard no more about it.

But my past was catching up with me in other ways. The next day after the Big Bomb, I was called into the office, together with Bob and Pete, to be told by the adjutant that we had to appear in court in Valletta to answer 'a number of charges'. He would defend us himself, Tom Tit told us; he'd been a solicitor in civilian life. Once again we dragged out our best blues and marched off to the courtroom, the image of clean and sober if rather nervous youth, where a judge in full rig looked down on us and asked us sombrely how we would plead.

'Guilty,' we said, just as we had been advised to do by Tom Tit ('You just plead guilty and leave the rest to me.'). The police gave their evidence – most embarrassing – and then Tom Tit stood up.

'These three fine young heroes,' he began with, and allowing that idea to sink in, he went on to expatiate to the court how we had been risking our lives daily to bomb the Sicilian airfields in a brave effort to stop the Germans as well as the Italians from bombing Malta. All under twenty-one we were, so young, non-drinkers more or less, who had been Led Astray by the officers who took them to a Christmas party and filled them with strong drink To Which They Were Not Accustomed. It was the Strain these fine young men were feeling in their constant operations to Save the People of Malta, etc etc.

Just when we were beginning to feel really good about ourselves, the air raid warning went off. Panic ensued and the entire courtroom scrambled for the door, the judge losing his fine robe in the rush. In moments all was empty except for the three accused and the adjutant. So we sat down and had a cigarette (everyone smoked in those days), and after about half an hour the all-clear went. The court, judge, policemen and all, began to trickle back in, rather sheepish. Tom Tit – not one to miss an opportunity – made the most of this, sternly pointing out to the reassembled court that we had been abandoned and might all have been killed. 'Humph,' was the only comment from the judge, but he called the police up to the bench and after some mutterings between them, announced that all charges were dismissed, but that we were to pay for the plate-glass window. He might have been about to add something to that but at that moment the sirens went off again, and as before we stood alone in an otherwise emptied courtroom.

'To hell with this,' Tom Tit said. 'Let's get back to Luqa. I'll sort something out tomorrow.'

And that was the last we heard of it from the Maltese point of view, but we did have to pay for the window. I suppose they could just about cope with windows being bombed by the Germans, but it really hurt to lose them to friendly fire, as it were.

But worse, far worse, came of it all the very next day. Bob and I were in with the adjutant and the CO, Wing Commander Stickley, when the phone rang. 'Good morning, sir,' the CO said. Pause. 'I'm afraid I must assume all responsibility for their actions. We took them to a squadron party forgetting they are so young and not used to drink, and I'm afraid we really should have taken them back to camp . . . Yes . . . Thank you, sir.' He put the phone down, then turned to us, his face stern.

I have to say that in those pauses we both died several deaths. We waited, my mind at least was full of my commission disappearing out the broken plate-glass window.

'That,' said the CO, 'was Sir Hugh Pughe. He has heard about your escapades and about the court appearance yesterday. I must tell you that he is not amused.' My stomach sank. 'But,' his eyes held our terrified ones, 'he has accepted my explanation, and this time will ignore your behaviour.'

We mumbled our thank-yous, and we meant it. Stickley had put his head on the line for us. I'd known him since Wyton, and to me he was a wonderful CO.

My four trips in January were to be my last from Malta and occurred on the 14th, 16th, 18th and 21st. On 16 January the operation was a kind of pre-emptive strike, dropping bombs singularly on any of the eastern coastal Sicilian airfields showing lights. A convoy with vital supplies for Malta was due in from Alexandria, and the idea was to prevent any German bombers from being able to take off to attack it. I honestly don't know how successful we were, but we spent three hours just flying from one airfield to another. The convoy had a rough passage, with most of it sunk, but managed to get 21,000 tons of vital supplies of food and ammunition through.

After my last trip – one to Sicily aborted because of thick cloud cover, what a way to end a tour as it turned out – I was called into the CO's office and informed that our crew, or what was left of it, had completed more than enough operations without a rest, so we were under orders to fly to Egypt and from there to return to the UK by ship. My heart sank; I knew this meant I'd be sent to an Operational Training Unit for a long spell of instructing. This dismay must have shown in my face, because the CO said quite sharply, 'To date you have been lucky. You have completed forty-eight operations without a break, and you're getting too cocky and over-confident. You're taking unnecessary risks, so it is for your own sake and the sake of your crew that you now take a well-earned rest.'

I suppose he was right. I considered for a moment the constant bombing, the terrible accommodation and food. During our time there the air raids had steadily got more frequent and heavier; in January after the Poor House was bombed we had been moved into the Naxxar Palace, which in spite of its grand name was appalling: crowded, lacking electricity or lavatories, the food disgusting (maconachie stew and corned beef still make me gag). I was fed up with all that, true, but I would miss the wonderful squadron spirit, the good friends I had made. These, I realised, were many. Although I had flown with my own crew, with trusty Joe Brogan as co-pilot until he got his own crew, there were numerous times when one or other members of the squadron had filled in, especially people like Keith Coleman and van Walyk, both rear gunners, and all first-class crew and good friends. Still, there was some compensation to be had: both Bob Munro and my flight commander Bill Craigan were tour-expired, and we were all to fly out together when the next transit Wellington passed through. My time in Malta had been both exciting and sad. Joe Arsenault had been killed, and several more friends 'missing'; in all six crews lost on operations during my time there. Another good friend, Frank Sunley, had been killed when the aircraft he was about to board for an operation was bombed, the rest of the crew injured but escaping death. Death was always right there next to you.

So, after many fond farewells in the mess and in the Gut, and many beers, we were off on 27 January taking over a transit Wellington, much to the annoyance of the transit crew, and with a last low-level run over the squadron huts we waved our good-bye and left Malta.

CHAPTER SEVEN

An African Holiday of Sorts

After a five and a half hour flight, we landed at LG 224 in the desert for refuelling, then it was forty-five minutes to 107 Maintenance Unit, where we left the Wellington we'd hitched a lift from. From there it was back to the Middle East Pool. We prayed it would not be too long a stay this time. In Kasfareet everything was exactly the same as before: the camp full of disgruntled aircrew from all over the world awaiting posting, the bell tents for six, with empty mattress covers for a bed and a lot of sand. Sighing, we picked the stones out from the sand, put out kitbags for pillows, and stuck up some nails to hang clothes on. Then we went down to the mess. Everyone hung around the mess; there was bugger all else to do, except talk or argue. It would be March before the powers that be were able and/or finally saw fit to ship us home. What a waste.

I have never been positive that there was any connection or any concern on the part of the authorities about having thousands of young men with lots of energy and only limited ways of expending it kicking their heels, but certainly within the space of about ten days Bob Munro and I were both promoted twice and our pay backdated several months. What could we do but celebrate?

So, sporting our new flight sergeants' stripes and crown, off we went to the mess for a little sampling of various beers from around the Commonwealth. One of the favourites was an Australian brew called 'Richman Bitter', better known by us as 'Richman Fighting Bitter' because of the troubles it caused towards the end of an evening. There were no glasses in the mess, so beer was either drunk straight from the bottle or, if you were feeling civilised, out of some improvised glasses made by tying a piece of string soaked in paraffin around the neck of a pint bottle, lighting the string, then knocking the top off. Of course it was a good idea to file it afterwards, you didn't want your evening to start off with a cut lip.

Three days and three hangovers later Bob and I were again called in to the Orderly Room, this time to be greeted by a pleased-looking flight lieutenant, who told us that our commissions had come through: we were both now fully-fledged Bog Rats. He gave us some pilot officers' stripes to put on the epaulettes of our shirts, so the flight sergeants' crown and stripes so recently acquired were pulled off to make way. Complete with new side-hats and accompanied by the rest of the crew who obligingly carried our kit-bags, Bob and I trundled over to the officers' lines. On the threshold of our new abode everyone was pulled up in amazement: compared to the rest of the Middle East Pool this was luxury indeed. Bob and I had a large square tent to ourselves, with two (made-up!) camp beds, canvas wash basin, table and chairs. We were now due besides all this the princely sum of seven and sixpence 'hard living' allowance, where before as lowly sergeants we'd got one shilling and sixpence. We were also allotted a full-time batman, an Italian POW we called Fred.

'Why don't you escape?' I asked him once. I couldn't imagine why he would stick around in a hole like this with the enemy when escape was so easy.

He threw up his hands in horror. 'I am very happy here. When we (I liked the 'we') have won the war I will go home to my wife and children.'

The officers' mess was excellent (and you didn't have to do funny things with paraffin and string to get yourself a glass). Food was much better, and the company pleasant, but life was still pretty boring, the only excitement being censoring airmen's letters, a job I hated. If you wanted to sit in the mess in the afternoon, though, you had to do it, reading through the frustrations of men as frustrated as yourself. Small wonder I was looking for any excuse to party.

Let me see. First we celebrated what I thought was my twenty-first birthday. Then we celebrated it again (having got the date wrong the first time). Then we thought it might be prudent to take a repairing lease into Cairo and get some new kit made by one of the excellent (and cheap) military tailors there. Of course you cannot leave it at that, not in a lively place like Cairo. There was famous Shepheard's Hotel[1] to visit, then a near-miss in Opera Square involving some drunken Australians hijacking a gharry, and of course, a hopeful trip out to the Mary's House by the Pyramids[2], where we were smartly disabused of our chances as two mere pilot officers: 'You might as well forget it. There's half the senior officers of three services queuing up.'

---

[1] One of the many stories about it concerned some fighter boys there on a stand-down. They were having a whale of a party. It was about one a.m., and songs were being sung, full chorus, unprintable lyrics, all enthusiastically led by an officer. Suddenly a figure, upright and resplendent in silk dressing-gown, appeared at the top of the stairs, furious. Silence fell. 'I am Major Sir Somebody-Something, MC,' he boomed at them. 'This noise must stop immediately!' 'Oh?' The wing commander who had been leading the singing got up and faced him, swaying slightly. 'Well, *I* am Wing Commander the Earl of Bandon, DSO.' Pause. 'I think that's got you fucked on all counts.'

[2] There is the famous story about the admiral killed when the Mary's House in Alexandria was bombed: the Admiralty didn't know whether to list him as 'killed in action' or 'killed on active service'.

'Next time,' I said, 'we'll bring our own girls and pay corkage.'

You might have thought that this would be enough for one trip, but no. Pushing to the limits, we hitched a lift from an Army lorry to visit an old rugby friend of mine in Alexandria, a doctor colonel in the military hospital there, who hospitably gave us a comprehensive tour of what I should think was every bar and hotel in and around Alexandria. The rest is rather a haze to me, apart from the massive hangover, which continued to hang on. I hate being ill. It wasn't until after a day and a night of sickness and stomach ache that I finally dragged myself to the MO.

After a brief examination he got right to the point. 'Jaundice. No alcohol for at least three months and stay away from the fried food. No fats at all.'

I suppose I felt relieved that it wasn't anything worse, but no beer and no wine for three months . . .? That did make me miserable. Obviously it was bad for the health not being on operations.

And still there was no sign of a boat. The adjutant assured us we'd have plenty of time to pay a trip to Jerusalem, so three of us, Bob Munro, myself and Pilot Officer Byrne, my former co-pilot, set off for the Holy City, hitching a lift from an Army truck. It seemed appropriate enough, given my abstemious condition, that we stay at the YMCA, which besides being cheap, had the added attractions of being in a lovely building and serving wonderful food, fresh vegetables and meat. But *anything* would be a big improvement on the Middle East Pool. It was a fantastic break. During the day we went round all the places God would want us to go, while at night we explored places definitely on His mustn't-do list. I feel we broke even. I enjoyed the peculiar feeling of trying to swim in the heavy salt water of the Dead Sea and felt the frisson of seeing oddly-familiar Biblical places such as Jericho, the Garden of Gethsemane and the Wailing Wall.

Still, it was to be several more dreary weeks in Kasfareet before finally in March Bob Munro and I embarked on the *Mauritania* for Durban. After that long wait we, all the waiting personnel and quite a few civilian females who had been stuck in Egypt, were indeed lucky. The *Mauritania* was one of the top luxury liners in the pre-war P&O, and I understand that it had been put on the Suez-Durban run to ensure its continued safety. That first night on board when we went down to dinner we simply stood in the entrance and gaped: none of us bumpkins, especially after the conditions in Malta and the Middle East Pool, had dreamt of such opulence still existing in the rest of the world. The dining-room was in pre-war livery, with chandeliers, pristine linen, silver and china. Each night a five-course dinner was served by waiters in monkey-jackets. We had died and gone to heaven. The only sign of its wartime role as troop-ship was found in the accommodation as our twin cabin was fitted out with bunks for six people, but as all the trooping was in the opposite direction there were only a few of us going to South Africa/UK, so it was only

Bob and I in our cabin.

Most of the troops on board were RAF who had finished a tour of ops. There were several from the Abyssinia campaign, others from the Greece and Crete fiascos, and even a couple from Iraq who had been there during the pro-Axis revolt, when the Iraqi army attacked RAF Habbaniya. Listening to them was like something from Biggles: they'd mostly been flying antiquated aircraft, biplanes. One fairly ancient – at least forty! – warrant officer I spoke with had finished a tour and still not flown an aircraft with a retractable undercarriage! When operations started in Abyssinia the RAF and SAAF were mostly flying Gladiators, Gauntlets, Vincents and Wellesleys, the Wellesleys being the only monoplane. I also had a long chat with a flight lieutenant just liberated from a POW camp in Abyssinia. We talked about his constant tunnelling activities; the memorable thing being that his tunnelling was through solid rock. I would remember this much later.

Apart from a few Army and Navy personnel, the rest of the passengers were civilians, mostly female (thank you, God) who had been trapped in the Middle East and were now on their way back to South Africa or the UK. It took Bob and I less than a day to find two young ladies playing deck tennis, enveigling them into a foursome and getting them to chat over drinks (soft). We learnt that they were on their way back to South Africa, accompanied by their mums. The mums, constantly in attendance (I can't imagine why), were going to prove an obstacle to be overcome. Our luck held out: two flight lieutenants came to our rescue and selflessly engaged the mums to themselves. Soon it was the mums trying to get rid of the daughters, so what could we do but oblige? The elders and betters bagged the cabins; we had snug little slots behind the lifeboats. I cannot remember their names; I hope to God they've forgotten mine long since.

That first part, at least, of the long trip home was an idyllic voyage, about ten days at sea in balmy spring weather. It got even better at Durban, where there was a real sense of occasion as the ship landed: a band was playing, and as we got off the boat we were surrounded by people offering us hospitality. I have no idea why they should do this but they did, and we were grateful. I am afraid that in the completely blissful social whirl that followed, including the Durban Tennis Club, convivial occasions at the Mayfair Hotel, the Cosmo and Stardust clubs, the delicious, cheap South African wine, the steaks and eggs and all the trimmings, picnics up in Pietermaritzburg, lovely sunny days . . . I don't think those words 'diet' or 'jaundice' once crossed my completely prepossessed mind. I got on with having the time of my life.

But all too quickly we were back in the real world. The *Empress of Russia* was a far cry from the *Mauritania*: an ancient and creaking pre-war liner, definitely non-luxury. She'd been converted for trooping from the

UK to the Middle and Far East, manned by European officers, with Chinese and Indian sailors. Myself, Brownie, Bob and one poor Army captain were four to a small cabin. At night when you lay sweating in your bunk, the infernal creaking would start at one end of the ship and slowly travel back while you lay awake listening to it, unable to sleep. Chinese water-torture. I felt really sorry for the other ranks sleeping jammed in together in hammocks. As there was a mixture on board of all three services, mostly RAF and Navy, there were always three duty officers, one from each service, doing the rounds together.

The second day out I was duty RAF officer when we were called to a disturbance down below, in the latrines. Further investigations made it difficult for me to keep a straight face. The latrines were simply a long row of cubicles, open in front, the seats over a long tin tray which ran the whole length of the cubicles and then, I presume, out to sea. It appears that after breakfast, when the cubicles were full, one of the Navy boys thought it would be a good idea to soak a piece of newspaper in cigarette lighter fuel, light it, put it onto the metal tray at the top end and flush it along. The chorus of yells which marked its progress was something that unfortunately sticks in the memory. One musical type compared the sounds to a kind of human xylophone, and thought that if only he could have shifted them around a bit he might have got a tune out of them. However, those with the singed bottoms and other equipment were less than amused; they went for whoever they thought responsible and a whole series of angry fights broke out. I couldn't really blame them; they were hoping their equipment would shortly be put to use back in the UK. Calm was restored, with many firm promises of no repeat performances. Lunch in the officers' bar afterwards was hilarious, with all kinds of lewd suggestions put forward for setting up a lower deck chorus, and a unanimous motion never again to eat sweetbreads while on this ship.

After only a few days of the *Empress of Russia* we put into Cape Town for a week. More holiday! On that trip to the Holy Land I'd met a nice South African army type, also on leave, who asked me since I was to travel home via the Cape to deliver a letter to his parents there. Not one to miss any opportunity I presented myself, together with Flight Lieutenant Brown, and the letter. We got our just reward: not only the parents but their very pretty daughter Kathleen fell over themselves to make us feel welcome. We were wined and dined and generally treated to real Jewish hospitality, and they insisted on taking us out and showing us around the Cape. Kathleen even found a friend to keep Brownie company.

We had a thorough introduction to that beautiful part of the world, visiting all around the Cape area, the quiet university town of Stellenbosch, the Paarl vineyards, and Kathleen's parents insisted on paying for everything, all the expenses of the daytime trips, as well as our drinks and food. Their generosity staggered us. All we were allowed to do in return was take them out in the evening. It wasn't until our golden wedding anniversary in 1992 that I finally returned, with Mary.

All good things must come to an end. Mine certainly did, with a vengeance. Even though the evenings had not been as heavy drinkwise as in Durban, once again I was beginning to feel rough. I suppose I really should have listened to the MO in Kasfareet and stayed off the booze for three months rather than three weeks, but it would have been such a wasted opportunity. Back on the *Empress*, a day out from Cape Town, I was put into the ship's sick bay, on the top of a three-tier bunk bed. The heat was terrible, the smell even worse. After only a few days in this sweaty cesspit I couldn't take it any more; I hauled on my clothes and told the Doc that I wasn't infectious and I'd rather, much rather, be in my own crowded cabin. 'I promise,' I said to him, 'not to drink, and I will keep to my diet.'

The journey as we crawled up the African coast was unremittingly wretched. We stopped only once, at Lagos, to take on coal for this antique tub, and there were two U-boat scares. I never did mind facing the enemy in the air, but the thought of being torpedoed off the coast of Africa and going down in this floating coffin terrified me, perhaps not least because I cannot swim well and I hate feeling helpless. I spent most of the rest of the trip sitting in the bar miserably drinking my healthy orange-juice. It must have done some good as by the time we docked in Liverpool I was feeling much better.

I wish I could say how pleased my family was to see me. I suppose they were really, but they couldn't get over the change in my appearance. After passing through Customs white, or should I say yellow, with fear because of the considerable amount of illegal tobacco and cigarettes I'd brought as presents for everyone, I rang father to collect me and Bob Munro, who had nowhere else to go. Father was farming, and so had enough petrol to ensure that we were picked up about two hours later by my two elder sisters, Marjorie and Betty.

'You left for the Middle East in July a rosy-cheeked, bright-eyed young pilot,' my sister Marjorie kept going on when they arrived, 'and look at you now. Only ten months on and you're hollow-cheeked, yellow-coloured and that awful moustache. You look terrible.'

'I've grown up, that's all.' I decided to take the moral high ground. "I've been to war, don't forget. I've endured the hazards of Malta and forty-eight operations . . .' I wasn't about to tell them that most of the damage had been caused when we were not on operations but enjoying ourselves. But we had needed such enjoyment. In Malta, you had to take your mind off the fact that when you weren't being shot at in the air, you were being bombed from the air. There are some things you can't tell your older sister.

CHAPTER EIGHT

Tied Down

Before going up to No. 12 OTU, Chipping Warden, as an instructor on Wellingtons, I had a fortnight's leave at the beginning of June. A good thing too, the good fresh farm food and general fuss I would get at home would help me get back some of my wrecked looks and health. Not everyone coming back from a stretch in the Middle East was as lucky as me – springtime on a Welsh farm means ham and eggs, spring lamb, fresh air – just what the doctor had ordered, in fact. And best of all, Mary was able to come up from her farm near Kenilworth. I went down there to lend her a hand with her milk round; the early risers there I think were a bit startled to find a pilot officer delivering their milk. What had the war come to? At first she was a bit horrified at my yellowish complexion and at my lovely moustache in almost equal measure. She was already having some difficulties in convincing her father that I wasn't too wild and my looks did nothing to help this impression, although I do have to add that we got on well eventually.

Maybe it was the cold, clean country air of spring and home and Mary; maybe it was relief and joy at still being alive and returning to my usual healthy old self; certainly I was happy now in a way I'd nearly forgotten about in the heat and dust and complete absorption of the Middle East war, with its frantic social life and constant threat of death in its many horrible forms. In any event it didn't take long for the big decision to be reached, and off we went, Mary and I, on a quick sortie into Birmingham. More specifically, to Goodrick's, a ladies' fashion shop owned by Mary's aunt, where her father was the accountant. When I was actually stood before him, though, I was brought up short by a bout of uncharacteristic terror. Eventually, stumbling over every word, I asked him if I could please marry his daughter. Wing commanders, that judge in Malta, no look from any authority I'd encountered in the last two years made me tremble like the one from Mary's dad at that moment. Then, to my complete surprise, he smiled (almost with what looked like relief, this did make me wonder) and vigorously shook my hand, pleased. With Mary's mother he set the wedding date for 3 October. Confronted by all this future bliss in store, though, I'm afraid the most consoling thought to pass through my mind was Still Three Months of Freedom.

It was my parents who put up the obstacles. They thought we were too young, and it was difficult to explain to them, without sounding too morbid or negative, why we were so keen to get married as soon as possible. At the back of my mind, at the back of everyone's mind, really, even though it was hardly spoken of, was the awareness that the chances of survival, especially in Bomber Command, were not good, and it would be some compensation at least to be able to spend some time as husband and wife.

'Anyway,' I told my parents, 'we're not exactly rushing things; we've known each other since 1937 and worked together at Gorringe's. We've been through a lot already.'

Marriage wouldn't make much difference on a daily basis, though, as service wives were not encouraged to live beside their husbands, especially on operational stations. I was the one who'd persuaded Mary to join the Land Army instead of the WAAF, thinking even then of some kind of possible future together on a farm. Hard luck on Mary that I later changed my mind.

When I arrived at Chipping Warden in late June 1942, not exactly pleased to be there, I was nevertheless relieved to see quite a few familiar faces already there, especially from 40 Squadron, including my old friends Dick Broadbent, Jim Whaley and my former rear gunner, Don Taylor. I also met for the first time fellow Welshman and rugby player Gwyn Martin, a good friend until his death in 2001. After only a week I was to be whisked off to Upavon in Wiltshire, for an Instructors' Flying Course flying Oxfords, almost like going back to the beginning again. I hadn't flown anything for months now, so this was a perfect way to polish up a few skills, and the countryside from the air was stunning, Salisbury Plain with Stonehenge. A lot of our flying time was spent with another student in the back to practise our instructing patter on; it was mostly a very pleasant, relaxed time.

But trouble is never very far away from where I am. I soon discovered that an old friend of mine, Howell Jones, a solicitor from Wrexham, was now a captain in the Army and adjutant (as many solicitors turn out to be) at an Army training centre in nearby Tidworth. Of course we got together; he came over for a dance, and we took him flying. I think the experience went to his head, because he suggested that the next day I should do a shoot-up of the mess at Tidworth. He must have known I couldn't resist. Next day I was up over the mess, and after having done a couple of nice low passes, very low, in the Oxford, I noticed a procession of smart cars with outriders all coming slowly down from the tank training area. This was too good to pass up. 'I can resist anything except temptation,' Oscar Wilde once said, and I think he must have had me in mind. I went down as low as I possibly could and raced to meet them head-on, practically at their level. Showdown. It must have been terrifying. At the last possible moment the outriders peeled off into a ditch, and as I pulled up it struck me that on the bonnet of the first car there was a flag still fluttering from the rather close proximity of my Oxford. Oh, dear. Top brass or royalty, either way it could be very nasty. 'I think we might have dropped a brick here,' I said to the co-pilot, Chappel, and we tooled off for home.

When I told all to my instructor, Flight Lieutenant Hatton, he didn't tick us off but suggested that we ring my friend Howel and hope for the best. Howell was most amused. It did cross my mind then that he had set us up, but again it seemed that luck was with me. The general involved had thought it a marvellous piece of flying and appeared to be more annoyed that his outriders had chickened out.

On 2 August I finished the course and returned to Chipping Warden a fully-qualified instructor of multi-engine aircraft. Our flight had just converted to Mk III Wellingtons, with the more powerful Bristol Hercules XI 1,500 hp engines with sleeve-valve radials, which meant that you could maintain height with only one engine, most important when you're trying to stagger home with one engine shot-up. With this model you could also feather the propeller (that is, when you lose one engine you can still rotate the propeller blades so that they offer minimum resistance to the air), and there was a little more speed and a higher ceiling. None of this made much difference in training, but it was a wonderful boost to the morale of an operational squadron.

Before very long, though, I was aching to get back onto operations. At only twenty-one, and after all the excitement of dodging bombs daily on the ground in Malta and flying through the streets of Naples, to me instructing was completely boring and dull, each day just like the one before. My later career in the RAF involved quite a lot of instructing which I enjoyed, but now I craved something more stimulating than the routine recital of cockpit drill. Being away from operations never did my health any good either; boredom makes you push the limits. And in wartime you did things that in ordinary life would get you arrested. To take the edge off a dull day I'd go off with Gwyn Martin into Banbury or cycle along a bridlepath to our local pub, the White Hart at Woodford. The return trip from the White Hart, late at night, could be quite hazardous, as, halfway along the bridlepath, just around a blind bend, was a gate that was sometimes closed. Feeling wicked, we sometimes would challenge the students who'd come out with us to a race back to camp. Then, as we hared on our bicycles down the bridlepath, Gwyn and I would let them draw ahead, then wait for the inevitable yells and crashing of bikes and after a decent interval, throw out the anchors.

It got worse, embarrassing, even. In mid-August, Gwyn announced that he had been invited to the summer ball at a station in Moreton-in-

Marsh, with some old friends from the 75 NZ Squadron, and asked if I'd like to come along. This offer of a free party was music to my jaded ears, and off we roared on Gwyn's motorcycle into the lovely summer evening. Moreton is less than a hour from Chipping Warden, and we got to the mess just as things were picking up. I threw myself in, accepted I don't know how many drinks, and cannot remember a thing about the rest of the evening. Gwyn has enjoyed telling me many, many times how the last he saw of me was when I had cornered Wing Commander Hughie Edwards and was telling him in the certain heavy tones of the truly drunk, that he really should get operational, that was the only thing to do. Gwyn dragged me off him, thank heaven. I really should have noticed, even in my highly inebriated state, the VC on his chest. The VC was earned after Edwards, having been in two crashes and still preferring to stay on ops, flew a dangerous low-level operation over Bremen.

But I still don't remember any of this. I woke up at dawn in a ditch. I do remember thinking what a nice, comfortable ditch it was, and that it was a clear and crisp summer morning with the birds chirping away and absolutely no sign anywhere of an airfield. Picking myself up and dusting off my hat, I was unsuccessfully trying to recall any of my doings of the previous night when a farm worker came along the road, presumably on his way to milking. When I asked him the way to the RAF station he looked puzzled, as well he might, but pointed to some wooden huts off in a field not too far away. 'I think that's part of it.'

It wasn't. Twenty minutes later I was staggering back to the mess with a big flea in my ear from the extremely cross WAAF I'd woken up with my hammering on her hut door. I had no idea where I was supposed to be billeted, and the staff were already cleaning up party debris from the anterooms, so I decided to lock myself in the loo and get a few hours' kip before anyone arrived for breakfast. It was getting on for midday when I finally met up with an equally hungover Gwyn, and we set off for home.

I suppose it was the fresh air and the ride through the sleepy Warwickshire lanes that did it; certainly by the time we'd come into a pretty hamlet with a real old country pub in it, all the residual aches and pains had dissolved as far as we were concerned and we were ready for a fresh start. 'Hair of the dog?' said Gwyn, and having parked the bike, we entered the low door of the pub where the four very elderly patrons greeted us.

It seemed that the landlord's wife was out shopping so he couldn't offer us any food. All he had, he said, was beer, plenty of beer. I have little real memory of those few hours, but we all must have been making serious inroads into the beer, the landlord included. I do recall the mighty crash as he collapsed on the floor, all the glasses he had been collecting up shattered around him. We rushed to his prostrate form, put his head up on the tray he'd dropped, brushed most of the glass safely away and tried to make him as comfortable as possible. 'Oh, thanks, boys,' he muttered at us. 'The wife'll be back soon.'

Well, the military always know when to retreat. In an alcoholic haze I vaguely remember walking uncertainly to the bike and trying to get on it behind Gwyn. I don't really know how much longer afterwards there was a hell of a yell from Gwyn and I was flying through the air into a field where I landed with a painful thump. It seems that having somehow failed to take a corner Gwyn had hit a telegraph pole. He was all right, sitting dazed beside the road, but I had to crawl through the very prickly hedge I'd been thrown over. I don't know what part of my battered body hurt the most, but the bike looked the way I felt: scratched, bashed but basically fine, but with the handlebars bent to an angle of forty-five degrees. We decided it would be good to have a little rest before trying to get back on the road and off again. I honestly cannot remember a great deal about the details of how we did it. I later heard what we looked like from a WAAF ambulance driver who followed us for a way near Chipping. She said she came up behind this motorbike moving very slowly up the road like a doddering old man, its steering erratic. She decided it might not be prudent to try and pass it, so simply followed it for a while, increasingly amused. Apparently my hat flew off and to her amazement I stepped off the moving bike after it and simply plopped into a ditch. Gwyn turned to see what had happened, and what with the wonky steering, he came off, too, and joined me in the ditch, where we lay, incapable of movement. With her assistant she managed to get us both up into the ambulance and back to sick quarters. The woeful story does not end here.

It was lucky, however humiliating for me, that we had a wizard MO, Squadron Leader Rees, with a sense of humour and who knew us both all too well.

'I'm going to have to put you under for some minor repairs,' he said to me lying there.

'I don't think I need much putting under,' I mumbled.

He did it anyway, and while I was under my flight commander had come down to see what had happened. As he was cleaning up my cuts and grazes the MO said to him, 'Let's teach this young bugger a lesson.'

I came round, still groggy from anaesthetic and whatever booze was still floating around in my system, pain all through my body, to see a hazy white figure at the end of the operating table with a very large carving knife in his hand. Holding my pride and joy in one hand this figure said briskly, 'Well, we'll have to have this off for a start.'

I screamed, he told me after. 'Don't! Don't do it, doc! I'm getting married soon!' Oh dear. I never lived this one down. And almost worst of all, the person holding my head was a WAAF nurse.

Our mess summer ball was towards the end of August, by which time I was nearly repaired enough to be able to face Mary, who was coming down by train from Kenilworth. I was supposed to meet her at Banbury station, and when she stepped off the train, my heart did a little flip: she was stunning, her dark-brown hair all neatly coiffured, with a very pretty bright floral full-skirted evening dress on, full of excitement at her first RAF ball. The only trouble was, I realised as soon as she laid horrified eyes on her transport, having to ride pillion in an evening-gown on a motorbike might not be the best start to a good evening. I tried to make it as quick and painless as possible, and as soon as we got back to the mess I smuggled her up to my room for a bit of damage-repair. Of course she looked gorgeous. The ball was a great success, not least for us. We had needed this all too fleeting chance to be young and having fun.

About one o'clock in the morning it occurred to me that I was going to have to get Mary back to Kenilworth in time for milking and her milk round, and that the only means of transport was Gwyn's motorbike. But when I announced that we were off, Mary had her milk round to do, everyone appeared to take strong exception. Gwyn and Dick especially pointed out to me that it might not be such a great idea. 'You're drunk,' was what they actually said. They were clear on that.

'But,' I hesitated. Thinking was not coming easily. 'Kenilworth. What will they do without their milk on a Saturday?'

Well, they did get their milk that Saturday in Kenilworth. Mary was driven home in a Wolseley I bought on the spot for a fiver from an armament squadron leader, with no tax disc, no proper lights, wonky steering and its tank filled with 100 octane aviation fuel.

The dull routine of instructing finally came to an end early in September, when I read in station orders that an experienced crew was wanted to volunteer to join 150 Squadron, Snaith, in what is now Humberside. Immediately, I talked it over with Gwyn, who was equally keen to get back onto operations, and we decided to ask two NCOs, Jim Whaley and Don Taylor, who'd flown with us before, to join us. Unfortunately, Wing Commander Morris, who commanded Training Wing turned down point-blank this marvellous proposal. 'You have only been instructing for six weeks, Rees,' he said to me, 'and I expect you to do a lot more.'

Furious at his attitude I tried to argue, which only got me thrown out of his office. I never had liked him, and I think the dislike was mutual, but that was no reason, in my view, for him to try to stop me. Nor was I stopped. I had a card up my sleeve in the shape of the station commander, Group Captain Davey, my old squadron commander at Alconbury, so off I went to station headquarters and persuaded the adjutant to let me see him. It had been a year since he'd laid eyes on me but he straightaway congratulated me on my commission, and then asked what he could do for me.

I told him. He was the kind of man you could be absolutely straight with. 'We're the only crew volunteering, sir. I really think we should be allowed to go.'

He looked at me. 'Well,' he said, 'if you are all foolish enough to volunteer for another tour I can see no reason to stop you.'

I grinned like a schoolboy, thanked him and ran off to tell the others, only just able to restrain myself from going over to Wing Commander Morris's window and raising two fingers.

That weekend before going on leave we threw a little leaving party at the White Hart, Woodford. It was very nearly a complete disaster on a Maltese scale. There was quite a large crowd of us, and at closing-time we all decided it would be a good thing to carry on partying at the dance in the village hall. At first it wasn't too bad. There was a basic sort of band playing, lots of girls and a jolly atmosphere, but the resentment on the part of the local lads was simmering. After all, we seemed to have taken over their pub, drunk all the ale and were now pinching their girls for a dance. Then Dougie Fox threw an apple-core out the window. At least I think he meant for it to go out the window, but by then his aim was not very steady and it hit one big lad smack in the eye. That was it. The whole place exploded. For once I was being fairly sensible and keeping at a safe distance from the sidelines. I was peacefully watching the battle going on when a fellow came up to me and declared that I was chicken, that I should come on outside and he would deal with me. (These were not his exact words, of course, but you get the idea.) Peacefulness never lasts long with me; I duly went outside. It was soon obvious that he wasn't really much of a fighter and I quickly had him down, but then the blighter pulled me down on top of him and started to wrestle. Humph. I turned him around, got an arm-lock on him and he gave in. About this time everyone else appeared to run out of steam or will or something, so declaring ourselves victorious we all set off on our bicycles, bells clanging, to finish the party in the mess. At the time I thought it was splendid, but I would hear more about it later.

I hadn't told my family and I hadn't told Mary that I was returning to operations. I honestly don't think it even occurred to me that they might have some feelings in the matter. The closest I came to admitting to myself that I might not have got it right was the fact that I never dared to confess to Mary that I'd volunteered. I was young, too full of the heady excitement of living day-to-day in danger. I was an addict. So, like any true addict I could stow my doubts somewhere else and throw myself into the complete enjoyment of my few days with Mary, making plans for our wedding in a fortnight's time.

CHAPTER NINE

Snaith, not far from Little Heck . . .

It was 19 September, 1942. I stood for a while in the middle of all my packed luggage and thought for a moment about loading it all up and taking the evil five-pound Wolseley up to Snaith. It still had only half steering to the right, a beer label in its tax disc, no insurance and was filled up with aviation fuel. I'd tried to sell it, but evidently no-one else was as desperate as I had been that night I bought it. Heaving a sigh, I abandoned it and went up instead on the train to the tiny village of Little Heck, the nearest station to Snaith.

Gwyn hadn't arrived yet, but we were sharing a room almost opposite the pub in Little Heck which quickly became our second mess.

The very next day I did all the usual things to do with moving to a new squadron, booking in with all the various departments who needed to know where we were on the station such as accounts, equipment, officers' mess, drawing my parachute, finally reporting to Flights, where I met up with Taylor and Whaley. Then came the interview with the squadron commander, Wing Commander Carter, a good pre-war regular officer who liked being on operations. He was strict but fair, and he and his wife were known to enjoy the odd wild party in the mess.

'I'm glad you volunteered, Rees,' he said to me. 'We've had some losses and I asked for an experienced crew. With your experience I expect you to set a good example to the rest of the squadron, and if you do, you'll probably be made deputy flight commander in the short term, and take over as flight commander from Squadron Leader Kirwin when he completes his tour of operations, most likely November or early December.'

Difficult not to grin at that. I was thrilled. Sergeant to squadron leader in less than twelve months. I was determined to do it, dead man's shoes or no. 'My navigator should be arriving in a few days, sir,' I said. 'And, uh, I had planned on getting married on the third of October. With permission, of course, sir.'

Carter smiled. 'I'd like you to do a little bit of local flying to get settled in, but you shouldn't have to go on any operations until after the honeymoon.'

That night the squadron went on a raid to Essen, and Sergeant Granville and his crew failed to return. So it is you are made to realise that you're back on an operational squadron.

Next day I had to go through it – new boy in town, wedding, etc – all over again with my A Flight commander, Squadron Leader Kirwin, a very English Australian, and the rest of my new colleagues. Kirwin became a good friend. I felt a bit awkward asking for leave almost as soon as I'd arrived, but he was fine about it, and Gwyn was also given leave to help get me to the church on time, as he'd promised Mary he would do.

It was a good thing he had, too. We set off on 1 October, somehow managing to get to Ruabon (with a railway warrant made out for London from Snaith), where we were joined by my best man, Bob Munro. You may well ask why we had to go to Ruabon when the wedding was to be in Solihull. I could say that of course I wanted to have a few home touches before my wedding, but really what happened was a monster bachelor party, completely unplanned, which began in my favourite pub, the Trevor Arms at Marford, and finished up at Acton Hall with Sydney Aston. Sydney, twelve years older than us, not as well trained at living it up the night before the day you have something important on, enjoyed himself so much he failed to make the wedding.

Next morning Bob and I motored down to Solihull in father's car. There was plenty of time, since the wedding was to be early afternoon at Olton Church, but really it was not a good idea, this being bright and early, more of a fatal mistake of the usual kind, since there was nothing to do in Solihull but wait in the hotel. Two pilot officers, a best man and a groom just about to get married stuck in a hotel bar is quite simply a recipe for a party. Drinks kept coming and who were we churlishly to turn them down? They cheered us as we wove away, off to the church. I have to say that when crunch time came, we pulled ourselves together, both best man and groom appearing steady and reliable and as happy as they should. Mary arrived on time, looking as radiant a bride as one could ever hope for, and in a way that boded well for our future life together, kept me more or less on line for the service.

We never made it to our honeymoon hotel. Bad weather and the usual newlywed preoccupations kept us in High Wycombe that first night. Next day I found out that because we hadn't contacted them the hotel had let our room, and the only vacant place I could find was at the Regent Palace. Now, the Regent Palace was the place in London to take one's girlfriend, no questions asked. So, when I met one or two people I knew there and introduced Mary as my wife, they burst out laughing. After three days of honeymoon, plus quite a lot of dancing and eating and drinking well, I received the signal to report back to Snaith. Dropping Mary off at her farm in Kenilworth, I kissed her, gave her a breezy 'See you next leave' and drove back up north. Little did we know how long that would be.

Back at Snaith I was quickly engrossed in work, learning all I could about the Mk III Wellington and how it differed from the older model I was used to. I had of course flown the Mark III at Chipping Warden, but now we really needed to be clear about any other variations from the Mark Ic. There was a spot, for example, to store the pigeons we now carried. The idea was that if you came down in the drink and you'd remembered to collect your pigeon before taking to your dinghy, you then sent him off with the good news and to alert the Air/Sea Rescue boats. Unfortunately when we were actually shot down the poor pigeons were barbecued. I should think that happened a lot. More useful, certainly from Gwyn's point of view, was the new radar Gee box which in these, its early days, meant far more accurate navigation. There was also more room to store ammunition. The heating was supposed to be more dependable, too, but it was not infallible. The other significant change was that there was no longer officially a second pilot on Wellingtons, a second pilot only going along for experience to train him up for when he took over with his own crew. I'd already trained Gwyn to fly straight and level, though, so that when leaving enemy territory I could actually get up to spend a penny. But the old smells remained the same, of engine fuel, cordite and the residual sweaty fear off our bodies.

As a crew we felt confident, ready to start our tour. There was a lot of collective experience: Gwyn and Jim had flown over thirty operations, and Don, at twenty-four the old man of the crew, had in excess of forty ops in Europe and in Malta. I'd done over forty, twenty in Europe and twenty-eight in Malta, while the only rookie was the front gunner, Sergeant Dalzell, an Australian in the RAAF.

It was quickly borne upon me that since my last operations in July 1941, Bomber Command had changed a lot. When Air Chief Marshal Sir Arthur Harris took over as AOC-in-C in February 1942, losses had been heavy and morale was very poor. This all changed as Harris slowly built up the bomber force. His three stated aims for the force were expansion, better training and better navigational aids. It was he who brought in the 'one-pilot' rule, which at once cut down on the number of pilots needed and allowed them to get more initial training, completing eighty hours at OTUs instead of the fifty hours we'd had, before being sent to a squadron. Harris also saw to it that some of the aircrew's various functions were revised and made more efficient. The Wellington navigator's sole responsibility was now to be simply navigation, the dropping of bombs assigned to the front gunner/bomb aimer. The wireless operator would have to be able to man a gun in an emergency, but the front and rear gunners would no longer have to be trained as wireless operators. This, of course, was sensible, as it meant each crew member could get better and longer training for his primary duty. In practice, though, there was no way Gwyn was going to give up his place as a trained bomb aimer to some sprog front gunner. This was fine with me. I knew Gwyn's capabilities, and I also liked to keep both gunners in their turrets at all times.

It was also around this time that Harris dictated a first tour of operations to be thirty operations, since it had been worked out by the statisticians that this offered a fifty-fifty chance of survival. A committee had in fact been set up in January 1942, which decided on several crucial points of number-crunching: 1) that thirty sorties was about right for a first tour; 2) a crew could be considered 'operationally efficient' after ten-fifteen sorties; 3) second tours were to be twenty sorties. It was not clear to me then how this left our crew, but as it turned out, the question was academic.

On 28 September we were introduced to our brand-new Wellington, BK309, with not a speck of dust on it and smelling of clean oil. That first test flight was a joy. Everything worked, and we set to getting it just the way we wanted it. Gwyn tested the new navigational aids and swung the compasses while Jim calibrated his radio and the gunners gave their Brownings several good bursts. We were fired up and ready to go.

The first operation in BK309 'N' for 'Nuts' was on 10 October, mine-laying off St Nazaire. Although it was the most common of operations this was my first mine-laying operation. It was a task to which the AOC-in-C gave his full approval, in conjunction with Coastal Command: he felt that such attacks would force the Germans to divert more of their war effort into anti-mine-laying devices to keep their sea-lanes open. On paper it appeared to be an easy trip; we were quickly disabused. We went out at low-level over the sea and were to drop our mines from 300 feet at about 150 mph, but when we got to the target area there was suddenly a lot of light flak coming from all angles. Yet again it happened that the first aircraft to reach the target attracted most of the flak, so coming in slightly later ours was a reasonable run. Coming back home that night, flying low-level over France in the clear, moonlit night, I felt again the joy and odd beauty of being in the middle of it all, the war. Below us a train popped into view. We flew alongside it for a while, doubtless terrifying the passengers inside. The gunners wanted to have a go, but really we couldn't; it was a passenger train probably full of Frenchmen. Instead, I winged us off home to de-briefing and bacon and eggs, then bed.

We were off again the next night, on another 'gardening' trip, this time in the Heligoland. There was some nasty rocket and light flak about, and we saw one aircraft going into the drink, but ours was a relatively quiet trip. We got back, bushed after nearly thirteen hours operational flying in two days, to find that two Wellingtons and one Stirling had failed to return.

One day off and on 13 October we were briefed to bomb Kiel, part of a major operation involving 288 aircraft that night: a hundred Wellingtons; the rest four-engined Lancasters (eighty-two), Halifaxes (seventy-eight) and Stirlings (twenty-eight). This was my first bombing raid over Germany since mid-1941, and much had changed. Briefing and planning were far better organised, more methodical. Instead of picking our own routes and directions of bombing, I now found that we had to stick to set routes and times. Although myself I preferred the old tactics I quickly appreciated the greater efficiency of the new, especially having the Pathfinder Force to locate and mark all the target area. If all went well, the Pathfinders made our jobs that much easier and more accurate. Also on board was Pilot Officer Vincent, here to get a little experience of ops before taking his own crew. When we arrived at the target, too, there were differences: the searchlight belts were more concentrated, the flak heavier. As we turned onto the target Gwyn went down to the bomb aimer's panel, and I asked him to keep me weaving until the last possible moment for his bombing run. We had already arranged the height and airspeed. It did fleetingly occur to me as we were running up to our aiming point and the flak around us was getting even heavier, practically in our faces, to wonder what had possessed me to give up my safe and easy instructing job and put myself back into a place like this, with people trying very hard indeed to kill me. Of course, there is no real answer. The truth is I craved adventure and pitting my skill, so hard-won, against anything those bastards on the ground could throw up. Doubts disappeared as I got on with the job, throttling back and starting a glide onto the target. By now the flak was so thick it seemed impossible to fly through, much less fly through and not get hit. Gwyn's calm voice came in on the intercom, directing me to the target, when the rear gunner cut in to say he had just seen in the searchlights a stick of bombs falling just behind us.

'Bloody marvellous,' said Gwyn. 'Bombed by the big boys flying 10,000 feet above us.' It did happen. But not that day, not to us. As for poor Vincent, the whole episode left him, well, gobsmacked.

Now we were at the correct height of 9,000 feet and correct airspeed, running up on target, always the dodgiest time; Gwyn took over directions while I kept it straight and level. 'Left, right . . . left . . .' The flak by now was nearly impenetrable and the stench of cordite all-pervasive as you flew through the bursts...an age of this agonising slowness and death before a final: 'Left . . . two degrees, steady . . . Bombs gone.' With relief so strong it was almost joyful I opened to full throttle and with a mighty weave, nose slightly down, got the hell out and into the clear air.

'Keep a sharp lookout for fighters, boys,' I called to the gunners. 'We're not out of it yet.' Although we hadn't seen any I knew the Germans now had a far bigger and better-equipped night-fighter force. Apart from the excitement of the target area it was an uneventful seven-hour trip for us. Eight aircraft, including five Wellingtons, were lost; none from Snaith.

Another day of rest, then we were off again on the 15th, another big effort, 289 aircraft to the much-bombed Cologne. Once again Pilot Officer Vincent was in the co-pilot's seat. This was not to go down as a very successful raid. The losses were high (eighteen aircraft, 6.2%). Bad marking by the Pathfinder Force meant that a lot of aircraft bombed a decoy fire site, not the real thing. On the 16/17th we had another gardening trip, to Lorient and other Biscay ports. Once again we were lucky enough to drop our mines while the enemy were busy shooting someone else down. Out of the thirty-four aircraft, four were shot down that night, one of which was from our squadron. After thirteen hours' operational flying in two days I fell into bed and slept right through the next day.

We then had a few days off before the tannoy called us to operations again, another mine-laying trip, this time an important target in Norway, and the top seven crews in the squadron were being dispatched. It appears that intelligence had found out that the *Tirpitz* was about to make a dash for Kiel, using the many inshore channels down the coast of Norway as safe havens en route. One of these was the Karmsund, north of Stavanger. If the *Tirpitz* could be kept out at sea the Royal Navy had a task force waiting for it, so the importance of our operation was obvious. We took off at 16:00 hours, in spite of bad weather and an even worse met report, making for Haugesund, the small town on the Karmsund. But after only forty-five minutes we received a QDR to return to base. I was annoyed. 'Here,' I said to Gwyn, 'you fly it and I'll navigate.'

I got up more with the intention of having a pee. I'd been letting Gwyn fly a little during air tests and some of the general flying around we had to do. It seemed useful insurance in the event of my getting shot, but it also meant that I could go for a pee if needed. Anyway he was pleased enough, and after ten minutes I took over again.

'That was great,' he said, resuming his place. 'Uh, where exactly are we?'

'Haven't a clue.'

He was less happy at that; it took all his skill to locate us and get us safely back to base.

First thing the next day, 22 October, I was called into his office by Flight Lieutenant Pugh. Great, I was thinking as I was shown through, my time has come: Acting Flight Lieutenant Rees. But when I actually asked him about it he blinked, then said, 'Oh, that. Sorry, Rees. It's been approved but it's not yet gone through. It's rather a more serious matter I had to see you about . . . There's a Detective Inspector of Police waiting to interview you over some altercation at Woodford, when you were at Chipping Warden. It seems a railway worker there is claiming you broke his thighbone.'

To say I was stunned by this is grossly understating the matter. Woodford. The fight with the apple core, the man who had called me 'chicken'.

Something in my face must have showed my distress because Pugh asked me gently if I could tell him exactly what had happened. I did, and when I'd finished he stroked his chin thoughtfully. 'Hm. Leave it all to me and I will see about it. I would imagine he's just trying to get some money out of you.'

I grunted. 'He'll be lucky, sir. I haven't got any.'

As I left his office the tannoy called me to operations. We were briefed to do a cloud-cover raid that afternoon on Essen. As we walked up to N for Nuts Gwyn was annoyed. 'What a way to spend your twenty-first,' he growled. 'Bloody cloud-cover over bloody Essen.'

I nodded. We all hated this kind of operation: setting off in daylight, using only the cloud for cover, flying either in or just above the clouds and keeping a sharp lookout for fighters, all the time fingers crossed that the cloud would not dissipate and leave us bright and clear, sitting ducks. 'N for Nuts might be unserviceable,' I said to him. But it was no good. All the checks went perfectly well and everything was in good order.

Even the weather was against us: we came out of our safe cloud into beautifully clear sky at 6,000 feet. As I certainly did not intend moving far from cover it meant that we would be doing the entire trip at this low height, well within the range of light flak. Still rather the flak than any fighters taking bits off us. As Gwyn announced the crossing of the Dutch coast a burst of flak confirmed it. Oddly, I found flak in broad daylight like this not nearly as frightening as night flak. In fact, I found myself becoming fascinated by the black bursts of flak shown off against the backdrop of brilliant white clouds, perhaps not the best time to be caught up by the aesthetics of it all. Otherwise I was trying to keep the gunners below occupied by keeping up with our constant weaving and changing height. Unfortunately all this weaving kept Gwyn busy as well trying to navigate, but his Gee, the newish navigational aid which when working well, projected a ground image onto a screen in his office, was working well, so we stayed on course and avoided the populated areas. As always, once over enemy territory, usually as soon as we hit the coast, engines were de-synchronised to make it more difficult for the gunners on the ground to latch onto us. They tell me it did work, but for us inside the aircraft it was irritating on the ear, and it made you feel that something was wrong.

In spite of all our efforts for an age we seemed to be awash in a rough sea of black flak, right up until Gwyn announced that Essen was just ahead. As he said this all hell broke loose. The object of such raids was not so much to bomb a particular target but to keep the air raid alert on and so disrupt industry, so our bombs were dropped through thick cloud and flak. Once they were off, so too were we; nose down and throttle up I threw dear old N for Nuts around, climbing gradually up through the cloud layer into the blue sky. Fighters or not, the bright, clear air came as a relief after all the murk and smell and noise. I warned the gunners not to relax but keep watch out for fighters, especially into the sun. This constant scanning after a long and stressful flight was terribly tiring, but really, we simply could not afford to let up. They all knew such nagging could save their lives.

As we had had barely a glimpse of any ground since leaving Snaith, I asked Gwyn to let me know as soon as we had cleared the coast. I wanted to let down through the cloud over the sea, come home low-level. But the wind must have changed abruptly, because after I'd got the all-clear from Gwyn and was letting down, passing through cloud at about 2,000 feet, a sudden burst of flak seemed to heave the aircraft up. There was a huge, orange-coloured flash and the ripping sound of shrapnel tearing through fabric, then more bursts immediately around us.

'For Christ's sake, get weaving!' I heard Gwyn yell. 'We must be over Rotterdam.' But I already had the nose down and was busy weaving madly, too engaged even to reply, and at full throttle hurtled out to sea.

'Everyone all right?' I called up to the crew. No-one actually hit, the only troubles cosmetic, thank God, but everyone had shat themselves silly. It was a very, very relieved crew that finally hit the Norfolk coast and cruised north over the fen dykes and up to the pretty fields of Yorkshire. Oh, it was good to hear that welcoming voice of flying control, to make a quick circuit, wheels down – no trouble there – flap down, and with a gentle rumble as the wheels hit the runway, we were safely down. My fifty-fifth operation, I thought, nearly my last. There was a silence in the aircraft as I taxied in, a little prayer of thanks being offered, I think. Mine was.

I can still easily recall climbing out of the aircraft, completely exhausted, and patting good old N for Nuts for bringing us safely back. Then I noticed the look of horror and pride on the faces of the waiting ground crew as they took in the many shrapnel holes in 'their' Wellington. The flight sergeant, pan-faced, said to me, 'You really must be more careful, sir, this gives us a lot of unnecessary work.'

But as the dispersal truck carted us off to Operations for de-briefing I couldn't help a retrospective shudder at events. As a crew we were old hands; we'd come through many operations and we felt in some measure fire-proof. There was a certain amount of truth in the theory that skill and confidence grow as each operation is completed. Experience helps one to deal quickly and efficiently with each emergency as it comes up. But regardless of all the skill and all the experience in the world, there is always the unpredictable, the good old fickle finger of fate like the one we had encountered that day, which can in an instant hurl you from the sky. In fact, statistics now show that Bomber Command had an overall loss rate of about 3% for night operations and 11% for day operations. In practical terms this meant that for every hundred crews going out each night, three were unlikely to return. The empty chairs at each post-op meal told their own sad tale. I suppose 3% doesn't sound too bad, but at this point we were operating with up to three hundred aircraft on a maximum effort, and by the time you had done thirty operations the loss of three aircraft and crew in every hundred had in effect become seventy-five from the original hundred. Nearly 60% of aircrew became casualties. Crews lost on their first operations did account for a high proportion, but the odds against survival to the end of a first tour were still not much better than even money.

So, as our second tour progressed the chances of being included in these grim statistics increased all the time, because there would come a time when skill and experience reached a ceiling and what you needed was a modicum of luck, plain luck. With one gunner on his first tour, the navigator, wireless operator and rear gunner on their second and myself on his third tour, it was not unreasonable to feel that our particular odds were shortening and that the next operation might be for us the end of the line. I am not being morbid, and I wasn't feeling morbid about it at the time, but it was inevitable that it crossed one's mind. These were the daily realities, and especially after this last trip, although we none of us liked to dwell on the fact of our being shot down and killed, it was a real possibility. What we did was mostly close our minds to that possibility: it would not happen to us, not us, even while we knew in our hearts that it could.

The funny thing about life in Bomber Command was that we fought our war while in the midst of a normal, peaceful everyday life. The Army and Navy both, when in action, live in an entirely warlike environment. They become conditioned to the ever-present threat of injury or death and learn to adapt. We lived between operations in complete safety, apart from the odd intruder raid, and life on a bomber station felt and was very remote from war. In the mess one still had afternoon tea, and station standing orders still announced such vital events as kit inspection. Between operations we all relaxed into this peaceful half-life, waking up with a jolt via the tannoy to the inescapable fact that within a few hours we might be flying over enemy territory, all alert for night-fighters, every muscle tensed-up and aching with your aircraft as it and you desperately and violently dodged the flak. Even when life was at its most relaxed however, in the pub or mess bar, in one corner of your mind you lived over and over again that run-up to the target when everything on the ground below was being fired up at you, concentrated on you. That run-up was the most deadly part of your job, as well as the most professional, when the whole success of the operation and the safety of your crew besides depended on the extreme accuracy of your flying. All distractions of searchlights and anti-aircraft fire had to be ignored in that moment when the slightest movement could misdirect the bombs by thousands of yards and onto hospitals and civilians. All that was on you.

Although I realised that things had changed in the past year – the flak, searchlights and night-fighters were all more formidable – this was to some extent balanced out by the fact that there were now three times the number of aircraft on major targets, and the raids were concentrated into shorter periods of time. The Wellington was now the smaller part of the bomber force, and more and more four-engine bombers, Lancasters, Stirlings and Halifaxes, were coming into service. Although this meant we were the 'lowest and slowest', I considered this to be a slight advantage. Rightly or wrongly I decided to bomb even lower, at about 9,000 feet, my theory being that gunners and night-fighters would be concentrating on the more numerous aircraft and the ones carrying the biggest bomb-load.

It took a while for the adrenalin from the Essen raid to subside; we were still pretty high after de-briefing. While we were climbing out of flying kit Gwyn suddenly started to sing, 'I'm twenty-one today, twenty-one today', and broke into a little dance routine, the details of which I refuse to go into. He was immediately promised a monumental party he would never, we averred, forget. I have to say, we were rather talented at throwing parties.

The first move was to secure the services of our gunnery leader, Flight Lieutenant Spud Murphy, and even more importantly, his sex-wagon, a large, black, antiquated Vauxhall. Spud was older (twenty-eight), an Irish barrister very quick on the uptake, a complete wild man, just the person to get any party going. His car had a secret tank beneath the rear seat, normally filled with illicit aviation fuel to supplement his ration of 'pool' fuel. The other members of the party were our flight commander, Squadron Leader John Kirwin, the Australian who had nearly finished his tour, and his wireless operator Flight Lieutenant Lew Cavanaugh, a large Canadian, very useful if things got rough. But of course, why should they? So: Gwyn's coming-of-age was to involve two Welshmen, an Irishman, a Canadian, an Australian and a big black car full of aviation fuel.

As I've said before, I suppose these wild parties were difficult to explain to our nearest and dearest, who saw us all as clean-living young heroes. There was the 'eat, drink and be merry, for tomorrow we die' view, a cliché, but close enough to the truth. I suppose there was the element of bravado, too, in pretending for a while at least not to be worried about operations, all those empty chairs in the mess. It would be foolish to say we were not frightened when we went off on operations, but you always hope that you'll be the lucky ones, and I think that the main definition of courage is your ability to conquer your fear, or at least not to show it, and certainly not to let it dominate you. It was always depressing in the extreme to encounter the occasional unhappy crew member who had obviously lost his nerve and tragic to see them labelled LMF (Lack of Moral Fibre), demoted or drummed out and sent to some backwater where their fear could not infect others. In some cases this came near the end of a tour, often after a terrifying or traumatic experience. With a bit of luck the CO would quickly spot it and arrange a quiet posting to instructional duties without the disgrace of a court-martial.

Tonight, though, we had other things on our minds. The affair kicked off at our local pub in Little Heck, where we'd arranged to meet up with the rest of the crew, our ground crew and some of the other crews from the squadron. It started quietly, as we exchanged stories about the Essen raid, but as the drink flowed the stories grew taller.

'That flak, you know, it was so thick,' Gwyn was heard saying, 'that we used those flak bursts as cloud cover.'

Shortly after we were belting out 'The Bomber Boy's Lament', with its chorus:

Stand by your glasses steady
For this is a world of lies
Here's to the dead already
And here's to the next one to die . . .

Each crew pointed at the other as they drank the toast. Little did I know. Then came 'Salome' and others in the rugby repertoire. I still carry the strong mental picture of a very ancient local, well into his eighties, singing 'If I was the Marrying Kind, and Thank the Lord I'm Not Sir!' as if he meant every word and might drop off with the effort. But then the landlord cut in to announce that we had drunk him dry. Groans. Gwyn gave a final, heart-rending version as only a Welshman can sing it, of 'The Minstrel Boy'. With that the five of us said farewell and went off in Spud's Vauxhall in search of more beer.

We had been driving along for some time when we suddenly became aware that what few vehicles we did meet were swerving violently as we approached them.

'That's all right,' said Spud, 'that's all right. I switched off the lights, you know, just to test the night vision of all those other fellows coming on.'

Groans. 'Put those lights on immediately, Murphy.' Squadron Leader Kirwin was not that far gone. 'That's an order.'

Finally we pulled up at a remote pub somewhere in the bleak fens around Goole, with a friendly landlord who had, he said, just got in a delivery of bottled beer. When he heard it was Gwyn's twenty-first he entered fully into the spirit of things. We left him, long after closing time, fast asleep in a sea of empties all neatly piled up around him.

So, all in excellent form, fortified and in good voice, we set off on deserted roads back to camp. At least they were deserted until a policeman suddenly appeared in the headlights carrying a red lantern, a clear indication if one was needed to pull up and stop. Spud put his foot down. 'Got no insurance!' he yelled. 'No licence, either!'

'You get him, Spud!' came the cries from the back seat as the poor copper leaped for his life into the ditch.

By now we were ravenously hungry, so when a transport café came into sight we decided to try our luck and see if they would take pity on a few young heroes in search of spam and chips. We were just finishing when a very angry policeman stalked in, covered in mud. It was a fair cop, our uniforms and the car parked outside dead giveaways. Slowly, deliberately, notebook in hand he advanced on us, trouble writ large on his mud-streaked face. 'This is very serious,' he said. 'Failure to stop when directed to do so.' He paused for effect. 'There might even be an alternative charge of attempted manslaughter.'

I decided to cut this one short. 'You are terribly wet and muddy, officer,' I said in my best RAF voice. 'Where on earth have you been?'

He blinked, furious. But by then John Kirwin was muttering in Australian something about 'rabbit-eating limey cops' and Gwyn and I began singing in harmony, 'All bobbies are bastards.' Everyone else was giggling. We were enjoying ourselves.

He was apoplectic. 'I've just about had enough of this! Down to the station, the lot of you!'

Off we trooped: one wet, muddy policeman on his bike in his cycle-clips, closely followed by five very cheerful officers in their car. It may have been his anxiety to hand us over as quickly as possible to his desk sergeant, or perhaps his residual fear of being run down again, but certainly he went along at some speed, his cycle-clips twinkling merrily in the headlights to our yells of encouragement and much horn-blowing. The locals must have loved it.

When we got to the station the barrister in Spud took over. John Kirwin, still muttering imprecations about 'rabbit-eaters', was being forcibly restrained in the back by Gwyn and me. We watched Spud's smooth Irish charm take over as he went straight to work on the sergeant with a fluent piece of cock-and-bull about how he had thought it was an airman trying to stop us for a lift and as we were full he had simply driven on. After a while the sergeant reappeared and told us that although we wouldn't actually be charged, the episode would be reported to the station commander, Group Captain Thompson. We nodded politely, relieved.

It was perhaps rough justice that we should run out of petrol, both illegal and legal, just as we reached the airfield boundary. Crawling under the barbed wire – so much for airfield security – we staggered across the field to the mess. John, Spud and Lew lived nearby, but since it was another mile to our huts Gwyn and I decided to collapse for the rest of the night in some armchairs in the anteroom. We slept soundly, happy in the certain knowledge that after two days of operations we would be left in peace. Oh, were we wrong.

At eight o'clock that morning our happy slumbers were rudely interrupted by the tannoy barking out its instructions: 'Would the following crews report to operations . . .'. Ours was one of them. Everyone kept spare kit in the mess for emergencies just like this one, so groaning, we set to repairing the ravages of the night before. It was a bit much, really. On the 21st there had been that abortive trip in terrible weather conditions followed by a lone daylight cloud-cover raid with near-fatal results on the 22nd, and here we were, off again on the 23rd, to God knows where. Sighing at the cosmic injustice of it all we trudged off to ops. All we could hope was that our luck would hold.

CHAPTER TEN

End of the Line

Gwyn and I sat in operations, heads thumping and guts grinding from the night before, to hear that for seven crews, including ours, the Norway op was definitely on: squadron commander, Wing Commander Carter; the two flight commanders, Squadron Leader Kirwin (also hungover), Squadron Leader Pinkham; two deputy flight commanders, Flight Lieutenant Dunn and me; plus two senior crews. It was 23 October. Take-off scheduled for 17:00 hours. Oh, joy.

Our ground crew, at least, were bright and chirpy, already at the aircraft, getting it ready for a routine night-flying test. They had of course gone off to bed when the pub ran out of beer. I ran my hand across the fabric of BK309 N for Nuts, now blistered with patches where the shrapnel holes from yesterday's Essen raid had ripped her. They had done a splendid job; she was as good as new. Jim and Gwyn disappeared into their 'office', the navigator's table and the radio position just aft of the cockpit, while the front and rear gunners checked their turrets and guns, that all was running smoothly and that the ammunition had been properly loaded. When everyone had reported themselves satisfied, we started up and took off for a thirty-minute test flight. By now my head was pounding savagely, and I would not have been too heartbroken if N for Nuts had shown herself unfit for service that night. But she lumbered along sweetly as ever. Even if she hadn't we would have been stuck with the reserve aircraft, and in such circumstances it's always better the devil you know.

We landed; the ground crew gathered round. A full load of fuel (750 gallons) was taken on, and the armourers arrived with the bomb-trolleys carrying two 1750 lb magnetic mines to be dropped off the Norwegian[1] coast. These they hoisted into the bomb-bay whilst Gwyn, a great perfectionist, checked the switches he would use later to release them. It suddenly struck me watching him that he was looking perfectly fine, not at all reflecting the way I was feeling. 'Oh,' he said cheerfully when I asked him, 'I spent the whole of the air test on oxygen.' Now that one had never occurred to me before.

---

[1] *Bomber Command Diaries* gets this wrong: it is listed there as off the Danish coast.

Lunch in the mess was soup, steak and kidney pie and some kind of sweet I avoided mostly because of the inevitable disgusting lumpy custard covering it. Had I known what was in store for me that day the custard would have been scoffed: this was to be the last decent meal Gwyn, Jim and I would have for years.

After lunch, thinking of Mary, wondering idly how she was managing at Kenilworth, I called in to see the accountant officer just to make sure I was now being paid as a married officer. Still thinking of her, really, I then went to see Pugh, firstly to find out the latest update on my encounter with the broken-thighed railwayman, but also to ask if he had any news of my acting flight lieutenant status. Nothing from the railwayman, but he said that my acting rank had in fact come through, backdated to 5 October, and would be promulgated on station standing orders the very next day. I was pleased then, and in a few days I'd receive the concomitant pay. In the event, I'd only held the rank for nineteen days when I was shot down, so was not entitled to all that back pay while I was a POW. You never know. Gwyn also went to the adjutant that day, to find out about some parcels awaiting collection, probably his twenty-first birthday presents. He signed for them and arranged to pick them up the next day. He still wonders what happened to them.

At 14:00 hours the crew met for briefing in the Ops Room, wondering what exactly was in store for us this time. This time was always the most anxious, with nothing to do but wait. The station commander, Group Captain Thompson, led the usual procession into the briefing room: operations officer, intelligence, met officer, technical, armament, navigation, signals, bombing and gunnery leaders, and on this occasion an officer in naval uniform who brought up the rear. 'Where's the padre?' I whispered to Gwyn. 'There's everyone else here.'

Crews were checked, maps unrolled for reference and we waited for the intelligence officer Roger de Casalis's usual opening style: 'Tonight, we are going to Norway.' He was forgiven the royal 'we' on the grounds of advancing years. 'The target will not be heavily defended . . . not a great deal of flak . . . element of surprise . . .' and so on.

Unfortunately, as I only recently found out, the Germans had neglected to tell our intelligence that they had only just completed a whole line of new fortresses along this part of the coast. The Artillerigruppe Haugesund HKAA v/977 commanded by Major Saeger consisted of about fifteen big guns: 75mm, 88mm, 105mm and a whole lot of 20mm AA automatic guns – all just waiting for us to show up. Perhaps that was the 'element of surprise' angle. In addition to this, the Germans had put up 20mm AA guns on almost every hilltop in the approach to Salhus Sound. They also had mobile AA batteries on trucks, not to mention a couple of barges moving to and fro in the Karmsund. Most unsporting of them not to have told us this.

The briefing was not much different from the one we'd had for Norway a couple of days before. The mines were to be dropped from low level (300 feet) in the shallows of the Karmsund, a narrow channel between the island of Karmoy and the mainland, south of Haugesund, which would provide a safe haven for ships sailing south for the sheltered waters inland of Stavanger. We did not know it at the time, but from intercepted German signals and reports from agents in Norway, intelligence knew that the *Tirpitz* had sailed earlier that day from Trondheim. If she sailed south, Stavanger could provide a well-defended anchorage on the way to the Baltic, so a few well-placed mines along the Karmsund would be an obvious precaution against that eventuality. As it happened the *Tirpitz* sailed north that day for a refit, but of course no-one told us that. Still, from this and from the briefing given by the naval officer it was clear to us that the operation was considered to be of vital importance.

How important was soon all too clear when we heard from the met report the terrible weather in store, far worse than it had been the night we were recalled on the 21st.

> It is estimated that at 9 pm there will be an occluded front from 51.16E to 57.15E. At home bases low cloud will be accompanied by rain along the front and to the south. Visibility will be poor . . . Low cloud will cause take-off difficulties . . . expected to experience 10/10 cloud below 1,000 ft, with showers and drizzle . . . conditions should get better further north.

The full horror of this became apparent when Gwyn looked at his tracks in his chart. If we got off course to the east, we could easily descend through cloud that had a solid centre, i.e. mountains. The maximum endurance of a Wellington with a normal fuel load at its economical cruising height of 12-14,000 feet was about seven hours. The distance from Snaith to our target area was less than 500 miles, so at our best cruising height and with a reasonably favourable wind, we would have enough fuel for the return trip. The efficiency of the Hercules engine at sea level, however, was at least 20% less, and if we had to stay below cloud – and the weather report made that a certainty – we would not have enough fuel to return to Snaith. When we asked, this point was acknowledged by the briefing officer, who told us that if we found ourselves short on fuel we should divert to Kinloss in northern Scotland, which would be ready to accept us. We nodded, but the weather report had only said that the conditions 'should be better further north'.

'Sir, what is the procedure if Kinloss is closed by the weather?' Gwyn asked.

'In that case, you'll have to bale out.'

I suppose he considered Gwyn's to be a silly question, but it was a very depressing thought, all the same. In the previous ten days we had been on four operations, recalled from a fifth, and – self-inflicted though it was – we were short on sleep. So the idea of having forcibly to descend through cloud by parachute into cold you-knew-not-what did not fill me with delight. Later on, seeing my crew inspecting their parachutes with rather more than usual thoughtfulness, I said, 'At least it should clear your bowels. No worse than prunes.' Not great wit, but it helped relieve the tension.

Preparations for the trip now complete, the crew went off for the pre-flight meal, which we all ate together, officers and NCO aircrew, and as always, any conversation was forced or silly, everyone too keyed-up to think about anything but what lay ahead. Fifty-six operations and still it was the same: the dry mouth, constricted feeling in the stomach, a tendency to try to show how light-hearted I really was, the futile remarks. I understand actors experience the same stage fright before every performance. It's considered to be a part of the process of winding-up necessary to give one's best performance, putting all that adrenalin to best use. Perhaps this was just what we were doing, getting ready for our part in an all-important performance, our very lives depending on it. The tension began to lessen directly the aircrew bus arrived, promptly at 15:00 hours, and now there was something to be getting on with as we picked up our gear in Flights and conversation became more relaxed. Our NCOs talked about the dance the sergeants' mess was putting on that night. All aircrew were invited to these very cheerful functions, besides wives, girlfriends and WAAFs and some officers. Jim Whaley, who had invited me, insisted that he had found two 'smashing WAAFs' for Gwyn and me. 'Just keeping you in practice, so to speak,' he said to me. 'Your wife would thank me.'

I suggested to him that it might be a prudent move to take the girls along with us, just in case. Then, once in the crew room, I was distracted by the fact that I could not find my flying boots. So, in a hurry now, I helped myself to a pair from a nearby locker, size twelves, I noticed. I was a size nine. I can only think now that some guardian angel was on duty that evening, pointing me in the direction of those oversized boots; later that night they saved my life.

By now the weather was far worse: 10/10ths cloud at less than 600 feet. We all felt certain that the operation would again be cancelled. Jim's eyes lit up, but at 15:30 hours we were on our way to the aircraft, all chances of a dance this evening far behind us. I watched the ground crew stow our gear and the two pigeons we carried. I don't know if such birds were ever sent successfully; our two were certainly to be unlucky. Then the usual quick smoke, and – contrary to station standing orders – a final pee on the wheels for luck. Everyone did it. The technical officer always protested bitterly, sending out many notices condemning 'this disgusting and deleterious practice'. It had been pointed out to him that Naafi tea was the strongest drink to be had within hours of flying, and even that was not enough to harm a Wellington tyre.

16:10 hours, and we climbed into the aircraft, ready for a take-off at 16:30. At 16:40 we were still there, waiting at the end of the runway. All checks had been completed, it lacked only the green light from the airfield controller's caravan at the end of the runway. The weather was by now even worse, the cloud even lower; the op was bound to be cancelled. But at 17:00, the green light shone brightly through. It was all go from now: starting trolleys already connected, engines primed, with first port, then starboard engines growling to life. Once the engines were warm and temperatures ok, I opened up each throttle in turn, checked the constant speed propellers, magnetos, etc. All checks complete I called to Gwyn to signal the caravan that we were ready to go. Just after 17:00 hours, after an hour's wait, we got our green to taxi off. Groans from the NCOs.

'Sorry, boys,' I said to them, 'but we're on our way. If it all goes well we could be back by midnight. Just think of all the money you'll save – all those girls well-primed at no cost to you.' They were not convinced.

We took off at precisely 17:09, trundling down the runway like a pregnant cow, off the ground at about 85-95 mph. I'd barely got the wheels up and the flaps in when we hit the cloud base at about 500 feet. Flying round the south side of the airfield I told Gwyn I would set course at about ten feet above the control tower, so with full throttle I buzzed the tower and set course. A stupid bit of showing-off, but they knew how annoyed we were. Or perhaps not: from inside the tower a WAAF was waving happily at us, oblivious of the two tons of magnetic mines passing so close by.

Our first turning-point was at the coast at Whitby, and I told Gwyn that I would stay below cloud, in visual contact with the sea. This put us at about 500 feet, which suited Gwyn, as he was able to get a good fix at the coast and check windspeed and direction. At Whitby, with a new wind, we set course for a group of islands just west of Haugesund. As this would all be over the sea, we would get no more visual checks on our position. Jim Whaley managed to get a couple of radio loop bearings from the Netherland Station at Texel, and later, another from the Norwegian radio station at Stavanger, both of which confirmed the new wind Gwyn had found, so we also dropped a flare for the rear gunner to take a drift reading from. At least we knew where we were and what the conditions were.

Gwyn was now happy enough with the course, but I decided to stay below the cloud, because the wind, I knew, could easily be much different at a higher altitude, and I did not want to drift to the east and into the mountains there. As I've suggested before, it's not a good idea to come down through a cloud into a hard centre. Flying low over the sea like this our only worry was that we might suddenly find ourselves right over a British or German convoy. Even though we had been given positions of likely convoys during briefing, these were at best only approximations and could be miles out. To fly near one was to invite trouble: escorting destroyers always shot first and asked about identification afterwards – an attitude with which I could sympathise. I told Dalzell in the front turret to keep an extra sharp lookout, and chatted to him from time to time to make sure he was on the alert.

By 18:30 hours we were flying in the dark. Such flying is always a strain, with nothing much but water to engage the tired eyes but with the constant need to keep watch for any convoys below. The cloud cover had got even lower, forcing us down to 400 feet, which was very bad for fuel consumption. I now felt that we really would have to land back in Scotland, and hoped the weather would improve. At least such real problems kept me very much awake in spite of the engines' dreary drone, and the constant sense of flying in a wooden box, going nowhere: two Welshmen, an Englishman, an Australian and a Canadian, suspended in darkness between dark cloud and dark sea. The dim lights of the instrument panel gave off a pale warm glow before me; also from time to time came a glint of light from the office as Gwyn flashed a torch or Jim moved a light above his radio set. The odd question or comment would be exchanged, only Don Taylor, the tail-end Charlie, remained mostly silent. At twenty-four he was the old man of the crew. I trusted completely his alertness, even though, so far from land, there was little risk of any fighters suddenly showing up.

We all knew our jobs. As I've stated, I had a great admiration for the gunners, cooped up in their freezing, cramped turrets, staring for hours out into the dark, hands often frozen to their guns, feet frozen in their boots. As pilot at least I always had plenty to occupy my mind, and as captain, the ultimate responsibility was mine as well as talking with the crew to keep them vigilant and involved, checking compass, speed, altimeter and routine checking of engine temperatures, oil pressures and fuel gauges. The navigator was also busy all the time, checking drift, applying radio bearings, calculating positions by dead reckoning and working out any changes in the ETA, while the radio operator had to listen throughout the flight for recall signals or diversions, and when asked by the navigator for radio bearings, he would get them on the directional loop aerial. But the gunners had none of these routine jobs to keep them engaged and on the *qui vive.* They were tough characters, proud of their role, and I never knew one who showed fear or the slightest reluctance to fly. Few were commissioned, and very few had the satisfaction of firing their guns in anger. Mostly, they just had to sit there, freezing and staring into the darkness, waiting for that sudden burst of gunfire which, unless they got their guns to work on time, meant almost certain death for them and a poor chance of survival for the rest of the crew.

As the time passed, about three and a half hours, our mood began to relax. It was tiring flying so low, but it gave us the twin advantages of being below German radar and therefore able to take them by surprise. There were the usual wisecracks from the crew: 'Might as well do my calculations in knots, pressure head's (which operates the airspeed indicator) probably under water,' Gwyn grumbled, while from up front Dalzell called down, 'Get me a pair of oars and I'll row us to bloody Norway.'

Nearer the ETA, 20:20 hours, the thick cloud began to break up; we could see a bright moon shining through the gaps. We were now getting very close, so I decided to maintain our low altitude, now much easier because of the sudden visibility. An early sighting of the islands about eight miles west of Haugesund would be the best thing right now. Confident that we were close, Gwyn came up with his map and stood beside me, looking out over the moonlit sea. To add an extra pair of eyes Jim went up into the astrodome, while the gunners traversed the sky, their turrets swinging from side to side. Then over the intercom, a yell from Dalzell: 'Coast ahead!'

About the same time we became aware of quite a lot of flak to the east, towards Stavanger. 'Looks as though some of the boys didn't detect that wind change and have finished up over Stavanger,' Gwyn said grimly.

The moonlight was now brilliant, the sea below shining, and as I pulled up to 600 feet, there were the islands below and ahead of us, lumps in the sea. Gwyn grinned. 'Dead on track.' I grinned back. It had been no mean feat of navigation to come up spot-on after a low-level sea crossing of more than 400 miles. We got down to business. Gwyn went forward to fuse the mines, and when he came back he gave me the directions for our run-up to the target: 'Turn on to zero-nine-zero for about two minutes, and be ready to turn on to one-seventy for the run in to the aiming point.'

I remember thinking, what a lovely night.

I set the new course on the compass and went into a gentle turn to starboard, losing height to 300 feet. This would take us to the north entrance of the Karmsundet, and we could then fly south along it to drop our mines near Salhus, which was at the narrowest point. Gwyn went down to the bombing-panel ready to give me my final instructions for him to release his mines. It all seemed so simple.

By now I could see every detail of houses, roads and chimneys in the bright moonlight, and realised that equally, we could easily be seen from the ground. I'd begun my final turn when we encountered our first burst of flak, Gwyn yelling 'Flak!' as it exploded around us. I increased the turn to a steep weaving turn to starboard; at this stage I wasn't particularly alarmed as I'd often met such light flak before. But then it got less light, red balls of tracer fire rising lazily towards us from the ground, accelerating viciously as they whizzed close by. Our sky was quickly filling with flak. 'Christ!' I remember thinking, perhaps I said it, 'Who was supposed to be surprised?'

We were obviously the first on the target – a pity, as if one of the others had already arrived we might have been better prepared for what we met. So much for efficient navigating. As I turned again towards the target the flak intensified, hitting us like dozens and dozens of sharp stones, and with a loud bang the oil tank in the fuselage exploded, taking the two pigeons out completely, our first casualties. We were now well alight, and some of the flak hit the cockpit, great balls of fire. Good job my legs are so bandy, I thought, as some of it passed right through them. Gwyn, always one to keep fighting, had shot back into the office to see if he could get the flames out, but it was no good. With the intercom and lights gone, all my instruments gone, I was struggling simply to keep us straight and aloft, when Jim Whaley, face all burnt, appeared in the cockpit.

He tore my helmet from my right ear. 'We've fucking had it!' he yelled, then disappeared.

I tried once again to turn on to the target, but we were now being hit constantly, battered to death in the way we had seen so many other aircraft being battered before. Suddenly, a massive thump, and the starboard engine was dead; it felt as if the propeller had been shot off. Automatically my hand went for the trimmer to counteract swing, and I opened up the port engine to full power and tried to gain some height. Although N for Nuts was still flying, I remember thinking, bale out! Bale out before it's too late! But how to tell the others, if they were still alive. I had heard the rear gunner Don Taylor firing away defiantly but now his guns were silent, and I had to assume the worst. The fuselage was now a mass of flames, and we were still being hit. The front gunner, Dalzell, was now lying on the bomb aimer's panel, not moving. Gwyn and Jim had taken up crash positions behind the cockpit.

Now I could hear explosions behind me: ammunition and flares going up. N for Nuts was not going to fly for much longer, and we still had the mines on board. All these thoughts and events were taking place in a matter of minutes or less. We were still over Karmsundet, so I opened the bomb doors and pulled the emergency bomb release. It came away complete in my hand, and I couldn't tell from any obvious lightening of the aircraft whether or not I'd been successful. I looked out below, thinking about the possibility of ditching in the narrows – at least then they'd be in the right place – but even as I looked, the sea gave way to land and that option was gone.

We had now left the sea behind, but Nuts was done for. Flames had already enveloped the starboard engine and spread to the starboard wing. I knew the whole fuselage was on fire, and our flames were lighting up the boulder-covered ground about 200-300 feet just below me. To buy a precious bit of time and keep the aircraft in the air I now went for maximum power, pushing the throttle of the port engine right through the emergency wires. With no instruments and the mines possibly still on board there seemed little hope of survival, unless I could find some water to land in. Douse the flames, douse the damned flames! – that urgent thought the only thing on my mind. Then astonishingly, slightly to port I spotted a lake, its surface shimmering silver in the moonlight. I aimed the nose to the edge of the lake and hoped for the best. It was our only hope. I now know that a narrow split of land divides Lake Langavatn, right where I was aiming, but then its sudden appearance came as a nasty shock. All I could do was to ease back on the control column and hang on. It worked. We slid over the barrier with inches to spare. Throttle off, and hard back on the stick. I felt Nuts sinking under me. My last conscious thought was, 'Oh God, I hope the mines don't go off!'

When conscious action has to stop, helplessness brings a kind of dull paralysis. I remember coming to and discovering that I was actually alive, nothing more than that, just a hazy awareness that I still existed. I could not believe it. I may even have smiled then at the thought of Mary, how glad I was for her, and for my family. Then physical sensation returned: it was late October and I was thrashing around for my life in freezing Norwegian water. It also hit me that I couldn't swim, and a fine thing it would be to survive everything else only to drown like a rat, so I kicked and thrashed and, spotting the wing just nearby, I grabbed out for it, just hanging on. More splashing off to the side; I gave a yell in its direction and Gwyn's filthy face hove into view. I helped him to heave himself up onto the wing with me, then Jim Whaley, face and hands burnt red raw, joined us and we saw Dalzell floating in the water nearby. We managed to pull him out of the water and up onto the wing, but he was hideously injured. At least he was unconscious. The tail of the aircraft was under water, and there was no sign of Don Taylor. He was either dead or had managed to bale out. I doubted it was the latter.

Some water had entered its stowage, so the dinghy had automatically inflated and was bobbing nearby. The three of us together managed to get it to the wing, and as gently as possible handed poor Dalzell down into it. The shore was not too far away, so we all went to work paddling with our hands. It would not move, no matter how frantic our efforts. 'Look,' I said, 'someone's going to have to get down over the side and push it free from the aircraft in case it sinks and takes us with it.'

No volunteers. Heaving a sigh, I thought that as I'd been the one to get them here it had better be me, so back into that icy cold water I went. I think the combination of being in water, freezing and everything else that day (at least my hangover was gone) made me panic a bit, kicking frantically and getting out of breath. Then I gave up and just let go. My feet touched bottom. We were in only about four feet of water, so I simply towed them all into shore.

As gently as we could we lifted Dalzell ashore and made him as comfortable as we could tucked up with his Mae West. I believe he was alive, but only just, and terribly smashed-up. Jim stood up and blinked around him. 'We'll never make that bloody dance now. WAAFs will be furious.'

It was now time to take stock. Gwyn was reasonably free of injuries but had only one boot. Jim had serious burns on his hands and face. I had a sore knee and some facial burns. But it would have been worse had I not pinched those size twelve flying boots. They were still stuck in the rudder bars when I went back to the site in 1969, and if they'd been size nine I would have been still there in them.

In the distance we could hear dogs barking. We looked at one another; we were all now fugitives, and the enemy was right below and would be looking for us. It was time to get the hell away from the lake and N for Nuts.

PART TWO

Captive

CHAPTER ELEVEN

'For You the War is Over'

Every film cliché about the barking of dogs with their German masters in pursuit of their quarry – you – is true. It is a terrifying sound; it makes you want to run like hell instinctively, any residual exhaustion and shock simply frightened off. But we had Dalzell to consider, unconscious and in a very bad state. There was really nothing we could do for him, only to hope that he would be looked after when the enemy arrived. They could get him to a doctor whether or not we were still there and captured. I have rarely had a more tough decision to make, but it was the only one. We had to leave Dalzell behind. Jim was badly burnt but still adamant about coming with us rather than let himself be taken, while my main thought, once the decision about Dalzell had been reached, was to get as far away as possible from the crash site. It was of course still night, and through the broken cloud the Plough was just visible, and the Pole Star. To the east was Sweden, and eastwards we struck out, but the going was not easy, climbing up steep, rocky slopes, then down on our arses into bogs. Tedious stuff, and Gwyn and I had only the one boot between us. When we stopped at last for a breather, I suggested we empty our pockets of any incriminating papers, i.e. letters or any information about the station or operations, in case we were captured. I found that I only had a mess bill, but the others tore up odd bits of paper which they hid under some rocks. Walking along we came to some cultivated fields, which appeared oddly comforting after all the rocks and wet.

Although I knew that really we should avoid any early contact, equally I felt that we needed help. It was now about three hours since we had crashed, and we were all now shaking with shock and cold, wet and bruised, with Jim badly burnt, any adrenalin rush now disappearing. I decided to risk it and knocked on the nearest door. After a time, it must have been about five minutes, but we were cold and anxious, voices upstairs could be heard, stirrings, a light came on and a head appeared at the window. Gwyn decided to try a few words of French, which had no effect. When I facetiously suggested he try Welsh, the man at the window must have understood. 'Vat you vant?' he said.

'Um. We are Royal Air Force aircrew,' I said to him as clearly as I could. 'We are injured and need help.' He told us that he couldn't help us himself, but pointing out another house about a hundred yards down the lane, he said that we might find help there.

So off we went down the road, passing three milk churns on a stand which gave me a pang, a sharp reminder of Mary and her milk round now so far away. Although I loathe neat milk, some deeper need, a handle on the old, real life, made me scoop some into my hands and drink it while the others trudged on past. It was delicious, creamy and tangible somehow in the middle of this unreal sense we had been catapulted into. We then went up to the house and knocked on the door, which was opened after a few minutes by a middle-aged man who did not appear to be too put out to be woken up by three battered foreigners who had just nicked some of his milk. His name, I found out years afterwards, was Knut Ronnevik. Although he spoke little English he realised who and what we were, motioned for us to come in and led us into a warm farmhouse kitchen, with a plain, well-scrubbed wooden table, a very large, free-standing wood-burning stove, plain wooden chairs and a kind of bench settee where his brother Hans was sitting at the table. He blinked at us, but was equally unperturbed, as if this sort of thing happened every morning with the milk round.

We must have been shivering with shock and cold and relief at this respite from the outdoors, standing in that warm, homely kitchen. At any rate we were invited to undress, and as we were placing our wet clothes around the large stove to dry, one of the brothers appeared with dry underwear for us. This was kindness indeed. By now Jim was in a very distressed condition, shaking severely, and with his badly-burnt hands barely able to undress himself. With difficulty I managed to get Knut to understand that I would like something to put on Jim's burns. He brought a bowl of hot water and scissors, but did not appear to have any disinfectant, so all I could do was bathe Jim's hands and cut away all the burnt skin. Through all this Jim managed to be stoical, but the moment I'd finished he wobbled over to the settee and passed clean out.

By this time, about an hour or so, our uniforms had partly dried out, and since I felt the urgent need to get moving as soon as possible, we put them back on, the wool still steaming with damp. Knut gave me a pair of boots which fitted pretty well, certainly better than the last pair I'd had, and Gwyn was given a pair of warm slippers. But just as I was trying to explain to Knut that what I'd really like was a map, the shock caught up with Gwyn, and with a little sigh he simply passed out, draped across the table. That was two of them out cold. Oh, Lord, I thought. Was I going to have to press on alone? We had to leave now or we'd have no chance at all of eluding the Germans and their dogs. But try as I might I could not get it across to the impassive Knut or his silent brother that what we needed was a map. Even today I could not say whether they were reluctant to let us go because of the Germans or because they thought we were too badly injured or they simply did not understand, but then I only felt increasing frustration. I was just about to go out the door myself and simply head east when it burst open, just like it does in every movie you see, and in poured about half a dozen German Combined Services with tommy-guns and revolvers all pointing at me: *'Hände hoch!'* My hands were already pushing at the ceiling. You don't fool around with all that ammunition directed at you.

Two American-style civilians in coats, portly and ordinary-looking, followed hard upon: Gestapo. I felt a barrel prod my stomach; a Luftwaffe hauptmann had stuck in his Luger. He looked me in the eyes. 'For you the war is over,' he said. I was not prepared to argue.

It was at this point that Gwyn decided to come to. I nearly burst out laughing at the completely comic look on his face as his eyes opened to find a Kriegsmarine lieutenant's Luger pressed hard against his temple, and those classic words said to him. Jim was roused, though, by the rather gentler attentions of a Norwegian doctor, a Doctor Lundewohl, who had no Luger in his hand. The doctor must have noticed my distress, because in hesitant English he assured me that Jim would be taken to hospital. In fact he was to spend many weeks in hospital, very well attended to, and we did not see him again until after the war.[1] I looked around the warm kitchen at all those men, all those guns, and realised for the first time that I was beaten, there was no way out of this one. We were in the hands of the enemy. There was no relief with this realisation, only frustrated anger. All Gwyn and I could do was, Lugers in our backs, allow ourselves to be ushered out to the waiting transport, several open, Jeep-type vehicles, bloody freezing now in our damp clothing.

In retrospect it must have appeared ludicrous, this impressive convoy, bristling with the latest armaments, taking two very dejected, damp, bruised airmen off into captivity. But we had obviously put the wind up the area; we were stopped by no less than three roadblocks of soldiers who had been called up to search for us. Still, I suppose it sent out a fairly unmistakable message to the locals, that no harbouring of fugitives would be tolerated.

Upon reaching what appeared to be the deserted streets of Haugesund, we were taken directly to the local military HQ and deposited on a bench

---

[1] I now know that the person in the first house we had called at, realising we were injured, had rung Dr Lundewohl. And it seems that whenever a doctor is called out in such circumstances he must inform the military.

outside the main office, in what felt like some kind of bare waiting-room where we sat, exhausted, the centre of attraction, two guards with rifles on either side of us. At one point a fat German major came to look us over, and started abruptly yelling at us and waving his hands about. In fact he was so much the rude caricature of the Hun seen in every newspaper and propaganda sheet – short, fat, square cropped head and angry red face – that I couldn't help it, I went off into paroxysms of giggles. One of the guards quickly disabused me, giving me a smart clip on the head with his rifle butt. Laughter was not on the current menu, but it was very difficult not to, rather like being stuck at the very stuffy funeral of someone you never liked. Not long after this a very young, baby-faced corporal came in to see us, and in broken English told us that it was his battery that had hit us first and set us on fire. He seemed so genuinely excited about it that I felt I must congratulate him, and shook his hand. God knows why.

A lieutenant now appeared and began to interrogate us. Gwyn responded in English even more broken than the lieutenant's, saying that we were both in fact Welsh, and being a Welsh-speaking Welshman from the Rhondda Valley, he could only answer questions in Welsh. I quickly caught on, and although a non-Welsh-speaking Welshman I could easily string together a dozen Welsh place names that sounded convincingly like a sentence. The lieutenant's polite face could just about cope with the strain of English, but the burst of Welsh did for him utterly. He was quickly replaced by the fat major, who after a few minutes of more Welsh gibberish looked ready to explode. By this time we felt we had nothing to lose in these tactics, and it made us feel as if we had one up on them. So red-faced and apoplectic was the major I thought he might actually hit us, but he threw in the towel in the end; after about half an hour he stormed out, while we were taken off to a nearby building and locked in a third-floor room with an armed Luftwaffe guard outside.

It had been a long day. We were given some water, but no food. Perhaps it had occurred to them that a bit of starvation might improve our English. After a time, perhaps another half an hour, I was taken out to an office and seated in front of an elderly Luftwaffe hauptmann wearing an Iron Cross, from the First World War, I should think. He was charming and elegant, spoke perfect English and was exceptionally pleasant. There was no question of any Welsh prevarication here, though. After a few minutes of charm he smoothly got down to business, asking me questions about our mission, where we had flown from, had we dropped our mines, and so on. Nothing I hadn't anticipated, and there was still enough bloody-mindedness left in me to keep going, so to each question I replied that I could only give him my name, rank and serial number, not answer any other questions. After several attempts he suddenly said, 'I quite understand. Our Luftwaffe crew receive the same briefing.' He gave me a little smile. 'I am so sorry that we should be fighting each other, when really, we should both be on the same side fighting the Russians.'

That surprised me at the time, but it was a sentiment I was often to hear from Germans in the years that followed. He went on, telling me that a bloody battle had started at El Alamein, and although both sides were claiming advances, he feared that the English had left it too late.

'This is what we have been waiting for!' I said with great enthusiasm. I'd never heard of El Alamein. 'It will be the turning-point of the war, mark my words!' Little did I know then how right I was. I always feel a bit aggrieved that from the night I was shot down the Allies went on to victory.

The interrogation finished on a fairly friendly note, with a handshake. He wished me well, he said, adding almost as an afterthought that any future interrogations might be rather more unpleasant, especially if conducted by the Gestapo. I left the room, feeling sick.

Early the following morning, starving, since we had been given no food at all, we were marched down to the nearby quayside and under the watchful eyes of the very suspicious crew put on board what appeared to be a Kriegsmarine minesweeper. That voyage, from Haugesund to Stavanger, was the roughest and most claustrophobic sea trip I ever endured, shut down in the hold, with little air and extremely rough seas. The crew were actually very curious about us, and like so many operational servicemen on both sides, seemed to appreciate our current awkward position. One of them was very proud of a wound he showed us, where he had been hit on the thigh by a bullet from a Blenheim. Another brought us both a bottle of beer. I would have drunk it much more slowly if I had known how long it would be before I would taste another.

On arrival at Stavanger we were shut in the cellar of the local Gestapo jail. With its damp, dark walls and dank stench, and a small barred window far up out of reach, it was more like a dungeon. There were two wooden shelves, each with a stained, smelly blanket. Not quite what we were accustomed to. 'We'll get used to it,' I said to Gwyn, who nodded, neither of us believing it. Stiff, filthy, exhausted, bruised and by now feeling really sorry for ourselves, we collapsed without another word onto our hard wooden beds. I lay there for a while thinking about Mary and my family. What a shock for them; they would have no means of knowing I had survived. Weariness soon overcame me and I fell asleep.

Next morning, they gave us a mug of something hot that vaguely resembled tea and a slice of black bread. Gwyn said thoughtfully, 'It's mad, but you know, I had the most erotic dream last night.'

I nearly choked on my black bread. 'Well, you'd better treasure the thoughts, that's all you're going to get for some while.'

We were taken to hospital for an examination, during which we found out that Jim Whaley had been retained in the Haugesund hospital and that Dalzell was dead. No mention was made of Don Taylor, and we decided to keep mum, just in case he had managed to bale out and got away. I doubted this really; the only thing that could have stopped him from firing his guns was being hit. (In fact, when we returned to the site of the crash in 1969 Gwyn found him still in the rear turret of the aircraft. He was buried with full military honours alongside Dalzell in the military cemetery in Haugesund, twenty-one years after having been shot down.)

Despite cuts, bruises and minor burns, we were pronounced fit enough to travel, and under the guard of two corporals, were taken by train to Flekkefjord, then by bus on a most spectacular drive via the fjords to Kristiansund, where we were put on a train for Oslo. There were times during this trip when it crossed my mind to try to make a break for it, but either the guards were too alert, the train too fast or the terrain too rocky. I suppose I was still a sprog prisoner, and still suffering from the effects of the crash, but I was soon to realise that I had missed the best opportunity I would have in the next few years. The Norwegians are most brave and patriotic, and had a well-organised resistance, and I'm sure that if I had only managed to make a run for it at that time I would have been taken in, sheltered and given every assistance to get to Sweden.

On arrival at Oslo's main station, Gwyn was taken off to get some boots, since he was still in the slippers that Knut Ronnevik had given him. On his return we were taken off to Gestapo headquarters, separated and then interrogated by two men in drab civilian clothing. Facing them, for the first time since being shot down I was really frightened. They were stereotypical Gestapo, hard-faced and cold, one with a scar down his cheek. They seemed to know exactly what our operation had been and were most keen to find out if we had actually dropped our mines. It occurred to me that although I knew we hadn't dropped them, it might be more useful to lie and say that we had. Apart from looking for them in the Karmsund, if they poked and prodded a bit too much around the wreck of N for Nuts they could get themselves blown up in the process. The rest of the interrogation, about fifteen minutes, was made up of lots of questions about the RAF to which I duly responded with name, rank and serial number. I have to say that at any moment I expected the rubber truncheons to come out or my fingernails to be painfully removed, so I was very much relieved to be dismissed at last and taken back to what I think was a room in the town hall.

After a couple of days during which there was no further questioning, we were allowed a most welcome primitive wash which barely addressed the dirt and itching, and taken to Oslo airport, where we were handed over to a Luftwaffe sergeant going home on leave, who'd been given the job of guarding us on the flight. As we were loaded onto a Junkers 52, I could see that most of the other passengers were army officers and either wives or secretaries, everyone loaded down with what appeared to be pails of butter, cheese and other such comestibles difficult to get in wartime. The weather was bad, the flight very bumpy. Our sergeant, who had spent a great deal of his time telling us what a terrific pilot he was and hinting broadly that having been shot down we ourselves couldn't have been all that good, was sick. So were several other passengers, and Gwyn and I found ourselves handing out sick bags and trying not to grin too obviously at our sergeant's plight. Our first landing was at Copenhagen. The passengers all got off, and we were left under the baleful eye of our guard and some ground defence crews. I think he must have learnt that he could not bullshit us and was possibly even a bit ashamed of himself, because he produced a sandwich and to our amazement, as it must have been most precious to him, a piece of milk chocolate, giving them to us.

After about an hour we took off again, and in late afternoon on the 28th or 29th, landed at Gatow, the Berlin airfield, new to me from any angle. It was odd to be sitting on an airfield with lots of Me109s and Junkers 88s, and I was very relieved when at last we left it before we could be bombed by any of our compatriots. To our delight we were marched off on a tour of Berlin, possibly as a propaganda exercise to show us how little damage had been done to it by our bombs. I must say, when I had last seen it London was in far worse condition, and had sustained far more damage. Eventually, we arrived at the Anhalter Banhof, the railway station, where we were forced to sit in some considerable discomfort under the eyes of passing Germans who viewed us with interest and in some cases outright hostility. We did manage to get a cup of tea from what I assume was the equivalent of our WVS, and even a sympathetic smile. Still, I was glad when our train arrived.

We arrived at the next stop, Frankfurt-am-Main, at first light, and changed trains to Oberursel, which I gathered was the transit camp and interrogation centre for new prisoners of war. By this time my groin was giving me terrible grief: itching so bad it hurt. Heaven knows what the civilian passengers on the train thought of my efforts to relieve it.

Dulag Luft was the interrogation centre for RAF prisoners of war. It was divided into two halves: the adminstration block contained the Kommandantur (the garrison headquarters), staff living quarters and the interrogation cells, while the other half, smaller, was a well-wired compound which housed several wooden huts for the accommodation of prisoners after they had been interrogated. We were booked in at the guard room and put in separate cells. The cells were about eight by five feet, and contained a bed, mattress, a small table and a chair, all painted white, with a small barred window high up at the end. The door at the other end had a peephole for the guard to keep an eye on us. I was given a small piece of soap, scentless and latherless, a razor and a stick of shaving soap.

About mid-morning I remember sitting on that tiny bed thinking about how my life had changed in only a few days. My room at Snaith had been a bit spartan, but compared to this it was a palace. As I sat there and scratched, the door opened and a Luftwaffe lieutenant came in with a folder under his arm. They don't give you much time to settle in, I thought. This was to be the friendly approach, made before you had time to think. He produced the well-known bogus Red Cross forms we'd been warned about in lectures during training. Seating himself in the chair, he smiled, said how sorry he was to have to disturb me so abruptly, but if I could only fill in the forms he would be able to let my family know that I was safe and sound. I looked at the forms; they seemed to be asking for a mass of information. Apart from my name, rank, etc, I was being asked for name and address of next-of-kin, what squadron I'd been on, which station and which aircraft type I'd flown. I filled in the name, rank and number and silently handed it back. He was very persistent, though, reiterating how hard it was on my family not knowing what had become of me, and how just by filling in that form I could put their minds at rest.

'Well,' I couldn't resist saying to him, 'we're a large family. I'm sure one won't be missed. Anyway, all you need to inform the Red Cross is my name, rank and number.'

He was not pleased. Gathering up his things in a huff he said, 'You will be interrogated again and next time it will not be so pleasant.'

If he had wanted to scare me he succeeded. I thought, Christ, I hope they don't start getting too rough, because if I told them all I know they wouldn't believe it was so little.

I sat there on the bed, scratching madly, fed up. If I cleaned up, I thought, I might feel a bit better, and perhaps a good wash would cure my terrible itching. It was some time before I could get the guard to come and let me have some water from the washroom, no doubt a bit of bloody-mindedness on his part. Eventually, I stripped, shaved – carefully negotiating the burn on my chin – and washed, paying particular attention to my lower equipment. I did a horrified double-take: my lower equipment was alive. I had often heard people making jokes about 'crabs', saying you had to shave yourself like a Windmill chorus girl. Oh, well. Windmill it was. Once more, a good lather, and a most painful, excruciatingly careful cold water shave with that useless soap, all the while cursing my luck and wondering whether it had been the longjohns from Knut Ronnevik or the dirty blankets in Stavanger to blame for my new little friends. I settled on the blankets, but just to make sure, decided to dispense with the longjohns.

I had now used most of the tiny, hotel-sized bar of soap and left its dregs in the washroom. This was a big mistake as I found out the next morning when I asked for another piece of soap and was told that I'd already been given a month's supply. For the rest of my time in the cells, about five or six days, I had to depend on my stick of shaving soap. The remainder of that day passed with me sitting on my bed, staring at the white walls, scratching and contemplating the future. The next three days were exactly the same. I hated it. I'm a gregarious kind of person, and simply having to sit there with nobody to talk to and nothing to read, just worrying about Mary and my family was real torture. I brooded over the operation at Haugesund, trying to think if there had been anything I could have done to save the front and rear gunners. I tried pacing the few steps up and down in my cell – not comfortable, since my knee was still painful and swollen from the crash. I did realise that this was meant to be a softening-up period, and sure enough, on the fourth day a middle-aged hauptmann came into the cell with his sheaf of bogus forms. Once again I filled in name, rank, number only, putting a line through the rest. I also told him that we had been warned about these bogus forms. To my astonishment he then produced a packet of Players cigarettes and offered me one, which I gratefully accepted. I can only guess that this was a psychological gesture to relax me, since he quickly proceeded to ask a lot of questions, some aggressively and some in a very pleasant, polite manner. Apart from saying that I had completed my mission, which I felt was the right thing to say, I kept silent.

After another two miserable days in my solitary confinement my interrogator came in again, this time with a couple of files under his arm. After a few of the usual questions, which I ignored, he paused, then said, 'Well, I'll tell you a few things.' Opening the file with an arch look he then to my amazement began to tell me that I was a very experienced pilot, that I had been on 40 Squadron at Alconbury, then with them in Malta (he seemed to have missed the short spell with 38 Squadron). He then told me how I had flown out from Snaith, and even said that the station commander, Group Captain Thompson had recently been awarded a DFC. Although I tried to keep a straight poker face at all this I should imagine my mouth was agape. He said he had lots of information on the squadron, and also in the other file, the location, type of aircraft and so on of most of the squadrons in the RAF. He tried to hand them over to me for a look, but I refused, saying I was not interested. Giving me another cigarette he said he didn't think I could help him any further; I would be transferred to the Lager (the area reserved for POWs) the very next day. I cannot express my relief at this: leaving this horrible cell and being with other POWs sounded like heaven to me.

After a reunion with Gwyn, we were both taken into the POW compound to be met there by a small crowd of welcoming fellow sufferers and the small regular English staff, all pumping us for any news from home. After an apparently informal chat with the senior RAF officer on the staff – who was, I assume, checking that we were not German stooges attempting to integrate ourselves – we were allocated a room which already contained six other POWs who had only recently, that is, in the last few weeks, been shot down. It seems we were being kept at Dulag Luft until there were enough of us to make up a purge, as it was called, to be taken to the main camp at Sagan. None of us knew exactly where we were going until we actually arrived and were briefed by the RAF permanent staff there. The six in the room were a mixed bunch: Shultz and de la Harpe – two South Africans shot down in the Western Desert – Jean Regis, a Free French Spitfire pilot built like a heavyweight boxer and Gordon Lindsay, an Australian fighter boy. One other Spitfire pilot and ex-racing driver was Gordon Brettell, who was to become a master forger and should have had a brilliant career in whatever he did had he not been murdered in The Great Escape. Finally, there was an American in the Canadian Air Force, George Harsh, older than the rest of us, a former rear gunner. More about George later. We all had our tales of woe to tell, and already were discussing how long we would spend in POW camp. The popular opinion, based most likely on simple optimism, was that we would be home early next year, but one thing about being a POW is that you have to work hard to keep up your optimism, in spite of everything to the contrary. I was to hear three times before release: 'This will be the last Christmas in the bag!'

Towards the end of November, Dulag Luft had accumulated enough assorted POWs for the purge, which meant simply that we would all be taken on to a permanent camp, Stalag Luft III at Sagan, in Silesia, far from the action. It was a pretty miserable journey, jammed together on hard wooden seats, closely guarded and cold, for several days. Food was almost non-existent: some sliced black bread and watery soup at lunchtime. Thirty-five scruffy, hungry, subdued officers marched in an unkempt column up to the gates of Stalag Luft III.

As the new arrivals were being counted, checked and handed over, a crowd of interested inmates collected around at the camp entrance, curious to see if any old friends might be among the new boys. I suddenly spotted Joe Noble, from the early days of 40 Squadron. Using a popular slang of those days I yelled out, 'Hey, there, Shag Noble!'

At that he turned, grinned broadly, and much to the amusement of the assembled crowd, yelled back: 'Hey, there, Shag Rees!'

My first lesson in being a POW: how you get your nickname. He was already called 'Red', so for the rest of my POW days I was stuck with the monicker 'Shag'.

CHAPTER TWELVE

Stalag Luft III, Sagan: East Compound

November 1942

Prisoner of War

It is a melancholy state, you are in the power of your enemy. You owe your life to his humanity, your daily bread to his compassion. You must obey his orders, go where he tells you. Stay where you are bid, await his pleasure, possess your soul in patience. Meanwhile, great events are in progress, opportunities for action and adventure are slipping away; hours crawl like paralytic centipedes, life is one long boredom from dawn till slumber. Moreover, the whole atmosphere of prison, even the most regulated prison, is odious. You feel a sense of constant humiliation in being confined, fenced in by railings and wire, watched by armed men, webbed about with a tangle of regulations and restrictions; one can only hate every minute of captivity.

Winston S. Churchill, 1899

It would be some time before I fully appreciated these sentiments, expressed by Churchill when he was incarcerated by the Boers in South Africa, but for now I was just relieved to be in a permanent camp, out of the hands of the Gestapo and into the hands of men who were at least airmen like myself, the Luftwaffe. 'Stalag' was short for 'Stammlager Luft', permanent camps purpose-built specifically for airmen of all the services. Stalag Luft III had opened in May 1942, and was under the command of Oberst Friedrich-Wilhelm von Lindeiner-Wildau, the holder of two Iron Crosses.

That first grim view of Stalag Luft III was not designed to make you feel anything but that you were miles from anywhere, isolated even if you were in company. You saw barbed wire and bare new-cut wood, a bleak vista of tree-stumps where what appeared to be endless woods had been cut down and this camp carved out of vast, unfriendly wilderness. I cannot say if actual walls might not have been an improvement on the bleak and uncompromising barbed wire which allowed you to look out but realise how hopeless it was to think about escaping into that bleakness. There were five miles of perimeter barbed-wire fencing, eventually enclosing fifty-nine acres when all the compounds were finished. By July 1943, Stalag Luft III would be a large configuration of three compounds, with two further compounds nearing completion. When I arrived there in November 1942, much of the camp was still under construction, the constant hammering and sawing part of the general background noise. What had already been built was a stark collection of large huts, a minimal roof-angle away from being simple boxes on stilts two feet above the ground, surrounded by a web of barbed-wire fencing, with a few guard-towers we called 'goon-boxes', just covered platforms, really, looming like malevolent spiders in a web of electric wiring above the whole scene. The overridding impression was of barrenness. The only thing which made it at all acceptable was the sight of so many men in familiar uniforms walking around inside the wire.

We newest arrivals were dispersed into different rooms in different huts around the compound, probably sorted out by the adjutant. Gwyn and I were separated, Gwyn going off to share a room with seven Czechs and an Englishman, while I wound up in a room with the other newcomers, Frenchman Jean Regis and an Englishman called Rogerson. We found already in residence there one Australian and six Englishmen, most of them having been prisoners since early 1940 and 41. They gave us a great welcome, sat us down around the small table and bombarded us with questions on everything from the state of the war to the quality of the beer and how everyone was coping. I quickly realised that apart from a genuine thirst for news of any kind, they were also making sure we were bona fide RAF and not an attempt by the Germans to infiltrate a stool-pigeon. I only ever heard of one case in our compound, but I believe it happened in other camps.

As this was going on I remember looking around this tiny room, no bigger than a medium-sized bedroom at home, which was to be my abode for the unforeseeable future. At one end were four double bunks, about a foot in between them, with the fifth bunk against a side wall. A small, free-standing wood stove was at the other end of the room, plus a table big enough for eight with eight chairs, besides a bench to sit upon, while a couple of food lockers completed the furnishings. I'd thought our rooms at Snaith pretty basic, but Gwyn and I had shared a room larger than this one. It was clear that in this claustrophobic environment I was going to have to keep a rein on my opinions and make an effort to be careful not to express too strong a view on anything, at least until I'd got to know my room-mates better.

That same day we were given all the basic gen of what it meant to be a POW. There were what might be called perks, but which under the circumstances only helped to make daily life a bit less miserable. The old boys told us it would be a few weeks before the Red Cross would be able to pass on the news that we were POWs, and that we would get two postcards and two letters to send each month – all censored, of course. Anyone could send us cigarettes at duty-free prices, and we could receive one clothes parcel from next-of-kin every six months. This parcel, however, could contain not just clothes, but toiletries (soap!) and made up to the approved weight with chocolate. Of course, it would be some time before we new boys actually received our first parcel. Although cigarettes were plentiful, matches were not; normally you had to cadge a light from another smoker, but in those days nearly everyone smoked, so this was easy.

After all this newness on top of a long, uncomfortable journey, I was feeling tired, and my knee was beginning to play up again too, the calf inflamed and swollen. After a glance at it, John Marshall, the senior member of the room, declared that I should go sick in the morning and let the doctors see to it. I'd been allocated a top bunk, above Johnny Bull, but decided that before climbing up and turning in I'd better make use of the night latrine which was in a small end room in the same block. We were locked in after dark, and these were for night use only.

The night latrine was narrow, about five feet wide, with two thunder boxes. I had just made myself comfortable when the door opened and in came someone with a group captain's stripes on his battle dress who without any ceremony dropped his trousers and settled in on the seat opposite. Now I had read the 'Customs of the Service' issued pre-war to all officers, but the etiquette of this situation had me completely stumped. What was I to do? Here I was, halfway through my business, trousers round my ankles: it would be undeniably silly at this point to stand up, although saluting in situ was obviously not on, either. Happily, he chose that awkward moment to break the ice himself, asking if I had just arrived, by which I assumed he meant in camp and not just on the bog. I said, yes, and he chatted on easily about things in general, and in between the odd grunt, advised me on how to settle in to POW routine. I suppose he was really demonstrating at least one aspect of POW routine right then and there, but still I couldn't decide whether to be polite and let him leave first, which would involve my standing up in a most undignified manner, trousers down, saying 'good night', feeling keenly the breeze between my knees. On the other hand, I could simply get the hell out. I did just that.

With full and genuine relief I returned to our room, put on my clean, warm, new Red Cross flannelette pyjamas, climbed painfully up into my bunk above Johnny Bull and simply passed out cold. Then I was back in my Wellington and on fire. This time I baled out, but my parachute wouldn't open. I struggled, then crashed hard onto the ground. I was just coming to terms with this when my eyes opened and I saw Bull's face peering down into mine.

'What the hell do you think you're doing?' he said pleasantly.

Bruised even more and aching now in every part of my body, I tried to crawl back up to my bunk. 'I just baled out and my parachute wouldn't open.'

'Oh? Maybe next time you should just stay in the aircraft and crash with it.'

Next morning everything was hurting like hell, so I reported sick, and was taken out of the compound and into the Vorlager, which contained the sick quarters manned by two Army doctors, one Australian and one New Zealander, assisted by a German-speaking Dutch fighter pilot, Bob van der Stok, who had once been a medical student. They put me in a three-bedded ward together with a Pole called something like Alexandrovich, and a Dutchman called Forwarda who spoke perfect English. Completing this international set-up were two Russian orderlies.

The medical equipment was pretty basic. All they could do for my knee and the infection in my calf where a bit of shrapnel had evidently pierced it was to give it 'heat treatment', where you stuck your leg under what looked like a plywood arch into which two electric light-blubs had been screwed, the whole thing covered with a blanket. Crude it may have been, and these days plain dangerous, but it seemed to work. A similar infection in my spine was treated with hot poultices probably made from bread. With a few days' rest my knee began to improve, and after about a week the Doc lanced both abscesses. That, I have to say, hurt like nothing else, but the relief that followed was almost blissful.

After about fourteen days I returned back to my room in the hut feeling much better in every respect, especially since the food in the sick quarters was much nicer than our normal rations. In fact, my own lifelong interest in cooking began in Stalag Luft III, perhaps because food was so much on our minds. I found on my return to the room the other two newcomers already settled in: John Regis, being French, had been appointed 'Cook Führer', and since there was no other obvious room job for me, they made me his deputy. It was quickly borne upon me that while cooking for a room in a POW camp was not a particularly arduous task, you did need to exercise considerable ingenuity to transform spam or our meagre Reich rations into something resembling real food.

I am often asked what the food in camp was really like. I can only say that it was both scarce and monotonous. The first meal I had there appalled me. God, I thought, we've got to live on this? We were hungry all the time. For those first months as a prisoner you spend all your time thinking about food, not the beer and women which had been our first priority before capture. The rations supplied by the Germans as laid down in the Geneva Convention should have been the same as for German depot troops. Instead, I understand it was the lowest grade, as supplied to civilians too old to work. The daily ration dished out by the Reich worked out at between 800 and 1400 calories, and when we were on that alone, most activities stopped. We spent most of our time 'pit-bashing' – i.e. lying in your bunk, or just sitting around. The Reich gave you ersatz coffee made from acorns, three slices of soggy, heavy black bread made from God knows what[1], a thin soup known as 'green death' made from ox-head or cabbage or even weeds, and some potatoes. In the evening you might get some bread and swede jam. A typical day would begin with a breakfast of ersatz coffee, a slice of black bread, margarine and jam, all rationed out by the Bread Führer. Lunch as supplied by the Germans consisted of two or three potatoes, some 'green death'; we'd eat the soup but save the potatoes for the evening meal. For tea there would be another slice of bread and jam and then oh, joy! – the small but eagerly-awaited evening meal. Everything had to be meticulously shared out. If there was even an odd piece of carrot or a spare precious pea, the cards would be dealt out and the first jack got it. We had to be terribly careful; you wouldn't want a punch-up over a pea.

What really saved our lives were the Red Cross parcels. On paper we were supposed to get one Red Cross parcel per head per week, and when this actually happened, and with the Reich rations, we would be fairly well off Unfortunately, what did happen was that we were on half-parcels most of the time, and when we had been bad boys caught trying to escape, the punishment was that our parcels would be stopped. On full parcels, together with Reich rations, we were getting about 2,600 calories a day, just about enough for normal activities, and which allowed us gradually to put aside small amounts of prunes, raisins and a little sugar, enough to concoct a 'brew', lovingly dished out by the Brew Führer. Other precious bits from our parcels enabled us to make 'kriegie cake', a mixture of crushed biscuits, powdered milk, margarine, raisins, Reich bread, and breadcrumbs. Add to that a little tea or coffee, mix, put it all into a homemade cake tin and bake. Kriegie cake was made as a special Christmas treat, with sugar icing but no candles. A small piece went a very long way, lingering around heavily in your stomach for days. Somehow we also managed to save enough prunes and raisins to ferment and distil

---

1 The recipe for black bread, as given in the official records of the Food Providing Ministry, Berlin, dated 24 May, 1941: 50% bruised rye grain; 20% sliced sugar beets; 20% tree flour (sawdust); 10% minced leaves and straw.

for a room party about twice a year, Christmas being the main one. The success of the party was judged by the number of days it took to get rid of the appalling hangover.

Johnny Bull took me under his wing. He had been shot down in 1941 flying Wellingtons. Like me he was married, but he also had a small child, born since he had become a POW. A rather serious man and a keen escaper, he had spent most of his time in captivity digging unsuccessful tunnels, and already there was a lot of tunnelling going on: before we left for the North Compound more than a hundred tunnels had been started under the East Compound. Together we would pound the circuit, 'circuit-bashing', which meant walking around the perimeter of the compound, just inside the warning wire, a popular form of exercise. While we trudged around the perimeter he would tell me about numerous escape attempts, most of which ended up in failure and the Cooler or worse, although Johnny himself had never been caught. Yet. It was soon brought home to me how difficult if not impossible escape really was from Stalag Luft III. Johnny was convinced that a tunnel, although tried on dozens of occasions, was still the best option. It also began to dawn on me that although escaping from the camp was difficult enough in itself, your troubles were only just beginning the moment you got the other side of the wire. If you couldn't speak German or another language that would allow you to travel as a foreign worker, you had to go 'hard arse', as we called it: keeping low, out of the way of police, guards, and virtually everyone out there, moving by night, carrying what food you had managed to scrounge, and several hundred miles to cover before you could find friendly territory. Almost impossible, but we didn't let ourselves think that way at the time.

One of the first routines we had to get used to was the call for 'on parade', or 'Appell', as the Germans called it. Normally this was twice a day, but if they wanted to be difficult it could be three or four times a day, and we all had to drop everything and stand on parade by our huts on the sports field. As we stood there in rows of three the guards would then count us, together with any sick who had remained inside the huts. These, morning and afternoon, usually took between twenty and thirty minutes, but could take ages, depending on our co-operation or other factors. They were very thorough. If the numbers failed to correspond to their list it would start all over again: not too bad in summer, but diabolical in the icy Silesian winter. We formed up by blocks, usually with reasonable discipline since we all wanted to get away as soon as possible, but occasionally we would be covering for someone who had escaped.

In fact, it was first through such daily routines that one gradually developed an awareness of how the camp was run. The Kommandant, von Lindeiner-Wildau, now in his early sixties, was as well-equipped as any to run Stalag Luft III with its large administration. A fluent speaker of English, he had been on Göring's personal staff when war broke out. Göring, himself a former WWI pilot, had a certain amount of sympathy for Air Force POWs, and when the camp was opened in May 1942, he had von Lindeiner posted in as its Kommandant, with Major Gustav Simoleit as his deputy. Von Lindeiner was a fair and honourable soldier who steered clear of German politics and dealt fairly with us, certainly within the guidelines of the Geneva Convention. The liaison between him and the senior British officer, Group Captain Herbert Massey, was excellent.

The Kommandant had several departments under him running the camp. One department was, I suppose, similar to the equipment branch in the RAF: they supplied food and furniture, and supervised the construction and kitting-out of the new compounds. Another department, most of which spoke English, looked after the file index-cards containing the personal history of each prisoner (before too long, Red and I doubtless had a few black marks on ours). Simoleit, a former professor, looked after this department. He was responsible for allocating two Lageroffizieren (camp officers) and several sergeants and privates to each compound, one of whose main duties was the twice-daily Appell.

Another large department, under Captain von Massow, was responsible for censoring all the Luft Camps' mail and checking books. There were about a hundred of these censors, mostly women, covering all the European languages, although I believe Major Simoleit was the only one able to censor the letters in Polish or Czech. I am pretty sure that no-one in that office was able to make any sense of Welsh; in any event that's what I eventually used to send the odd bit of useless information home, asking my mother, for example, to send me a book entitled *The Food Here is Rotten* by Somebody ap Something. Gwyn, who like my mother, spoke fluent Welsh, supervised this bit of subversion. In my later tunnelling days I also managed to let them know that I was studying to get a job after the war at Hafod. Hafod was a nearby colliery.

The department that excited our main interest, though, was the one whose duty it was to maintain security and prevent escapes, headed by Hauptmann Brioli. Brioli's people were the ones who searched us when we first arrived in the camp and who did the routine searches in the blocks. These were the ones we called without a grain of affection 'ferrets', easily spotted from the blue overalls they wore designed to allow them to crawl under huts and probe around there with their steel prodders, searching for any signs of tunnelling activity. One officer and six NCO ferrets were assigned to each compound; they could enter rooms unannounced, listen at windows, and generally spy on inmates. In charge of the team in our compound was Oberfeldwebel (Warrant Officer) Hermann Glemnitz, a large, genial but very shrewd and experienced character, who was ably and enthusiastically supported by my arch enemy, Gefreiter (Corporal) Greise, known to everyone as 'Rubberneck', for all kinds of reasons.

After my spell in hospital I soon met up with Gwyn and my old friend Red Noble, who had been shot down a few months before us. In those early days we mostly talked about the camp personnel, our activities and what our chances might be of escaping. Pretty much from the outset escaping was high on my own agenda. From discussions I learnt that kriegies tended to sort themselves out according to their interests. Quite a few of them, the majority I suppose in fact, decided straight off that enough was enough, and they were simply going to sit out the rest of the war. In most of these cases being shot down had been too traumatic in itself, and since the war seemed now to be turning our way, why push your luck? Although I did not agree with their sentiments, as a new boy I found amazing hospitality and friendliness. The general attitude seemed to be: we're all in the same boat so we've got to help each other.

In a camp of this size, populated by RAF or Navy officer aircrew, there was a wide diversity of talent. There were graduates and lecturers in almost any subject you could name, from mining engineering to tea-planting, languages and law. In the early days I tried about three of the languages on offer – French, German and Spanish – but only lasted about a week with each. Sitting still never has been my forte. With the help of the Red Cross and YMCA sending materials, some of the eggheads studied hard and gained their degrees whilst in captivity. I personally did not think that a POW camp was the best place to study; once you started a course it was very difficult not to get completely taken over by it. One person I knew gained his degree and with nothing to occupy him any more promptly went round the bend. This was enough excuse for me to avoid such mental activities, although I did attend lots of lectures with interest, ones such as gold-mining in South Africa, cattle-ranching in South America or farming.

The other main activities on offer were sports, theatre and escape planning, or perhaps I should say, dreaming. These were much more to my taste, although with my bad knee I had to leave off sport for a while until it had completely healed. With the help of the Red Cross from various countries we had proper equipment for nearly every sport imaginable, even golf clubs, but without any golf balls which had to be manufactured in camp. We made a pitch for rugby and football, with a rough bare patch for cricket. We also played volleyball and softball, both very popular with the Canadians and Americans. When winter came the Canadians built an ice rink. It was great fun to watch the British trying to play softball and ice hockey, and the North Americans trying to play rugby and cricket. But generally, the standard in all these sports was exceptionally high: Gwyn and I managed to get into a compound rugby side that included an All Black and a Springbok besides many future first-class players. The biggest problem with sport was the lack of food. Even on our optimal diet, in the more strenuous sports we could only play fifteen-twenty minutes each way at most.

But all this was to change. By March 1943, the camp was getting hopelessly overcrowded. The Germans, efficient as ever, had anticipated this, and by April a new compound, called the 'North Compound' had been completed. This was only a few hundred yards from our present camp, but it was on the other side of the German adminstrative and living quarters.

The move gave us all the opportunity to select roommates, whereas before we had all been spread around randomly as we arrived. We would be six to a room, at least, to start with. Gwyn rejoined me, together with two squadron leaders – Irishman Bren Hooper and New Zealander Clive Saxelby – besides Johnny Bull and Red Noble. The move took place, perhaps ominously, on 1 April, and as the seven hundred of us entered the new compound, carrying our few but very precious possessions – Red Cross food, cooking pots, eating utensils – we were carefully checked and strip-searched. Although in this processing we lost quite a few maps and compasses, all the really essential *verboten* equipment like our distilling equipment got through. This small victory over the ferrets made us buzz like excited schoolboys.

CHAPTER THIRTEEN

Stalag Luft III: North Compound

The vaulted dome of Heaven, china blue,
That cups the gleaming diamond of the sun,
Where swallows soar and swoop in silent fun,
And rainbows build an arch of brilliant hue,
Calls from its boundless depths that man should view
The miracle of flight that he has won,
And guard it, lest he finds that he has undone
The benefit and good he sought to do.

God never meant that we should desecrate
The quiet beauty of the sky with flame,
Or urge our gallant youth to dedicate
Destruction to the glory of a name;
And those he spared see justice in their plight,
The pain of caged birds observing flight.

Harry Crease RCAF, from a log book

The six of us had been allocated a room in Block 119. There were fifteen blocks (or huts) in the North Compound, each block consisting of twelve rooms, six on one side of a long corridor, four on the other side, with two single rooms at one end and at the other end the night latrine, plus kitchen and washroom. Single rooms were normally only allocated to wing commanders and above. Each block had a small kitchen with a sink and a cold tap, and a solid fuel stove, but two men from each block had to collect any German food such as the bread, potatoes and prepared green death soup, from the cookhouse, carrying it across the compound in a large metal jug with handles. Even the water was awful. Water from the tap was 'kein trinkwasser'. Rather than go through the painful exercise of shaving in freezing cold, smelly water, many of us had beards: it was less trouble and it kept you warm in winter. The room itself smelt pleasantly at first of clean new pinewood and was generally a vast improvement on the East Compound room, but this soon would change. Bunks were quickly sorted out using the tried and fair method of cutting the cards. Although there

Top left: Ken with his first car, a 1934 Austin 7, in March 1939.

Top right: Ken as a U/T pilot, September 1939.

Bottom left: Sgt Dick Broadbent RNZAF, who took Ken on his first operation on 14 April 1941.

Bottom right: On leave from 40 Squadron, 1941.

Top: A 40 Squadron Wellington photographed whilst passing through Gibraltar on the way to Malta.

Bottom: Taken whilst visiting the pyramids, Cairo, August 1941.

Top left: In Malta, October 1941.

Top right: Ken and Mary on their wedding day, 3 October 1942.

Bottom: With 40 Squadron in Malta. Back row, from left to right: Bob Munro, Smith, Banks, ?. Front row, from left to right: ?, Ken Rees, Harrison, Keith Coleman.

Top: Gwyn and Ken in 1983 by Lake Langavatn in Norway with some of the remains of BK309.

Bottom: Gwyn Martin and Ken laying wreaths on the graves of Sgt Dalzell and Sgt Taylor, who were killed when the crew crashed in Haugesund in October 1942. Taken in 1985.

Opposite page: Stalag Luft III, taken from the air.

Top left: First POW postcard home.

Top right: Chums in Sagan, 1943. From left to right: Joe Noble, Larry Somers, George Smith and Harry Pearson.

Bottom: A purge of prisoners arrives at the North Compound of Stalag Luft III in 1943. Drawn by Ley Kenyon.

Top left: Ken and Gwyn after they lost a bet and had to have their hair shaved off. Taken in 1943. From left to right: Myers, Ken Rees, Gwyn Martin, Lister and Douglas.

Top right: The author's precious log book.

Middle left: The four rogues – Gwyn Martin, Bristow, Joe Noble and Ritchie.

Middle right: Johnny Bull.

Bottom left: Building the theatre in the North Compound, 1943.

Top: Arsenic and Old Lace. Harvey Vivian on the right.

Middle: One of the many rugby matches played at Stalag Luft III.

Right: A boxing match in camp. 'Tommie' Thompson in action.

Top left and right: Cartoons drawn by Bill Fordyce RAAF.

Bottom: A group of RCAF crew. Back row, from left to right: Larry Somers, Harry Crease, Floody, Buckham, George, Sweanor, Guilespei, Leggo, Jack Fry. Front row, from left to right: Butch Adams, Hank Hanlan, Hegwhite, Ogilvie, Brackenbury, McRae.

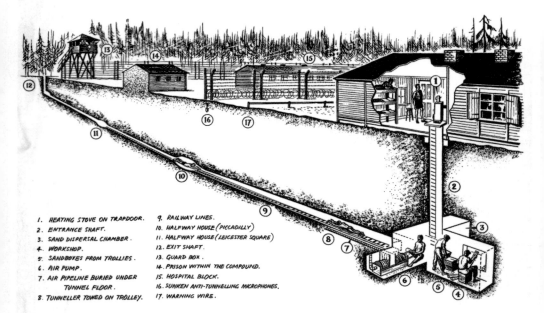

1. HEATING STOVE ON TRAPDOOR.
2. ENTRANCE SHAFT.
3. SAND DISPERSAL CHAMBER.
4. WORKSHOP.
5. SANDBOXES FROM TROLLIES.
6. AIR PUMP.
7. AIR PIPELINE BURIED UNDER TUNNEL FLOOR.
8. TUNNELLER TOWED ON TROLLEY.
9. RAILWAY LINES.
10. HALFWAY HOUSE (PICCADILLY)
11. HALFWAY HOUSE (LEICESTER SQUARE)
12. EXIT SHAFT.
13. GUARD BOX.
14. PRISON WITHIN THE COMPOUND.
15. HOSPITAL BLOCK.
16. SUNKEN ANTI-TUNNELLING MICROPHONES.
17. WARNING WIRE.

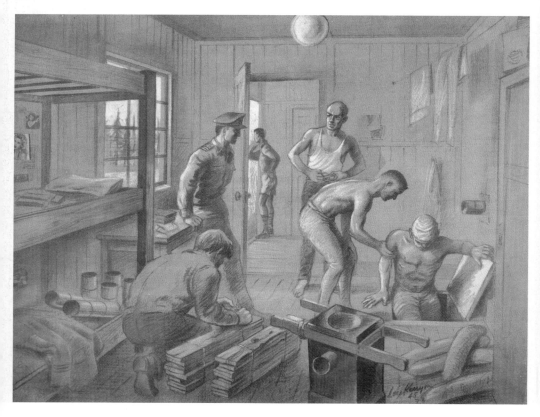

Ley Kenyon's drawings showing (top) the tunnel Harry and its location within the camp; and (bottom) a typical scene. The stove has been lifted away showing the entrance to the tunnel shaft. A lookout is standing in the doorway, one of several who would have been shielding all approaches from the guards.

This drawing, also by Ley Kenyon, shows the workshop in which the wood and metalwork for the tunnel was carried out. Bedboards are being prepared for shoring the tunnel, and hanging from the ceiling is a tin can containing pebbles which could be rattled as a warning.

Top: A box of sand is being transferred from one trolley to another at a halfway house, on its way to the sand dispersal chamber.

Bottom: A tunneller clearing away sand after a collapse of shoring boards. This vividly illustrates the cramped conditions of the tunnel. Both by Ley Kenyon.

Top left: Rubberneck with the air pump from Harry after the escape.

Top right: All that now remains of the entrance to Harry.

Middle left: Two ferrets inspect the trolley from Harry.

Bottom: Memorial to the Fifty murdered after The Great Escape.

In Memory of Those Who Gave Their Lives. — At Sagan 1944 —

F/Lt	H	BIRKLAND.	RCAF.
F/Lt	G	BRETTELL.	RAF.
F/Lt	T	BULL.	RAF.
S/Ldr	R	BUSHELL.	RAF.
F/Lt	M	CASEY.	RAF.
S/Ldr	J	CATANACH.DFC.	RAAF.
F/O	A	CHRISTIANSEN.	RNZAF.
F/O	D	COCHRANE.	RAF.
S/Ldr	I	CROSS. DFC.	RAF.
F/O	H	ESPELID.	RAF.
F/Lt	B	EVANS.	RAF.
F/O	N.J	FUGELSANG.	RAF.
F/Lt	A	GUNN.	RAF.
Lt		J.H.GOUWS.	SAAF.
F/Lt	W	GRISMAN	RAF.
F/Lt	C	HALL.	RAF.
F/Lt	A	HAKE.	RAAF.
F/Lt	A	HAYTER.	RAF.
F/Lt	E	HUMPHRIES.	RAF.
F/Lt	G	KIDDER.	RCAF.
F/Lt	R	KIERATH.	RAAF.
F/Lt	A	KIEWNARSKI.	RAF.
S/Ldr	T	KIRBY-GREEN	RAF.
F/O	J	KOLANOWSKI.	RAF.
F/O	P	LANGFORD.	RCAF.
F/Lt	T	LEIGH.	RAF.
Lt	N	McGARR.	SAAF.
F/Lt	G	McGILL.	RCAF.
F/Lt	R	MARCINKUS.	RAF.
F/Lt	H	MILFORD.	RAF.
F/O	J	MOUNDSCHEN.	RAF.
F/Lt	K	PAWLUCK.	RAF.
F/Lt	H	PICARD.	RAF.
F/Lt		PEJ POME.	RNZAF.
Lt	B	SCHEIDHAUER	FFAF.
P/O	S	SKANZIKLAS.	RAF.
F/O	C	SWAIN.	RAF.
Lt		STEVENS.	SAAF.
F/O	R	STEWART.	RAF.
F/O	J	STONER.	RAF.
F/O	E	VALENTA.	RAF.
F/Lt	T	WALENN.	RAF.
F/Lt	J	WERNHAM.	RCAF.
F/Lt	G	WILEY.	RCAF.
S/Ldr	J	WILLIAMS.	RAF.
P/O	J.E	WILLIAMS.	RAF.
F/Lt	D	KROL.	RAF.
F/Lt	D	LONG.	RAF.
F/O		TOBOLSKI.	RAF.
F/O	D	STREET.	RAF.

JAS. T.R. TAYLOR
SAGAN 1944

Previous page: The author's own handwritten tribute to the Fifty.

Top: The last camp, on a farm near Lübeck. From left to right: Joe Noble, Bren Hooper, Ken Rees, Larry Somers, ?, George Smith.

Middle left and right: The accommodation in the Trenthorst Estate for the last few days before liberation.

Bottom left: January 1962. Ken at Wrexham RFC whilst on leave, with his nephew Lt Tim Rees (left) and son Officer Cadet Martyn Rees (right).

Top left: Mary and Ken at their son Martyn's graduation from Cranwell in 1965.

Top right: Ken and Mary at the Officer's Club HQFEAF, 1966.

Bottom: Ken with his wife Mary, son Martyn and daughter Sue in 2000.

were only six of us, there were four double bunks, doubtless anticipating new arrivals. But now we were all still like excited schoolboys, comparing notes on how we'd outwitted the ferrets and storing away our various items of *verboten* equipment.

The room, which served as our bedroom, living-room and dining-room, was about fourteen-foot square, like all the rooms equipped with a solid fuel stove sitting on a tiled base. In winter we got a very small ration of so-called 'coal', small brickettes made from coal dust and – as I understand it – a little cement, collected from a coal-store near the cookhouse (and sometimes extra bits pinched in between, Joe Noble was adept at this). Each room donated a small amount to the kitchen stove for the use of those cooking an evening meal, but we only cooked when there was Red Cross food from the parcels. That first winter we were allowed to dig up any tree stumps left behind when the goons had cleared the compound area. Joe Noble had the bunk above me, and imprinted on my mind whenever I wake up in the morning even today is that vision of a pair of hairy ginger legs dangling in my face every morning as he had his first cigarette of the day. Each bunk had a set of twelve wooden bed-boards about thirty inches long and six inches wide which were to become a godsend: around 10,000 of them would be used to shore up tunnels.

The new compound was about three hundred yards square, with fifteen huts in three rows accommodating about 900 men, rising to over 1,500 by the end of the war. Four large latrines, wooden twenty-seaters, which served us all had been built over a large pit and were emptied by a workman we called the Scheisser Führer. There was of course no water there, only a foul smell. The kitchen block cookhouse completed the arrangements. As in the East Compound the North Compound was surrounded by two barbed-wire fences, about nine feet high and five feet apart, the middle filled with coiled barbed wire. About twenty-five feet inside the main perimeter fence ran a warning fence about two feet high beyond which it was strictly forbidden to go. On the north side of the wire was the Vorlager, containing the sick quarters, the Cooler and the Red Cross parcel food store. The main security fence ran right round the Vorlager. The entrance to the compound was on the north side, with one guarded gate to enter the Vorlager and another to enter the main area. For the entire circumference at intervals of about every hundred and fifty feet the goon-boxes manned by watchful sentries stood above the wire. At night more sentries patrolled outside the wire, while inside it a Hund Führer patrolled with his dog. Beyond the wire all you could see were endless pine-trees.

Still, it was almost as soon as we had dumped our few belongings that Joe and I went out to see if we could find any weaknesses at all that might give us the chance to escape. However, the first impressions were not promising. I even lifted a manhole cover only to find not enough room for a terrier to get down it. So, on first inspection it appeared that this compound was at least as secure as the one we had just left. In fact, we discovered later, the Kommandant, Oberst von Lindeiner-Wildau, told the SBO (senior British officer, Group Captain HM Massey) that now we were in this nice new compound he expected us to behave ourselves, not try to escape and instead settle down peacefully to await the end of hostilities. Some hope. We were officers, and because of the Geneva Convention, which prohibited any forced labour, we had a lot of time on our hands. At least half of us wanted to put that time to good use carrying on with our duties and fighting the war by other means. We were caged birds of prey and craved our freedom. We got started pretty much straight away.

By 1 April 1943, the date we moved in, the North Compound was complete apart from the area which was to become our sports field, still partly covered with pine-trees. Each day a party of Russian prisoners came into the compound to fell the trees, then the branches would be trimmed and loaded onto a cart pulled by oxen and taken off between the huts and out through the main gate. One enterprising soul whose name I forget noticed that as the cart passed one of the huts there was a blind-spot from the goon-boxes, so climbing onto the roof of the hut, as the cart passed by underneath he flung himself into the middle of the pine-branches, burrowing down until he was completely hidden. He made it out the gate. The next one to try this was also successful, but he got caught by the guard when he tried to climb out of the cart, and was marched back to the Cooler. After this, the guards were issued with long spikes to probe the fir branches.

That was my first encounter with Rubberneck, Gefreiter Greise, who was one of the guards fooled by the pine-branch routine and not at all amused by it. I was having a good laugh at his obvious discomfiture, and when he looked up to see who was laughing, he fixed my gaze, narrowing his eyes in a way that told me as clearly as if he had said it outright that he was going to take note of me. 'I've got your number, laddie,' he seemed to be saying. I think he hated me from that moment on.

In those early days there were several ingenious, daring escape attempts, successful and unsuccessful, none of which, to my chagrin, involved me. One kriegie clung on the underside of a lorry delivering coal, only to be discovered by a diligent guard at the gate. A small New Zealander, 'Digger' Carter, and an equally diminutive American noticed that all the laundry sacks were being loaded onto lorries by kriegie orderlies. They got themselves into the laundry room, wiggled into the sacks, their size being an advantage here, and were simply loaded onto a lorry. They nearly made it, too. Having cut themselves out of the sacks and got off the lorry, they had made their way by train to Stettin on the Baltic coast, only to be caught there just before they could board a boat for Sweden.

Although the ideas for escapes and tunnels had been under constant discussion before the move, it was only after we arrived at this new compound that it all became much more organised. Group Captain Massey decided that escape attempts should no longer be so hit-or-miss or undertaken on such an individual basis. Escaping was to be more organised, more planned. Each idea should be submitted to an escape committee headed by an escape leader known for security purposes as 'Big X'. It then was to be scrutinised, and if it had any chance of being successful it would be given the full backing of the escape organisation, the reasoning being that any really promising attempt would now get support in the way of papers, maps, money and route briefing, whilst the foolhardy attempts that endangered lives would be stopped. With such concentrated efforts at solving the problems involved there was more chance of success and less risk to individuals.

Massey appointed as Big X Squadron Leader Roger Bushell. Born in South Africa, Roger had been a barrister, CO of 92 Squadron (Spitfires), and was shot down over Dunkirk on 22 May 1940, aged thirty, highly-respected by both senior and junior officers. Tall, broad-shouldered, with chilling blue eyes, he spoke fluent French and German, and was a talented sportsman at the kind of sports which require daring individualism, skiing and bobsleighing. He was just the person to take on the job. By this time he had already made two spectacular attempts to escape. In the first one he was caught right at the Swiss border; in the second one, also made before my time, with a Czech named Zafouk, they made it to Prague, where they went into hiding for some months while arrangements were slowly being made for them to get out through Yugoslavia. Unfortunately for them, around that time Gestapo chief Reinhard Heydrich was assassinated by Czech partisans, and in the subsequent mayhem and reprisals both Bushell and Zafouk were rounded up. The Czech family who had sheltered him were shot, while Roger himself wound up in a Gestapo cell in Berlin, where for months the Gestapo tried to pin on him charges of spying and sabotage. Using all his barrister's skill he managed to outwit them, and at the end of 1942 he was returned to Sagan. I well remember him telling me that if he was caught escaping again he would undoubtedly be shot, but this never stopped him. By then he had developed a cold, unyielding hatred for all Germans – Gestapo, ordinary guards and ferrets – they were all the same to him. Whenever he managed to compromise a guard he was merciless; he had them trembling with fear as he threatened to expose them to the authorities if they did not comply with his requests for such things as railway timetables, passes, and various other useful items. He was the mastermind of the X Organisation.

Bushell had an executive committee of resourceful and varied characters, many of whom, like my old roommates Gordon Bretell and George Harsh, had arrived at Stalag Luft III with our purge. Others were Wally Floody, a Canadian, and Lt Commander Peter 'Hornblower' Fanshawe RN. Bushell now collected together a group of exceptionally skilled forgers, tailors, map-makers (including my former flying instructor, Des Plunkett), tunnel engineers, and surveillance experts and announced that he intended to get 250 kriegies out of the compound via a tunnel. In the meantime, though, the X Organisation would give every assistance to any other feasible escape attempts.

One such scheme was put forward by Johnny Stower shortly after the move. He was beating the circuit when it struck him that the goon-boxes above the security fence had been built protruding over the wire by about four feet, so that the guard could look down the inside of the wire, otherwise a blind spot. He realised that if he could get himself under the box it would be impossible for the guard to see him, and he could then quietly and simply climb over the fence using the underside of the box to get over. The plan was accepted, and the X Organisation arranged for the very necessary diversions – usually a punch-up or some sudden, rowdy sport – which allowed Johnny to step over the trip rail and calmly climb the fence. If seen he would have been shot; we all knew that. In fact he made it over the Swiss border, but in the dark he got confused and crossed back again into German territory and was caught. He was sent back to Sagan and was sadly one of those murdered in The Great Escape. Each goon-box subsequently had a suitable fence constructed around its base.

Although escape fever had quickly spread all over camp, smaller acts of defiance continued to flourish, too. One day soon after settling in the new compound I was passing the kitchen block, where I noticed a German guard just leaning his bicycle against the kitchen wall before disappearing inside. I couldn't resist it; those tyres were crying out to be let down. I was just starting on the second wheel when around the corner came the large figure of the head security guard, Oberfeldwebel Glemnitz. 'Vot are you doing, Mr Rees? Off to the Cooler!'

'Oh, I'm just trying to pump the tyres up for this poor guard . . .' Pretty feeble. I didn't have a pump. And even if he had a bit of a sense of humour Glemnitz also had a revolver. Off I went for seven days in the Cooler.

This was the first of many trips to the Cooler. You are incarcerated in a small, whitewashed stone cell about ten by five feet, with a bed, a small table and a chair. No heating. The tiny window is barred, with wood rising from the base at such an angle as only to let in light and a view of the sky, nothing else. I hated the solitude – I cannot begin to describe how much – with nothing to read, nothing to look at, nobody to talk to. Even the food was punitive: a thin round of black bread for breakfast, thin 'soup' and a few potatoes for lunch, and another piece of bread in the evening. One lunchtime I had a bit of extra protein in the shape of grubs in the soup. Although very hungry, I passed that one up. You were allowed no books and smoking was *verboten*, but luckily that first time I had managed to conceal my cigarettes and some matches by palming them while they searched me on arrival. I knew they'd smell the smoke, so I asked if I could go to the toilet, and once there and alone, I took one cigarette out of the packet and hid the others on top of the high-level cistern. This precious cigarette I cut in half and spent the rest of that day and most of the next gouging out a small hole in the bottom of the table leg, just big enough to conceal a half cigarette and a couple of matches. To stop them from falling out I jammed the hole with a piece of potato peel. The whole procedure became a main source of amusement. They would catch me smoking, confiscate the butt, search the cell and frisk me and find nothing. Later on they would again catch me smoking and have to go through the entire process again. On my last day I retrieved my last two cigarettes from the cistern, rang the bell, offered the guard a fag and asked him for a light. To my delight he simply shook his head in disbelief, accepted the offering and gave me a light. This apart it had been a miserable seven days. When I returned to my room I found my roommates had saved me extra rations. It felt like Christmas.

That June 1943, the first of several particularly audacious escapes was organised. The Germans were very well aware that any lice found represented a potential typhus epidemic, so to avoid this they had a de-lousing unit set up in the administration area. In order to get the wind up them and set a de-lousing programme into operation it was decided to manufacture some lice or find something that looked like squashed lice. The ploy worked, and a number of us were smartly put down for the shaved hair and powder treatment. After several of the bona fide de-lousing parties had departed for the unit, another party was formed, escorted by two 'Unteroffizieren', in fact two fluent German speakers convincingly dressed by our own clothing department. Carefully judging the timing when at midday the guard on the gate was changed, and using a forged pass, the ersatz de-lousing party passed right through the gates and once out of sight, dispersed into the woods.

Almost immediately after this lot had disappeared out of camp, a group of several senior officers, including the senior American officer, Colonel Goodrich, and Wing Commander Bob Tuck, headed for the gate, escorted by Bob van der Stok, the German-speaking Dutchman dressed as an 'Unteroffizier', ostensibly looking for the administration block as if on their way for a meeting with the Kommandant. They managed to get past the first gate with their forged pass, but at the next gate the guard was a little more conscientious, turning the pass over and spotting some mistake there. He shouted, and immediately half a dozen guards came running out of the guardhouse to the scene of the crime. Brioli, the chief security officer, was quickly on the spot, happy to gloat, thoroughly delighted with the guard's perspicacity. He congratulated him warmly, but when the guard ventured to add how unusual it was for two parties to leave so close together, Brioli's happy expression collapsed entirely. Two seconds later the place was livelier than a real louse-hunt.

In spite of the head start most of the de-lousing party were rounded up pretty smartly. Three, however, evaded immediate capture. One Czech walked to Czechoslovakia but was caught trying to cross into Switzerland. The other two, Walter Morison and Lorne Welch, were caught trying repeatedly to steal a German aircraft, a Junkers W34, and banished to the notorious Colditz, the camp for really bad or really important bad boys. Brioli, not a happy man, kept his guards on the hop steaming around the camp, with the rest of us standing on parade for about seven hours while the guards counted and recounted and checked our faces against our photographs. As usual after such episodes our food parcels were stopped for the following week. We all hated this, of course, but it was the price paid for taking that joyous risk.

Soon after this, Red Noble and I were beating the circuit, when he noticed an ox-drawn waggon into which was being emptied the incinerator where we put the rubbish and cinders from our stoves.

'Look,' he could barely contain his excitement. 'There's only the one guard. All we have to do is distract him, then I could get into the waggon covered up by the rubbish. It's dead easy.'

He put the idea to Big X and it was passed. The next time the ox-cart was drawn up to empty our incinerator Red was ready. A German speaker from the X Organisation drew away the guard, while another diverted the attention of the worker loading the stuff, and Red quickly jumped up into the contents of the waggon while the work of emptying the incinerator was still being carried on. The one catch in all this became quickly apparent: we had not taken into account the fact that the contents of these incinerators actually retained their heat long enough to make things pretty uncomfortable for him right now, covered in it. We could hear his voice yelling out that he was burning and help, for Christ's sake! But as we rushed to his aid the guard brought his rifle to the ready. God only knows what might have happened to poor Red had not Paddy Byrne, a quick-thinking Irishman, shouted to the guard to get a ferret, go on, do it! It was all too much for the guard, who rushed off, giving us the chance to haul Red out from under his hellish cinders. He was very hot to the touch, but unharmed, and we had him away and into the hut and changed before the guard came back with Rubberneck, the chief ferret. Another failed attempt.

Still, such attempts made the Germans feel that we were in there trying, and diverted attention away from the main projects.

Several attempts to get out going through the wire had been approved, the X Organisation giving out money, passes, wire-cutters and suchlike – items which had either been manufactured on the quiet or obtained through tame or compromised goons. These escape attempts were generally made on a moonless stormy night, or when there was an air raid in the vicinity to divert attention. They never seemed to work. Jack Probert, from our hut, and a New Zealander, Jack Rae, decided that the reason these failed was that at such times the guards were actually more alert, and the numbers of Hund Führers increased. They had also noticed that just inside the warning wire, where the track was that everyone walked on and the carts working the camp used, there was a slight depression, not surprising given the sandy soil. Jack reckoned that anyone crawling up through this slight dip in the ground would be more or less hidden in the shadow of the searchlights. Just to make sure they would appear invisible, they soaked their palliasse covers in a mixture of surface soil and water.

The night of the escape was dry and moonless; we got them out of the hut window and wrapped in their palliasse covers they began their long, slow crawl through the dry sand. It worked, but every time the searchlights came on they had to freeze. It took them over five hours just to crawl to a position between the two goon-boxes from which they could make the very dangerous final ten yards from the track to the wire. They were caught in the act by the guard patrolling outside the wire and marched off for a month in the Cooler. I think this incarceration was too much for poor Probert, who tried to make a hopeless dash for the Cooler door and was shot in the shoulder by the guard. We all understood the desperation that drove him.

After all this, Red and I decided that the only way out for us was going to be via one of the big tunnels, and that's what we worked on from that moment.

CHAPTER FOURTEEN

Kriegies

Only those who have been prisoners have any conception of the horror of being a prisoner, or of the ineffable joy of release, of the terrible rise and fall of the spirit, the fluctuation between delirium of happiness and the madness of despair attendant upon the fluctuation of hopes and fear, and the possibility of release, advances and retreats.

P.C. Wren

From my own attitude and that of most of my friends one could easily imagine that everyone spent all their time thinking about escape or actually attempting it. But this is far from the truth, and I think that for most kriegies, the traumatic experience of being shot down and subsequent feelings that being shot down and surviving had been a lucky escape in itself, led to a kind of resignation that they had after all done their duty and would now sit out the war. There was justification for this philosophical view, especially after the Battle of Alamein in October 1942. All the news garnered from our clandestine radios was good, and most of us had no doubt what the outcome of the war would be. As I've said, I was shot down on the night of Alamein and I always felt rather put out that once they had got rid of me, the Allies went on to victory. Although most people in camp settled down to pursue their own interests like sport, theatricals or education, I always found that even if they were not themselves interested in escaping, they gave every support to those who did, in spite of the fact that escapes meant trouble for everyone, usually in the form of extra Appells and food restrictions. This attitude was, I suppose, understandable: everyone knew that for each one of us who became prisoners many of our comrades had given their lives.

It is as well to try to understand what many, if not most, kriegies had already gone through before their arrival in Stalag Luft III. The people I shared a room with provide example enough, and such stories formed at least part of the topics discussed when circuit-bashing.

Squadron Leader Bren Hooper, an Irishman, had joined the RAF in 1939, and by June 1942 he had completed over fifty operations and received a DFC. On 27 June he was returning to base after having just bombed Bremen, when a night-fighter attacked his Wellington, shattering the instrument panel and setting on fire the port engine. With the intercom dead he was unable to get the crew to bale out, so, to evade the fighter and with any luck put out the fire, he dropped the starboard wing, applied rudder and went into a screaming dive. This was not enough to put out the fire, and as he plunged into cloud the whole of the starboard engine was streaming flames. The cloud meant that he was getting dangerously low now, so Bren applied himself to the massive task of pulling the Wimpy out of its dive, frantically heaving and playing with the trimming tabs on the tail which controlled the fore and aft movement of the aircraft, and bit by painful bit it began to level out. Just about now, I think, Bren's guardian angel decided to come on duty, because the moment the aircraft levelled out it smacked the ground at what must have been 300 mph. The results were dramatic. Screaming through the Dutch lowlands, the Wimpy and its wing parted company, as did the tail unit, complete with rear turret and gunner inside it. Miraculously, when the blazing aircraft finally did come to a halt, all four remaining crew members evacuated the wreckage, the only injury between them being a nasty cut across Bren's forehead. They found the very shaken rear gunner about half a mile back; he had got out of his turret, staggered into one of the deep ditches all around there and nearly drowned.

Joe Noble, my friend Red, was a navigator in the RCAF, almost at the end of his second tour. He had been in Bomber Command, first with 40 Squadron, then with 214 Squadron flying Stirlings. It was his fifty-seventh operational sortie, and appeared on the surface to be strictly a 'no sweat' trip, bombing the railway yards at Osnabrück. After completing the task with very little opposition they headed for home. About ten minutes from the target a Me110 attacked from below, which is in Stirlings a blind area for the gunners. The initial attack set the aircraft on fire, while two subsequent attacks finished off both the Stirling and the Me110, which was brought down by the mid-upper gunner's fire. They were falling and out of control when the order came to bale out. Two of the crew were already dead, four had jumped clear, and the captain – Squadron Leader Peter Nixey – and Joe were ready at the escape hatch, parachutes on, when the whole thing exploded, blowing itself to bits at about 1,000 feet. Joe was thrown clear of the debris, and despite the short descent, landed safely with his parachute in a cemetery, with only minor burns on his face and hands. Nixey was not so lucky; he never got out. Of the crew of eight, now only four survived, two to become captured and POWs. Joe met up with Flt Sgt Bailey, and between them they worked out that they must be seventy miles east of the Dutch border.

Travelling by night, on the fifth night they made it out of Germany and into Holland, where they decided the next day to try to get help for Joe, whose right hand was by now very painful, swollen and infected. No-one appeared to speak any English, and although people seemed friendly enough, they were all too terrified of the Gestapo to offer any assistance other than the odd bit of food or drink. So, Joe and Bailey pressed on for a few more days, and as they approached the Belgian border they encountered two Dutch police officers on bicycles. One was friendly and appeared willing to help, but the other did not, and after some discussion which seemed to be getting nowhere, Joe and Bailey decided on desperate measures, launching themselves at the two policemen. But the policemen were fitter, better-fed and didn't have burns on their hands, so Bailey was forced to run off in one direction, leaving Joe there on his own. Although Joe managed to grab his man's gun and bicycle and pedal furiously away, his hand was by now in very bad shape, the pain nauseating, and the only way forward involved crossing a lot of guarded bridges over canals. He might still have made it, approaching each bridge at full speed and hoping for the best, and in fact he made good progress for about a day, but he'd already left a trail behind him filling up with Dutch policemen alerted from the previous night's episode and his hand was now completely useless. They caught up with him at last, four policemen and some bridge guards, and he was forced to admit defeat.

Then there was Bob Nelson, a flight lieutenant in the RAF, who had arrived at Stalag Luft III at the same time as Gwyn and me, even though he'd started his journey into captivity about a month earlier when his Wellington caught fire over the Western Desert, approximately fifty miles south of Sollum. By the time he had baled his crew out, the aircraft was too low for him to get himself out, so he crash-landed the burning plane in the desert. There was just time enough to grab emergency rations and bundle himself out through the escape hatch, when it all blew up, fuel tanks and bombs together. He struck out for the east, towards El Alamein, 200 miles away, with some water, the emergency rations and just a small pocket compass to guide him, with no shelter and only the clothes he'd come down in. His idea was to walk at night and sleep during the infernal heat of day, but the heat and the flies made sleep impossible, if not actual torment. At sunset on the seventh virtually sleepless day, by this time out of water and rations, he saw on the horizon a herd of camels with a young Arab driver. He was given some water and later, when they had set up camp, some bread made over the campfire. Next day, the driver took him to an encampment where he was treated with great courtesy and given a tent furnished with rugs where he flopped down and enjoyed the first really good night's sleep in over a week. The following morning, when he asked the chief for some help to get back to the British lines, some fourteen days away, he was told that with all the Germans around this would be too dangerous for them, but in the end they sent him off with two additional water bottles and a haversack filled with British Army biscuits!

Bob has some difficulty recalling the exact sequence of events after leaving the Arab camp. He did return to walking in the evenings and at night, but his feet were so swollen and blistered by now that he had to use sticks for support. It was a painful, slow progress, but he did make it to twenty miles south of the coast and was soon caught up in all the signs of a war going on. Day and night aircraft flew overhead, and he was forced to hide from the many passing German trucks and armoured cars by concealing himself in the numerous remains scattered about of crashed aircraft and abandoned vehicles. One morning, he later found out it was 6 October, the battle of El Alamein, he was catching up with the rear of the German lines, beyond which lay the British. There was a great deal of activity, so he decided on the bold approach, walking purposefully straight through everything going on. Although it must have looked as if a scarecrow had suddenly put in an appearance, no-one stopped him. That afternoon he came to within range of the British guns, where he decided to stop and take stock of what on earth to do next. There were not many options. Walking forward was now dangerous as well as painful; he was a solitary figure in no-man's-land, with shells whining overhead and constant bursts of machine-gun fire. In the end he decided simply to crawl into a slit tent and wait for darkness, when he might be able to sneak through. When night did come he made his way through the barbed wire entanglements and the mine fields, and just when he thought he'd made it through he was challenged from behind. He fell flat on his face in the sand, bullets whistling above him, but it was no good. They sent out a patrol to pick him up, less than a quarter of a mile from the British lines.

Another occupant of the room was a cheerful young Canadian wireless operator called George Smith, known as 'Junior'. On 24/25 July his RCAF crew aircraft was hit just after they had attacked Duisburg. The pilot was wounded and for whatever reason did not bale out the crew but managed to crash-land, killing himself and the front gunner Radcliffe, while Westwood, the rear gunner, lost a leg. George, too, was badly wounded, and spent several months in hospital, where he met another wounded man who was to live in our room, Larry Somers, also RCAF.

Larry had been shot down in a Spitfire over the North Sea. His aircraft in flames, he managed nevertheless to bale out, and landed in the sea with his flying suit still burning and his face so terribly burnt he could not see. Somehow, he managed to get to his dinghy, only to be machine-gunned, presumably by the same German who had shot him down. He survived the attack, and after three agonising days adrift was at last picked up by a German patrol boat, then spent many months in the hospital where he met

George. He regained his sight eventually, but his face and body were very badly scarred. In spite of this Larry was the most cheerful soul imaginable; he threw himself into most of the sports available in camp, especially ice-hockey and softball.

And there was Squadron Leader Clive Saxelby DFC, a New Zealander who had come over to England in 1939 with a short service commission. On 7 September 1942, during his sixtieth operation, the last of his second tour, he was shot down over Düsseldorf in his Halifax. Although they had already been set on fire, everyone managed to bale out, apart from the rear gunner, already dead. 'I'd already received my new posting,' Sax used to say, 'but I reported to the Third Reich instead.' Like many of us, he had his twenty-first birthday party in captivity.

Just about all POWs had similar stories to tell, so one could well understand the attitude of many prisoners who, after such traumatic experiences, felt that they were exceptionally lucky to be alive and simply wanted to make the best of a boring but relatively safe existence. And boring it certainly was. There was a huge amount of time to fill each day; you could only spend so much on sport, lectures or even escape planning, and the meagre diet left you lethargic. Because there was so much of it, one quickly lost all sense of time. I think any real sense of urgency and purpose only came from escaping activities, especially when we were working so hard to finish the last tunnel, Harry. Some of us needed that exhilarating rush of adrenalin more than others.

A typical day was based around very dull and basic routine. One woke up to the morning Appell, with the guards marching through the huts, exhorting us with shouts of 'Raus, raus! Schnell!' to hurry up and get out onto the sports ground, where we would be counted. After the morning count, breakfast, i.e. a piece of the disgusting Reich bread smeared with margarine and turnip jam, followed by our daily chores: cleaning the room, taking it in turns to clean the communal parts, queuing for hot water to do one's dhobie. The dhobie was done in a bucket with two tins, one smaller inside a larger, stuck on the end of a pole to act as an old-fashioned Dolly to swish the clothes around. The rest of the day was clear until the afternoon Appell, when once again we were counted.

As I've said before, in a compound of over 1,000 aircrew coming from all walks of life and from all over the world, there were experts on just about any subject you could think of. Harvey Vivian, a former master at Clifton College, was in charge of education, and thanks to the relief agencies there was a comprehensive reference and lending library. The Germans fortunately could see the practical value of keeping us occupied; preoccupied, we were far less likely to try to escape. Serious students were able to study even to degree level, the examination papers arranged through the Red Cross. But being stuck in school had never been a favourite pastime with me, so I had no real desire to stay the course. Besides, I was busy enough elsewhere.

Being a POW, I sometimes felt at the time, really was like being at some University of Life, not least because I was surrounded by people from so many different countries and backgrounds and talents. All the Commonwealth countries were represented, as were most non-German European countries, as well as South America and South Africa. We also had all the American Air Force POWs until they were moved to their own compounds, then under construction. In between sport and digging I did a lot of visiting the people I had got to know: Norwegians Jan Staubo, Peter Bergsland and Jens Muller, who managed to escape to Sweden; then there was the theatre crowd – Peter Butterworth, Rupert Davies, Kenneth Macintosh, the producer and director, Tolly Rothwell, who wrote and produced several West End plays as well as the *Carry On* series, and another actor, the son of Sir John Casson and Dame Sybil Thorndike, John Casson. Amongst the Americans I remember best Major Jones, known to us all as 'Tokyo' Jones for his part in the famous bombing raid on Tokyo led by Colonel Jimmy Doolittle, and Major Jerry Sage, larger than life and built like what we call in Wales a brick Ty Bach (i.e. outhouse). Jones became commander of the USAF, while other kriegies became air marshals or senior politicians. Of the latter, two kriegies who studied accountancy in Stalag Luft III were Tony Barber, later Chancellor of the Exchequer, and Harry Williams, town treasurer of Belfast. It is difficult to describe the strong bond felt by all of us disparate specimens of humanity, but it was certainly stronger than any old-school feeling: what we had in common was the enemy and our experiences of him, being shot down and imprisoned by him. 'Living Well is the Best Revenge', and that's what we let them see.

When we were moved into the new compound, an area on its southern side had been designated as the sports field, but before it could be put to use, those of us interested in sport spent many back-breaking weeks clearing it of dozens of tree stumps before we could get on with any playing. As I said, sport was one of my main interests during my time in Luft III. Both Gwyn and I played for the compound rugby team against the East Compound, and the standard was amazingly high in spite of our starved state. We had a New Zealander who'd had an All-Black trial, Jimmy Edgar, who played for Natal; Gwyn, who later had a Welsh trial; another New Zealander, Pete Kimberly, who captained Cambridge after the war; I later captained London Welsh; Tony Bethell, who played for Barbarians, and several other first-class players.

North Compound v. East Compound, May 1943
Mike Gummer (Eng)
Johnnie Stower (Argentina) Bob Herrick (Eng)
Gwyn Martin (Wal) Kimbly (NZ)
Jimmy Edgar (SA) Ken Doran (Eng)
Harvey Vivian (Eng) Gerricker (SA) Polly Theron (SA)
Pete Kimberly (Eng) Sgt Brown (NZ)
Ken Rees (Wal) Bush Kennedy (SA) Tony Bethell (Eng)

(I don't remember who won but it was very physical.)

We arranged all kinds of matches – sevens, fives – all well-supported. Gwyn even got up a Welsh team, but had some trouble finding fifteen true Welshmen. He decided that anyone called 'Williams' or 'Davies' was eligible; Tony Bethell it was decided was obviously 'Ap Ethel'. Rupert Davies, later of *Maigret* fame, refused to play as he was currently treading the boards as Macbeth and didn't want to get hurt, but he volunteered to run the line as referee. It was sod's law that he tripped and sprained his ankle doing this, so we had a limping Macbeth that evening.

Rupert, or 'Pud' as he was known,was one of the leading lights in the camp theatre, which did so much to keep up everyone's morale. When we were moved into the new compound, the Germans surprised everyone by agreeing to the SBO's request to put aside one of the huts for recreational purposes, under the aegis of the SBO. A popular wing commander, Digger Larkin, was put in charge of building a theatre. Larkin was a keen entertainer himself, a guitarist, and under his enthusiastic supervision the project took shape. He enlisted the help of an architect POW called Callwell, while the rest of us were put to work digging out hundreds of tons of the local sandy soil to make a sloping floor for the auditorium. Thousands of bricks went into the foundations, the projection room and fire wall. It was a proper job. On top of this was set the prefabricated hut. The auditorium had a seating capacity of three hundred and fifty individual seats made from Canadian Red Cross crates, each seat with an armrest. The interior was decorated, and under the supervision of two RAF NCOs, lighting was installed. Stage lighting was ingeniously constructed out of biscuit tins, bits of wood and quite a few bribes; there were even dimmer switches on the control panel. Lt MacKay, a South African who was wizard with a homemade blowlamp, managed to produce all kinds of metal work out of Red Cross tins, including ornaments for the stage like lamps, furniture or mantelpieces and stage swords. The carpenters, equally ingenious, devised dozens of props from scraps of wood obtained God knows how and cardboard. I well remember seeing on stage a wonderful wrought-iron gate of the most intricate design, actually made of cardboard and painted black. From a tiny room behind the stage, under the supervision of Flt Lt Smallwood, a small band of kriegies turned out a stunning range of costumes, especially female dresses, from old shirts, pyjamas, handkerchiefs and any other material they could beg or bribe from the Germans. The end results would have made Christian Dior envious, and were the source of a great many erotic dreams after the show!

The theatre was a huge success, and went from strength to strength, giving enormous pleasure to everyone involved in the productions as well as the appreciative audiences. Even the Germans enjoyed it. Many of those involved, like Rupert Davies, Ken Macintosh, Talbot Rothwell, Peter Butterworth and others, went on to successful postwar careers in theatre and film. I remember an American pilot arriving in the compound still in possession of a ticket for *Arsenic and Old Lace* which he'd given up as a lost cause. He was astonished to find that it was on the bill for that evening, and since he was the only man with a real ticket, was given a front seat. Needless to say my own contribution to all this was either as labourer shifting sand in the construction or else sitting in the audience. My only stage part had been at school, when as one of the spear-carriers on the first night of *The Merchant of Venice* I managed to faint, landing on Shylock's back as he was pleading with Portia.

One of the best things about the theatre was the excellent pit band. In fact we also had a full classical orchestra conducted by a Canadian, Art Creighton, and a Glenn Miller-type band lucky enough to have as a member an American major who had been with the original Glenn Miller Orchestra in earlier life. Instruments were miraculously supplied through the Red Cross.

Yet another source of interest and enterprise was started up by a Flt Lt Douglas, a sort of barbed-wire department store he called 'Foodacco'. With all the inhabitants receiving a Red Cross parcel per week, or as was much more usual, one parcel between two, a lot of different types of food came into each room, the parcel contents varying according to country of origin, such as Great Britain, Canada or the USA. Every six months each of us also had a personal parcel from home which usually contained clothing, but which could be made up to the approved weight with chocolate. After the first few parcels we requested fewer clothes and more chocolate as it had such nutritious value (and a lovely sweet taste). Whenever a personal parcel arrived in the room the chocolate would be shared out, with some being kept back for trading or bribes. Anyone at home could send cigarettes, so there was always an abundance. With all the regional variations, the personal likes and dislikes and the abundance of certain items, Douglas decided it might be a good thing to trade it all around. Since the goons didn't allow any currency in the camp, a system of valuation was devised using points, the points allocated depending on the popularity of the item, and each individual had his own account. Apart from its Food Department, Foodacco had its Tobacco and Miscellaneous Departments; thus one could put in an unwanted item of clothing and use the points accumulated to purchase something else. As I was Cook Führer for our room I opened a room account to enable me to vary the meals. It also proved useful if we wanted extra prunes or raisins to make up a brew for a party.

A room had been allocated to Foodacco, also equipped with a large notice-board which kept us all up to date with camp activities such as lectures, sports, plays and concerts. Also posted, I could never understand why, were a section of extracts from letters, some amusing, some rather sad, especially the 'Dear John' letters written to break off a relationship. One I remember said simply: 'I am fed up with waiting for you and am marrying your father!' Another told the recipient that since he was a POW it was now all off, adding that the least he might have done was to die for his country! One American got a letter from his wife to say that she was having a baby by an army major, but that this would be all right since the major would send him cigarettes regularly. One from a rather pessimistic wife in 1944 said: 'I am enclosing a calendar, which will be useful since it has several years on it.'

But for me the days were still difficult to fill. One can only spend so much time playing sport or even digging tunnels. Playing bridge or poker without money was no fun. Neither was strip poker without any women. I pounded the circuit endlessly, discussing everything under the sun, especially the war, wives, women and what we would do after the war. It was mostly boring, boring, boring. Many like myself had been keen to fly, to be in on the action, to be active and useful, and were instead now stuck and confined for an indefinite future. We felt confident we would win, but when? Small wonder some were desperate to get out any way we could.

CHAPTER FIFTEEN

Tom, Dick and Harry

April/May 1943

Roger Bushell, Big X, oversaw the whole escape committee, and actually masterminded the big plan, which was to concentrate all the efforts and dig not just one but three tunnels, called 'Tom', 'Dick' and 'Harry', and get out of camp around 250 prisoners. There had already been many attempts to tunnel out of Stalag Luft III, more than thirty in the summer of 1942 alone, but a number of problems had to be solved. The soil was loose sand, a different colour from soil around the compound, and any tunnel through such loose stuff needed to be heavily shored up. Secondly, the distance from any of the huts to the wire was never less than sixty yards, and finally, the Germans had devised microphones which could detect any digging activity to a depth of fifteen feet. But the ingenuity and expertise which had produced out of practically nothing theatrical productions, lectures on any subject, and much of what kept us all alive and sane was certainly up to such a challenge.

Roger set up a tunnelling executive committee. Wally Floody, a Canadian mining engineer, was to mastermind the sinking of shafts and the tunnelling for all three tunnels; Peter 'Hornblower' Fanshawe RN was to organise the dispersal of the sand; and Flt Lt George Harsh, the American in the RCAF I'd shared a room with in Dulag Luft, was to be in charge of security. Security began, Roger emphasised to us all, with care at the most basic level: if he heard any bastard mentioning the word 'tunnel' he would personally crucify them. It wasn't any lack of trust; rather making absolutely certain there was no loose talk.

When after the war I read George's book, *The Lonesome Road*, the revelations in it astonished me. When I knew him he was a quiet, reserved man, at thirty-three rather older than many of us, and he had come even further than most. He had grown up with wealth and privilege, but was wild; while at university for kicks he took part in a hold-up which went wrong, and he gunned down a security guard, for which he was sentenced to death, later commuted to life in a Georgia chain gang. Only the toughest survived; he gained a certain amount of respect when he killed another prisoner over a bar of soap. This aggressive attitude changed; he changed. For good behaviour he became a 'Trusty', working with the doctor in the prison hospital, where he became interested in medicine, reading all the medical books he could find. Then one stormy winter day in 1940 the electricity and phones were cut off. He was alone on duty when a prisoner was brought in with acute appendicitis. George operated, using some ether as an anaesthetic, and the man survived. For this extraordinary effort he was granted a full pardon, and on his release went up to Montreal to enlist in the RCAF as a rear gunner. No-one in camp knew then about his past, but he was the perfect choice to be in charge of security.

Wally Floody was supported in his tunnelling outfit by four keen and experienced tunnellers: 'Crump' Ker-Ramsay, John Marshall, Johnny Bull and 'Conk' Canton. I'd shared a room with both Marshall and Bull in the East Compound, and still shared with Bull, so as a main digger and team leader he invited Bren Hooper, Joe Noble and myself onto his digging team. They rationalised that since I was Welsh I was bound to be good at mining. I hadn't actually ever done any, but I was thrilled to be asked and willing to learn. There would be plenty of opportunity, since a lot had to be done before the main digging could begin.

The escape committee had decided where to place the three tunnels. Tom was located in Block 123 on the west side of the compound and would have about 150 feet to get to the outside. Dick was also on the west side, but starting from Block 122, one row in from Tom; it needed about 250 feet to get beyond the wire. By far the most ambitious, Harry would start from an end room in Block 104 on the south side of the compound, pass under the Vorlager and into the wood, the overall distance a staggering 350 feet. It did have the advantage of being the least likely place, from a German point of view, for a tunnel.

Some Polish officers headed by Minskewicz were the trap experts, par excellence. Since the huts were raised two feet off the ground, only the concrete from the stoves and the washrooms actually touched the ground, so somehow we were going to have to go through the concrete. Tom's trap was to be situated in a dark corner of the concrete floor just ouside the kitchen. The Poles had liberated some cement left behind by careless German workers, and this was used to cast a concrete slab in a wooden mould about twenty-four inches square. Minskewicz chipped out the concrete in a darkened area outside the kitchen in Block 123, the exact size of the slab he had made. He handled the chisel with great precision, and when the block was finished, with two lugs set in its sides, it fitted in the hole perfectly. When it was laid in place, any minute cracks filled with cement paste and dusted with dirt, it was almost impossible to detect.

The trap for Dick was the most cunning I ever heard of. In the middle of the concrete washroom floor in Block 122 was an iron grating about twenty inches square, into which water flowed from showers and washing clothes. Under the grating was a small chamber about three feet deep with a pipe about a foot from its bottom to carry away the water, which meant that there was always about a foot of water in the chamber. Minskewicz lifted the iron grating, baled out the water and chipped away one blank side. Once again he cast a slab to fit the side he had chipped out, and when this was put in place, the cracks filled with soap and sand, and the chamber again filled with water, it was, we considered, impossible for the ferrets to detect. I worked on the other two tunnels, but for some reason never went down Dick.

The trap for Harry was under the stove in Room 23 of Block 104. Conk Canton and his team had carefully lifted the stove up off the tiles it stood on, then reset the tiles into concrete on a wooden frame. This he hinged, and when the stove was off it could be lifted up. After using a pick to get through the bricks and concrete it was ready for the shaft to be sunk.

Under Wally Floody's expert direction the tunnellers now got to work to sink the three shafts simultaneously. Johnny Bull was one of his team, and he assured us that we would be called upon as soon as the actual tunnelling started, but first the shafts had to be sunk to a depth of thirty feet, shored with wood the whole way down, and a ladder nailed to one wall. At the foot of each shaft three compartments were dug out: one for storing sand ready for dispersal; one as a small workshop; and one for the air-pump which would be needed as the tunnel progressed.

Whilst these activities were getting under way, Big X had been busy setting up the rest of the vast organisation necessary to ensure a successful operation. The two most important at this beginning stage were security and sand dispersal. A 'Little X' was appointed for each block, and he recruited volunteers for these teams. If anyone had special skills such as tailoring, carpentry, engineering and so on, he would be allocated to the appropriate section.

Security was now under the joint direction of Lt Col Clark, George Harsh and Tom Kirby-Green, a squadron leader from 40 Squadron who had been shot down just before I had joined it. The compound was divided up into 'safe' and 'danger' zones, the east side of the camp being the 'safe' side, since it was furthest from the compound entrance. The goons were also identified according to how dangerous they were considered to be. Some of the guards and ferrets could always be diverted into a room for a coffee, but others like Rubberneck and one we called 'Keen Type' were incorruptible. Sight-lines all around the compound were worked out so that signals could quickly be sent about any threatening movements. In a room in the block nearest the entrance-gate a 'duty pilot' was positioned to book in and out anyone who came into the compound. These were then constantly monitored and if any threat suspected, especially when the traps were open for business, the traps could be shut down in a matter of minutes.

Snap Appells and block searches were a constant danger, but the highly-efficient intelligence department generally got advance notice of these. Formed and run by Czech Flt Lt Ernst Valenta, intelligence was comprised mostly of German speakers who had managed to control several tame goons through either bribery or blackmail, a valuable source of information as well as a source for railway timetables, maps, passes, identity cards, bits for the radio, and travel documents that could be copied. Over a period of time, using the cigarettes, chocolate or coffee then almost unobtainable in Germany, intelligence managed to compromise certain goons. This was done very gradually, beginning when they had pinpointed some weak character who craved some goodies for a wife or girlfriend. It would start off with asking for something relatively trivial, but once the goon had been compromised Roger Bushell would take over and get the poor unfortunate man into his room for a masterly and completely ruthless going-over. With Roger's cold blue eyes on him the goon would hear how he would be exposed to the Kommandant, which meant he would be shot or at least sent to the Russian Front. You almost felt sorry for the poor sod, watching him leave Roger's room a quivering wreck, off to risk himself obtaining whatever it was we needed at the time, but for which he would be recompensed. Chocolate came expensive, however you looked at it.

The major problems in digging the tunnels became quickly evident. At about six inches below the grey surface loam Wally discovered the rest was a sand much paler in colour than anything in the compound. Any such sand dispersed on top would show up immediately. Hornblower and his team set about overcoming these difficulties.

When work first started on the tunnels, soon after we moved into the North Compound, it was decided to disperse the sand around the surface of the compound itself, by making use of the many sandy areas already created by the Germans during the digging of latrines, drains, the fire poll and so on. Some trees had been uprooted, and these also left sandy patches. By using such patches it was decided that sand could be mixed and buried there without it showing up, but the first problem was how to get the sand to these areas? Most of them were well inside the compound and out of sight of the goon-boxes. The first idea was to carry the sand in specially-constructed bags slung around the chest under battle-dress and supported by a cord around the neck, but the hitch here was that it was impossible to drop the sand without taking off the battle-dress or greatcoat, and further, the weather was getting warmer. Pretty dubious wearing a greatcoat in high summer.

So a new method was devised which, although successful, was very slow. The German-issue towels we had were sewn into a narrow sock-shaped bag about twenty-four inches long, the top being slightly larger than the bottom, and two of these were joined together by a cord. These sacks were carried inside each leg of the trousers, suspended by a cord around the neck, the bottom of each sack secured by a pin on a length of string extending inside the pocket. The carriers found that they had to practise walking normally when moving fully-loaded into the dispersal area, their characteristic lolloping side-to-side gait earning them their inevitable nickname, 'penguins'.

The sheer amount of sand to be dispersed was enormous: Hornblower's team had calculated about one ton of sand was being produced for every three feet of tunnel. It was estimated that the shafts and the three underground chambers *each* produced about twelve tons of sand, and since each penguin could carry only sixteen pounds of sand, the task assumed frightening proportions. It was worked out that during the course of the whole operation, right up to the successful completion in March 1944, a total of 250 tons of sand had been dispersed[1]. I understand from Hornblower himself that the maximum amount of sand disposed of in one day was four and a half tons.

The method used to dump the sand was firstly to pick sandy sites that were obscured from view of the goon-boxes by buildings. A camouflage party would man each site, and when the penguins arrived and jettisoned their loads these were immediately covered up while appearing simply to be going about ordinary business. Another area used a lot was in the so-called gardens outside the blocks. In this case, the gardeners would dig a trench, the penguin would jettison the sand and it was immediately covered up. When working to capacity several of these sites would be used simultaneously, thus avoiding the suspicious sight of too many penguins heading in any one direction. Any way you look at it, it was an extraordinary feat of organisation. From all this it can be seen that the rate we could dig the tunnel was entirely governed by the speed with which the sand could be got rid of, and this in turn governed by the clearance given from security.

While dispersal was going on, as an extra precaution diversions were organised under the supervision of Jerry Sage, the larger-than-life American paratroop major. Such diversions might be an 'impromptu' volleyball match or just a general mêlée with the odd penguin in the middle of it all with sand flowing from the bottoms of his trouser legs.

Dispersal and security employed the majority of men, probably about 200 working in shifts, but there were other departments essential to the escape plan and the building of the tunnels, and involving craftsmen of the

[1] 'The Dispersal of Sand in North Compound at Sagan.' Unpublished paper in author's collection.

highest calibre. The clothing department was run by Tommy Guest and his team, who produced or helped people make workmen's clothes or other civilian attire ready for the time when they found themselves on the outside. Tommy converted uniforms into fairly convincing civvy clothes. Johnny Travers, a Rhodesian mining engineer, was a genius with his hands, and together with Bob Nelson organised a department which seemed able to produce ingeniously all the needs of the diggers. They made fat lamps from tins with boiled-down margarine for fuel and wicks made from pyjama-cord and shovels from Red Cross tins. This team also included the carpenters, the ace carpenter being Digger Macintosh, and between them they designed and built an air-pump made of klim tins and kit bags with wire inside to get air all the way into the tunnels, and a railway with trucks to bring the sand from the face. It was they who dovetailed every one of the 10,000 bedboards needed to shore up the tunnels.

Another, most important set-up was christened 'Dean & Dawson' after the well-known pre-war travel firm. It was run by Flt Lt Tim Walenn and his team of forgers, working in conjunction with Valenta, who obtained all the necessary documents by bribery from the guards he now controlled. These included such papers as the Dienstausweise (permission to be on Wehrmacht property), Urlaubscheine (leave passes), identity cards, passes for foreign workers travelling on leave and many others from the security-conscious Germans. Copying these was done by hand, even the tiny typefaces, and each took weeks. Photographs were taken by Chas Hall, a keen amateur photographer, using a camera and developing materials which had to be kept carefully hidden.[2] All the official Nazi stamps bearing the eagle and swastika had to be cut out using the rubber from the heel of a shoe, and the right kind of ink used. The Germans had a habit of changing such passes, and photographs were needed on some – all in all it was breathtakingly difficult, arduous work.

Des Plunkett, my former EFTS instructor, and his team were the mapmakers, the most essential piece of equipment for those of us intending to travel on foot, 'hard arsers', as we were called. Another team led by Al Hake had a production line making compasses. The casing was made from '78' bakelite gramophone records – of which there was a wide collection in camp – by breaking them up and heating them until the material became pliable, then pressing them into a mould. The points of the compass were drawn onto a circle of paper that fitted into the base of the casing. A gramophone needle was fixed into the centre of the base, and on this was a slither of razor-blade which had the one end magnetised. Glass for the finished article was cut from small pieces of broken windows. Of course,

---

[2] But many of the extant photographs of camp life were actually taken by Hauptmann Pieber, the officer in charge of Appells, himself a keen photographer, who also provided many of the prints.

much of the work being done needed soldering, solder being obtained from silver cigarette-paper, or from melted joints of bully-beef tins, while any resin came from the few pine-trees still standing in the compound.

By May 1943, the X Organisation involved nearly everyone in the compound in some capacity or other, and when one slip-up could mean total ruin the need to keep secret the ever-accumulating stockpile of materials was paramount. Although the ferrets would often search the blocks, through his tame ferrets Roger usually knew in advance when a search was to take place, so there was enough time to stow everything out of sight. Still, the many hiding-places, especially in such cramped conditions, were cleverly conceived. The wooden walls of the huts were of double thickness, perfect for storing away slender items like maps through loosened panels. We hollowed out the odd chair or table leg, and even put things in tins and buried these outside our rooms. Some of the bigger items had to be hidden in the roof of the outside latrines, which for some reason – doubtless the stench – the Germans never searched.

That May the shafts and three compartments for all three tunnels were ready, the first few feet of tunnel dug, about two feet up from the bottom of the shaft. I was thrilled but I must say at the same time apprehensive when Johnny Bull said he wanted me to start work with him the next morning on Harry. Welsh or not I was not at all sure how I would react to being shut in down a shaft thirty feet below ground, and having to burrow through sand in a two-foot square hole. It was to be some time before I got to sleep that night.

Next morning after Appell I set off for Hut 104 with Johnny and Joe Noble. We arrived in the room the same time as the trap operators. This was the first time I had seen the shaft entrance, and I was amazed when they deftly removed the stove and hinged back the tiled trapdoor to expose the shaft. We took off the few clothes we were wearing, and followed Johnny down the shaft ladder, wondering all the while at the high quality of workmanship that had gone into its construction. At the bottom, thirty feet under ground, we pulled on the grubby long johns and long-sleeved vests that were kept in the shaft for working. In fact, these became so damp, smelly and disgusting that most of us preferred to work in the nude, much easier to clean up afterwards, too.

There was some sand piled in the one chamber, and for the first time I saw the pump installed, not yet in use, as the tunnel was only about four feet long. Johnny started to dig, looking for a moment ridiculous with his feet sticking out into the shaft. Well, soon enough we'd all look like that. He pushed the sand back behind him and we loaded it into the sand chamber. This wasn't a lot to do, but it was a good initiation for Joe and me. But I still had my fingers crossed that the claustrophobia which was always so close by would not get to me as the tunnel grew.

CHAPTER SIXTEEN

The Summer of 1943

Day follows day in dull monotony
The sun hangs heavy in a changeless sky,
Dust devils eddy down the sandy road.
The long, drab rows of huts lie mute within
The shadow of the all-encircling wire
And this is the life.

The hours slip silently to eternity
The days stretch into weeks: the weeks to years.
Time ages, but its features do not change.
Time sweeps along on feet that never move
Feet tethered by the wire's weightless bond.
With night comes sleep
And night runs sweetly as it did before.
Bright eyes, sweet lips, cool drinks, good food, soft beds
The thousand fantasies of vanished peace
Till morning's light returns with hopeless hope.

Harry Crease

It was early May, the weather much more pleasant after the bitterly cold continental winter. We knew the spring really was with us when one day Bren Hooper took off several layers of clothing, and looking down at his chest said, 'Okay, you can come out for the summer now!' Feeling the heat at last I realised what I needed was a pair of summer shorts, but realised equally that my only hope was to make them myself. My mother would have been proud of me, not to say astonished. I got Smallwood, the wardrobe king of the theatre and escape clothing department, to measure me and cut out a pattern for them from the lining of my greatcoat. With great difficulty and involving a lot of bad language, eventually a fairly reasonable pair of shorts emerged from my needle. With constant servicing they lasted me for two summers.

That May and June, between the ceaseless work on the tunnels, life in the compound went on; especially now the weather was so much better, we could be outside more often and for longer. It was around this time that I spent my second big stretch in the Cooler. I was sitting outside our block when a working party of about a dozen Russian prisoners who had been felling trees in the sports area were being marched out of the compound. The poor beggars looked utterly miserable, thin and hangdog, so feeling really sorry for them I thought I'd take the risk and throw them a couple of packets of cigarettes. My aim was good, but one of their guards spotted me doing it. He shouted and came after me, rifle at the ready, but I was already away and sprinting like hell for the latrines, to shouted encouragement from all the other kriegies. I ran around the back with the guard right after me. After a couple of circuits though, I misunderstood the instructions being yelled at me from the onlookers and thinking that the guard had doubled back the other way, I did the same and at the corner ran smack into him. The chase over, to cheers from the crowds I was marched off to the Cooler, a rifle stuck in the small of my back. In the confusion I understand that the Russians got away with their cigarettes. I got twelve days solitary without any.

Oh God how I hated the Cooler. I could only hope that the Russians really appreciated the sacrifice which had been made and enjoyed their smoke. It was twelve long, miserable, lonely days spent simply pacing up and down the tiny cell, broken only by periods spent lying on the bunk day-dreaming about Mary, wondering how she was getting on in the Land Army and moving on to what we would do when I finally got home after the war – that of course after we had completed our interrupted honeymoon. At that time I was still thinking of returning to farming. My thoughts moved on: I was furious with myself for getting shot down, and then for not having taken the odd opportunity, even if the chances were very slim, to escape our escort on the bus and train to Oslo. At the time it had seemed foolhardy to jump from a moving train or risk getting shot, but now given the same slight chance I would do it. I was also depressed at not being able to take an active part in the war, especially now we appeared to be winning it. These teasing thoughts would be countered by the sensible ones that told me how bloody lucky I was to be still alive and what a good innings I'd already had. Most kriegies entertained all these thoughts at some or other time, but a stretch like this in the Cooler gave you too much time to brood over them.

When they let me out I returned to a good meal my roommates had prepared for me. Johnny said, more or less straight away, 'Well, you've had a good rest now, you can visit Harry tomorrow.' So, the next morning found me following Johnny backwards to the tunnel face, now about ten yards in. He would push the sand back to me and I would then pull it to the front of me and get it into the box on the trolley, ready at my signal to be pulled to the entrance. He also briefed me on the procedure in the event of a cave-in if he was covered in sand: 'Just pull me by the legs and don't stop until I'm clear!' This was the first time I had spent time right up the tunnel, and I must admit I was more than a little apprehensive; if you allow yourself to dwell on how truly buried alive you are, panic will follow. It was murky down there, and stifling, and you felt like a rat up a sewer-pipe, but from my position I could still see the reassuring light at the shaft entrance and kept it in my line of vision the whole time. After that first session, though, I never felt the slightest panicky sickness of claustrophobia, and I was soon too used to the conditions to think about it at all. And there was much to get used to: 'Smell, sweat and sand,' Dick Churchill called it, and that about sums it up. Down in the tunnel it was pretty disgusting. If you weren't actually digging at the face you lay there at the halfway house – or, in those early days, in the tunnel itself – waiting for more sand to be pushed your way, listening to the creak of the supports and hoping the whole damned thing didn't actually cave in. Before we got electrified there was light only from the fat lamps, which also gave off a sooty smoke. You could tell when the air from the pumps was getting too low because the fat-lamps would flicker and go out, leaving you in the thick darkness, choking and stinking of sweat and fat and any residuum from any tunneller who'd been caught out down there. If you were caught short, you dug a little hole in the sand and did your best. It was no joke when someone had a dicky tum down there in the tunnel. When you got back up to the surface you needed a cold shower to get the sand off, and sand clung to the filthy rags you used to tunnel in. Eventually, as I said, most of us went down the tunnel in the nude, it was simpler. In spite of all this people like myself were keen to dig, to be doing *something*, and often we dug more than the penguins could disperse.

That summer, in between sessions digging down Harry I kept myself busy with my various interests: sport, some lectures and a lot of general discussion. I pounded the circuit with friends, especially 'Skid' Morley and Gwyn. Skid was one of the compound newsreaders. The news would be written down from the clandestine radio, and when the coast was clear and our security people were keeping watch at each end of the hut, Skid would go round the blocks and read out the latest news to a hungry assembly. News-reading was one of the important events, and what was going on in the outside world certainly formed one of the subjects of conversation during our walks, as well as when the war might end. The other ones were home and family and what we would do with the rest of our lives.

Gwyn talked about having run away from home at fifteen. This drastic step was due to the combination of feeling he didn't measure up to his father's expectations and knowing he never would measure up to his mother's. She wanted him to follow in his grandfather's footsteps and enter the Church, while his own desire to go to sea or into the RAF had been stewing inside for a time. Crunch time came during Christmas 1936, after a term at school where he'd had an altercation with a couple of his masters in which he told them he disliked them at least as much as they disliked him. A generous aunt came to stay over Christmas, and on New Year's Day, his pockets full of cash from his aunt, he set off with just a clean shirt and not much else on his bicycle for London, where a friend lived.

Wales to London, on a bicycle. When you're fifteen and you've never been out of the Valleys you think nothing of the distance or of what you might find when you get there. The weather started out fine and cold, and Gwyn's spirits were high, but these dampened as rain set in, only pride and stubbornness keeping him from turning around and going home. As night fell he was pushing his bike up a hill outside Chepstow, when a transport lorry pulled up at the top of the hill to let his engine cool, and seeing Gwyn panting away, the driver asked him in a friendly way where he was going at this time of night. Gwyn lied about a job in London, but on the strength of this cadged a lift right to St Paul's, where he stood for a few moments amazed; for the first time it hit him just what he had done.

'Here I was, in London at midday,' he told me bashing the circuits in Sagan, 'on a BSA pushbike, with a clean shirt, some hankies, a toilet bag and six pounds on me, and no idea in the world how to get to my friends in south London. I lasted six weeks, though.'

He managed to find his friends, who got him some digs, and he talked his way at the Labour Exchange into a job at a local garage at fourpence an hour, which was not enough for him to live on. He reckons the Labour Exchange, smelling a runaway, must have contacted his parents, because one day they simply showed up to collect him. There was no mention of his enterprise or initiative, but his father made sure Gwyn was transferred to a school where he was himself a teacher. No escape; he went on to win an Empire Scholarship to Loughborough in 1940. 'Lucky for me,' he said to me, 'war interfered.'

One room of eccentrics I knew well and often visited were a most amusing bunch, one of them a Welshman called, believe it or not, Hardy-McHardie, and known to everyone as 'Foo'. When I called by there one morning for coffee, I was handed a mug of hot water. It appeared that the room had solved the difficulties of brewing up the instant coffee which came in American parcels, often in a solid lump. Usual practice was to put it in a tin of hot water on the stove and let it slowly dissolve, rather like Camp coffee. Not in Foo's room, that was too simple. Instead, they had bored a hole through the solid coffee, hung it on a piece of string suspended from the ceiling and you held your mug of hot water in the coffee dangling above it until it was strong enough for your taste.

How Foo had been captured was equally unstraightforward. About the time of the Battle of Britain he was engaged in a dogfight over the Channel with a Hun, who he managed to shoot down. Foo said it was his first kill, and he was so elated he felt like doing a victory roll over Dover. He was a bit surprised when the anti-aircraft gunners seemed to be joining in the celebrations, and really astonished when a shell hit him! Only then did he realise that he had been doing his victory roll over Calais, not Dover at all. He managed to crash-land in a field, knocking out some front teeth.

One afternoon it was announced that Foo was to give a lecture on a new theory in mathematics. I was a bit taken aback at this, since it didn't seem to me that Foo was at all the academic type. It turned out that the entire room had been fed up with the large number of arcane lectures taking place, so they decided to do a spoof one. Trench, the maths boffin in the room, supplied the lecture, complete with a series of prepared questions and answers, and the necessary equations and calculations. Foo was introduced, and it was explained that he had been a lecturer in mathematics for a brief time before taking a short service commission in the RAF. Before a large outdoor assembly, armed with easel and chalk, he launched into a profound lecture, delivered at speed and amply illustrated with equations that were erased almost as quickly as they appeared on the board. The intellectuals and sceptics alike were nonplussed, but then came the question-and-answer session, when they could make mincemeat of him. But Foo was up to this: he'd already seeded the audience with his stooges, primed with their questions, and as each sceptic put up his hand, Foo would take a question from a stooge, and with his swift, complicated equations produce the right answer then, before anyone could begin to double-check it, wipe the board clean. It was splendidly frustrating, and goodness knows how long it might have gone on for when a few drops of rain began to fall. Grabbing his papers, Foo apologised and abruptly disappeared, leaving behind a rather puzzled audience besides at least one or two who felt that they really had learnt something.

By this time – May – I had received my first parcel from Mary. One parcel every six months isn't much but it was certainly appreciated. What a thrill to open it and find inside all sorts of welcome goodies: shirts, underwear, sweaters, socks and much-needed toiletries, and Mary had thoughtfully made the parcel up to its maximum weight with milk chocolate. After keeping back a little for trading purposes I shared the rest around the room. Ever-hopeful, I also kept a little on the side ready to make a concentrated escape ration bar. The bar was made to a formula worked out by Eric Lubbock, a Royal Navy officer who was also a dietary expert, and it consisted mostly of chocolate, dried milk and porridge oats, made into hard little bars easy to carry. There were always plenty of cigarette parcels arriving from friends; oddly, these were not limited and could be sent duty-free. My best man Bob Munro, family and friends kept me well and truly supplied. I always passed any excess on to new kriegies who hadn't yet got their parcels, but because there were so many they didn't have much value in Foodacco.

It was around this time that we were lucky enough to be on full Red Cross parcels, and – foolishly, as it turned out – the room accepted a bet that our most able trencherman, 'Ish' Somers, could devour the entire contents of a parcel in one day. This may not seem like much, but it did contain such items as half a pound of margarine, a tin of powdered milk and a tin of jam, and our kriegie stomachs were not used to large amounts of food. But Ish was always hungry, he declared, and was ready to be trained up by Red Noble with me, as Cook Führer, concocting how he was to eat the stuff. The room had Red Cross parcels riding on this big appetite, besides 'D' bars from the American parcels, cigarettes, various articles of clothing and quite a lot of cash.

The day before the great event we managed to persuade Ish to forgo his evening meal. We got right in next morning at 8:30, when breakfast consisted of a tin of sardines followed by thirty prunes covered in a chocolate-cream sauce made with half the tin of cocoa and dried milk plus a small portion of pineapple pie, the crust made with biscuits and dried milk. Oh, we were cunning. At 9:30 Red took him for three brisk circuits of the compound, Ish declaring the while that he still had a 'good edge' to his appetite. More chocolate brew at 11:15 plus a few circuits. At 12:30 I prepared a lunch for him, the menu consisting of two tins of stew, half a tin of pâté and half a tin of spam, with quite a lot of margarine in it to spread the load. This was followed by more pie and cream and a strong coffee. He duly consumed all this, and although he was now looking a little pale, Red hauled him off for a couple of circuits, after which he had a sleep. At 3:30 I called him for his coffee with biscuits, marg and jam, covered with yet more cocoa-cream and the rest of the pie. Disaster fell. He simply sat and stared at the feast put before him, tiny beads of sweat began to form on his brow and he was promptly sick. I must report that he exercised great forbearance as none actually passed his lips, but the umpires declared that he had been most definitely sick. Poor Ish sheepishly accepted defeat. I think for him it was a relief, really, but to us it was a sad blow indeed, since most of the block had supported his case with £500, five parcels, 1,200 cigarettes and thirty-five D bars (Foodacco value £4-10-0 each). After this there were no more such bets.

But it was not the last bet we ever lost, either. Bren Hooper, ever the optimist, made a rash statement in front of witnesses ever-ready with the book, that if Sicily were not invaded by the end of June, all the members of our room would shave all their hair off. This was duly noted, and on 1 July 1943, Private Peter MacNeil, the very affable Scotsman who was camp barber – a pre-war bus driver from the Isle of Lewis – appeared at our room armed with his shears and a big smile. We very publicly had all our locks shaved off, Sax and Gwyn going even further and having a clean shave. They looked ghastly with their dead-white scalps dripping blood from the blunt blade. Although I looked and felt a bit strange hairless, in the warm weather it was in fact very comfortable, and I quickly learned to appreciate the added advantage of being able to wash out the sand much more easily after any digging session. The results were recorded for posterity in a photograph.

With their increasing involvement in the war, by now the numbers of Americans had grown rapidly; they occupied three huts on the west side of the compound. Early in July as we were walking around the circuit, all hell seemed to be coming from one of these huts. It hit us then that today was the Fourth of July, and the Yanks were celebrating. In fact, they had been plotting this for some time, and the resulting brew was strong and plentiful. As the afternoon progressed they decided to have a parade through the compound. It was led by Jerry Sage doing a Paul Revere, dressed in a tricorne hat and what appeared to be knee breeches, and riding two other Yanks done up as a horse, followed hard upon by a column of very drunken US airmen yelling 'The British are coming!' and singing 'Yankee Doodle'. They finished up by the fire pool where a group of kriegies had been quietly sitting. This quickly changed, and most wound up in the water. But just to make sure it was all friendly, the Americans threw in a couple of their own senior officers. It didn't finish there.

When we fell in for Appell later that afternoon on the parade ground, all in ranks, with Pieber and his entourage beginning their routine count, up trotted Major Sage, still on his 'horse', passing Pieber and Co, where the horse proceeded to urinate before taking its place with the rest of its block. Another American staggered in wearing only his service hat and his tie. Pieber, to do him justice, took it all in his stride, even announcing the numbers in that block, 'plus one horse'.

This episode apart, I felt that in general the Germans had not got a very well-developed sense of humour; they usually failed to understand or appreciate the silly antics they often saw around the compound. For example, people were apt to make rash statements, generally about the progress of the war, which would immediately be written on the wall of the room – our instant way of taking a book. I think it was Digger Carter, the pint-sized New Zealander, who threw out the remark that if Italy was not invaded by early June he would carry his bed around the whole compound. The day came. He lost, and the guards were open-mouthed to see this diminutive figure staggering around the circuit, a bunk bed on his back.

Alec Bristow bet he could walk around the circuit backwards quicker than Pop Green could walk it normally. Pop was an elderly rear gunner, well into his fifties, who had served with distinction in the First World War. How he'd managed to bamboozle his way into the RAF as a gunner I will never know. (In fact Pop's son was awarded a DFC later in the war, while Pop himself got out in The Great Escape.) Pop could be seen every day, regardless of the weather, head down, pounding the circuit at a very steady, deliberate pace. Pop was of course – we thought – ignorant of the bet, so he was being surreptitiously timed as he did what he always did, while Alec set off to the cheers and boos of the assembled kriegies. Halfway along he was well up on time, but tiring. Red, his trainer, began to put the pressure on, causing several falls. He did finish the course, but well behind Pop's time: more D bars lost.

In late July I think it was, a German general paid us a visit, a sort of AOC inspection, I assume. A large, sparkling black Mercedes pulled up inside the compound, and he got out of it, together with the Kommandant, von Lindeiner. As they left for their tour of the compound, von Lindeiner, seeing all too well the prisoners who had surged up around them, told them smartly to keep their distance. But the general, brimming with self-confidence, said, 'No, no. The driver will keep watch.' Like his boss the general, the driver didn't know much about POWs; he was far too polite, fielding a constant stream of questions from two German-speakers while the rest of the rabble scrambled over the car, in evident awe and admiration. After giving the driver some cigarettes the crowd dispersed, together with the general's gloves, torch, maps and tool-kit, and a handbook optimistically marked 'Secret'. Although the driver, poor sod, was probably already on his way to the Russian Front when von Lindeiner came into the compound next day and suggested to the SBO that if the handbook were returned the other losses would be ignored and no reprisals taken, we all knew that really, the general was far too embarrassed about having been so easily taken in, and would be only too glad for every reference to be hushed up. And there was no point in keeping the book anyway, as the German speakers had been through its every nook and cranny, finding there very little of interest or military value. Roger Bushell quickly arranged for a special stamp to be made and applied to the front pages. The general got his book back stamped: 'Passed by the POW Board of Censors.'

With summer slipping away the number of American POWs was still increasing dramatically. As their daylight bombing offensive became heavier, so did their losses. Although American losses were much greater even than those of Bomber Command, the survival rate of those shot down was much greater than that of the night-time bomber crews, and now the Americans were often having to share as many as twelve in a room intended for six people. But these large increases had been anticipated by the Germans, and they had been building what was to be an all-American compound on the south side of our compound. This was nearly finished, and yet another compound begun on the west side. This fairly imminent move of the Americans to their own camp and the felling of the trees on the west side created a major problem: Tom went right through the west side. We were now going to have to risk it and blitz Tom in order to give the many Americans who had been working with the X Organisation a chance to escape.

CHAPTER SEVENTEEN

Digging for Victory

Roger made the big decision to take our chances and concentrate all our efforts on completing Tom. To this end, work on Dick and Harry would be put on hold. Taking chances meant of course that we would have to increase the speed with which the sand could be dispersed, and this would not be easy. But as Roger said, 'If we get caught out, we've still got Harry to fall back on.'

Roger also devised several schemes to confuse the ferrets. He organised parties carrying empty Red Cross parcels into and out of Hut 119 on the opposite side of the compound from Tom, hoping that this might con any nosey ferrets into focusing there. He then got one of the minders to mention 'in strictest confidence' to his tame ferret (already suspected of working for both sides) that there wasn't a tunnel at all, and that all this was being done out of sheer bloody-mindedness to cause confusion. Unfortunately by now the German security organisation was pretty well-versed in the ways of POWs and not so easily fooled.

I think Glemnitz and Rubberneck were convinced there was a tunnel somewhere in the compound. After all, we had been in the compound for some months without them finding any trace, and this was longer than they had ever been before without finding one. They knew us well enough to realise we had not given up. It was also entirely possible that one of the ferrets might have found some tell-tale sand.

Despite all these problems and pressures we had to press on with Tom, since the date for the Americans' move was obviously getting much closer. As the trees were already being cleared for the new West Compound, it was decided that if Tom were discovered, it would not be practical to carry on with Dick, as by the time Dick was finished it would emerge in the middle of the new compound. Not a good idea to do all that work and wind up still inside the camp! So from now on Dick was going to be reinvented as a workshop-cum-hiding-hole, the eighty-odd feet of tunnel already dug used to disperse some of Tom's sand. This shift of emphasis meant that work on Tom was going forward much faster, the ace diggers now concentrating all their efforts on the one tunnel. I still worked on Johnny's team, but not quite so often, only about twice a week now, as there could only be so many bodies at one time in the tunnel. And although there was a surplus of volunteers to dig, apparently I was considered to be one of the best, since not everyone was able to dig straight and level. I still wonder if the skills involved in flying straight and level were somehow transferred under ground.

But having as we thought found some traces of sand, the ferrets intensified their activities. Security spotted some of them with binoculars hiding behind the bushes outside the wire, and also trying to conceal themselves under the huts, watching and listening. All of Roger's attempts to lure them over to the other side of the compound failed. I think that Glemnitz was convinced that one of the three huts on the west side would mean the shortest route, and of these, Hut 123 was the most likely, as it was farthest from the main gate.

But the ferrets did not confine their constant probings to Hut 123. Coming off Appell one day in August we found that we had been locked out of our block, 119, whilst a search was being conducted inside it. I think this was really a bit of double-bluff, as they were much quicker than usual, the rooms not left in the usual disarray. They were probably far more interested in examining the maps of the Russian Front we kept on the room walls, the movements kept constantly up-to-date by the BBC news. It must have been difficult for them, knowing that we had a radio but being unable to find it, while at the same time wanting themselves to know what the news was. We all knew that they could get a better idea of the progress on the Eastern Front from our maps than from the more official sources like the *Volkischer Beobachter*. My own, far more urgent, fear was that they might have taken exception to the brew I had going behind the stove in our room.

It was to be our Christmas brew, which gives an idea of how long it took to get up a reasonable quantity of the stuff. The process involved only a small amount at any time, since the container we used – a round glass lampshade – could only hold about a gallon of the fermenting liquid, including prunes, raisins and sugar, all saved from parcels over months. When fermentation was finished, we distilled it with a contraption straight out of Heath Robinson, comprising a large Reich jam tin, capacity about a gallon, with two smaller tins soldered on top, the smaller one on top containing some baffles. From the top tin a small bore-metal tube, salvaged from a broken wind instrument (thank you, Red Cross), ran through a wooden trough containing cold running water.

The distillation process is not difficult. Put your fermented brew into your large Reich jam tin and this onto the stove. Bring it almost to the boil, then dampen down the heat to try and keep it just below boiling-point since, as every schoolboy knows, alcohol comes off at a lower temperature. If it gets a bit too near boiling, the baffles in the tin will cool the vapour so that the evaporated water drops back into the tin. Taste regularly. Red and I had become pretty expert distillers. In fact, we undertook to do a bit of freelance distilling for other rooms in return for a percentage of the resulting clear 'fire water'.

Luckily, the brew was still there safely bubbling away.

Glemnitz had a great respect for POW cunning, and from one of the tame ferrets we heard that he was musing on the possibility of our actually tunnelling on the north side, as the least obvious side, and that on 1 September he had ordered a search of Blocks 104 and 105. At the last moment the cunning old devil switched his search back to Block 123. Roger, alerted by George Harsh, took up position together with Floody in Block 122, and from a window they silently watched the search going on next door. 'If we can get away with this search,' Roger said to Wally, 'I really think they'll give up on 123 and we'll succeed in the long run.'

As one we held our breath. When after about two hours of searching some of the ferrets began to leave, standing outside the hut and looking fed-up, our spirits began to rise. Then disaster struck.

The last of the ferrets had just finished their search and were standing around outside the kitchen, when Herman, idly jabbing the concrete floor with his metal probe, suddenly found it had gone into a crack in the concrete. That was it. The concrete slab was quickly prised up, revealing the shaft underneath. Glemnitz was over the moon. Even glum Rubberneck was seen to crack a smile. The Kommandant and Brioli were sent for, and soon the place was full of happy Germans. Rubberneck gleefully went down the shaft, just enough to have his photo taken, not all the way. The only ferret who ever seemed happy to crawl down tunnels was Charlie Pfelz, a cheerful, wizened little character who was everyone's friend.

Charlie must have been about half an hour down there, crawling with the aid of a torch, to the end of the tunnel. When at last he resurfaced, some of the elation was gone from Glemnitz's face as he realised how near the tunnel had been to completion. I think it must have hit him forcibly how much of a near-miss it had been to a mass escape, a lucky probe by Herman between discovery and what would have been most dismal failure.

Bushell and Floody, devastated like all the rest of us, nevertheless were almost immediately off to see the SBO to start planning the next move. Some of the older prisoners like Johnny Bull were very despondent. If you had been working on tunnels for years, you do begin to wonder at such points of failure if you ever are going to succeed. The X Committee judged that Harry should be kept closed for an indefinite period. Roger, ever alert to such details, pointed out that Glemnitz and Rubberneck would have noticed how the tunnel was shored up with bedboards, and would certainly be on the lookout for any futher disappearance of these. So, Roger ordered an immediate collection of bedboards from all the rooms, to be stored down Dick and Harry for future use. He rightly assumed that the ferrets would believe that they had all been used on Tom. With this massive collection we now had about 2,000 bedboards safely stowed away.

By now the bunk beds were suffering from a real shortage of support, so some of us made a kind of hammock from string plaited into a net which we fixed between the side boards. I found this very comfortable, and with two of us having these string beds it meant that the rest of the room had enough boards under them for comfort.

The goons were now faced with the destruction of the tunnel. The normal method was to collapse them by flushing them full of water, but it was felt that this tunnel had been too well shored up for this to work on its own. They called in an explosives expert who, after having given the tunnel the flushing treatment, laid his explosives down the shaft. Unfortunately, he rather overdid the explosives. With an enormous roar the concrete trap, plus any other bits of concrete went right up through the roof of the hut. We gave him a cheer as he went on his way through the rubble.

Although we were all demoralised by the loss of Tom, it was even worse for the Americans who had worked so hard all the way with us on its construction, and especially for Jerry Sage's team who had done so well with the sand dispersal. Quite a few of the real movers in the X Organisation would now be gone – Tokyo Jones and Jerry Sage among them – as they all moved on 8 September to the new South Compound. To our delight, though, they took Glemnitz with them. But we were still left with Rubberneck in charge of the ferrets in our compound and ever keen to do a good job, he became even more obnoxious.

CHAPTER EIGHTEEN

Harry is Completed

Buried in Germany
Willingly, courageously, his young life he gave
Far from home where none could go in sorrow to his grave
In the strange and alien soil the British airman lies
He fought and fell; a hero in the battle of the skies
He sleeps amongst the enemy in hostile company
But the grave could never hold the soul so brave and free
His spirit has come home, in fond remembrance to abide
Happy in the knowledge of the cause for which he died.
As recited by George Smith after kriegie 'hooch'

For a while that autumn there were a lot of very cheerful goons around beside quite a few mournful kriegies. Roger encouraged the glum faces. 'Let them think they've got us beaten,' he said. 'They won't think about the other tunnel.' He started another double-bluff, letting it be known via the tame ferrets that he personally was shattered by the discovery of Dick, and had given up all hope of ever being able to get a tunnel out. I don't think Rubberneck bought this version; he continued to dog Roger's every move. To help allay suspicion Roger even took a part in the play *George and Margaret*, produced by Ken Macintosh.

Johnny Bull told me in confidence that Roger had decided not to open up Harry until sometime after Christmas. As team leader and senior digger Johnny didn't want his team to feel any anxiety about when or whether. We knew now that we'd have a target again, but until the time was right we could simply settle down into the usual kriegie activities. With summer almost over, cricket and softball gave way to soccer and rugby.

Besides this, everyone was feeling much more optimistic about the progress of the war. North Africa and Sicily now had been conquered, and at the beginning of September, Italy was invaded by the Allies and soon sued for a peace agreement. This news, together with the recent advances being made by the Russians made the over-optimistic cry yet again, 'Home for Christmas!' Lovely thought, but most of us were more sceptical. Still, it gave us some satisfaction to display prominently such advances on the maps in our rooms, knowing the ferrets would see them. Others phrased it differently. 'Well, it's home or homo by Christmas,' Bob Tuck had said in 1942. When reminded of this by Red Noble, he replied, 'Well, do you want to keep me to it?'

I had now been a kriegie for almost a year. Letters arrived regularly from Mary and from my family, and I had received my first two parcels, plus plenty of cigarettes. Letters from Mary telling me how hard she was working in the Land Army were sometimes a mixed blessing: here I was stuck behind the wire and stagnating while she slaved at home. I felt useless and helpless. It was around this time that we were given our 'Wartime Logs' by the YMCA, in which we could record all sorts of things going on around camp but without being indiscreet, and for which I have always been grateful. Mine stayed with me right through to the end. Many of the drawings and photographs reproduced here came from my Log.

That autumn, too, the tunnel was always on our minds. Once, I was walking with Red back from visiting a block on the far side of the compound, when he spotted a labourer doing some electrical work near the cookhouse. Next to him was pure gold dust in the shape of a couple of drums of electric cable. Two Canadians also passing by, Ted White and Gordie King, spotted it as well. It was too much to resist, so quickly Red and I got the labourer's attention diverted (a quick scuffle usually did the trick) while Ted and Gordie liberated the cable, stuffing it all under their greatcoats, over 800 feet of it. Red was able proudly to deliver it later to Big X. Now instead of fat lamps we would have proper electric lighting in the tunnel, and it was all installed in time for the breakout. Meanwhile, nothing more was heard of the missing cable, the labourers obviously too terrified to report the loss. They were to pay dearly for this later.

Without any underground work to do I had plenty of time in my role as Cook Führer to concentrate on preparations for Christmas. I'd already been putting aside small amounts of raisins, biscuits, sugar and suchlike for some time, to make a Christmas cake, kriegie-style, and a powerful brew. The cake recipe, I say with some pride, was my own: not exactly Mrs Beeton, but at least it looked a bit like cake.

Rees's Finest Kriegie Christmas Cake
Ingredients: biscuits from Canadian Red Cross parcels; raisins;
klim milk; sugar; Reich breadcrumbs (for bulk).
Roll out your biscuits, then mix with all the
other ingredients, then bake.
(NB: do not drop this cake on your toe.)

We also had several brews on hand, plus a reasonable stock of distilled alcohol put on one side for what most of us thought would indeed be our last Christmas as POWs. Just to be sure, we'd done a small amount of lethal double-distilled to see us well into the New Year.

Just before Christmas, Gwyn rushed in one day and told us how Foo McHardie's room really had excelled themselves: they were court-martialling a mouse. The mouse had been eating some cheese which did not belong to it. The affair, they decided, was altogether too heinous, too repulsive to be anything less than full court-martial. A Board was convened, with a president, senior and junior members, a prosecuting officer and a defending officer – who, since the mouse was German, must be German-speaking.

The prosecution opened with a strong case, stating how the mouse had been caught red-handed – or red-pawed – nibbling the aforesaid cheese. The defence (speaking in German) could only plead guilty, but with compelling mitigating circumstances. His client, he declared, was a passionate anti-Nazi, and had only come into the compound to escape persecution for his beliefs. He had intended to move from room to room, only taking enough food for basic survival. The Board, after some consideration, found the defendant guilty, but taking his personal circumstances into consideration, the death penalty was waived. He/she was to have twenty-one days detention on bread and water, after which he was to be released at dusk near the boundary wire. At least they helped the poor beggar avoid being shot by a bored goon in the goon-box.

When it came we were ready for Christmas: the cake was baked, and a substantial amount of hooch had been stockpiled. I must say that I cannot remember much about it, but as it took three days to recover from it, the party must have been a success on some level. That the entire compound must have celebrated in some style can be extrapolated from the following letter written by the Kommandant to the SBO:

Stalag Luft III   Sagan, 27th December, 1943
Kommandantur

To Group Captain H.M. Massey – North Camp
Colonel Goodrich – South Camp

On my return here I have established with regret that in spite of my most earnest admonitions, the trust which was placed in the POWs, the way in which requests were met halfway, and the special concessions given to the POWs over the Christmas period have led to intolerable incidents.

1. Nine British POWs of North Camp climbed the barbed wire separating North and South camps on the night of 25/26th.

2. On the night of 25/26th thirteen POWs of the USAAF climbed, without permission, the barbed wire fence separating the North and South Camp.

3. I am punishing the officers concerned in para 1 and 2 each with 14 days Stuben-Arrest, the sentence to begin on 26th December.

4. The special privileges allowed in connection with the close of year are withdrawn. Closing of barracks and appells will now take place as usual.

5. The possession and use of drinks containing alcohol is forbidden with effect from today, instead of as hitherto ordered, with effect from 4th January, 1944. Existing alcohol will be confiscated and destroyed.

von Lindeiner

New Year's Eve 1944 was rather more restrained than Christmas had been, but still, we'd managed to hide the remaining small amount of hooch, so in spite of the Kommandant's admonishments, it was nevertheless celebrated in due style. A few days later, on 4 January, Johnny Bull was called to an X Organisation Committee meeting. He came back into the room, an excited grin on his usually sombre face, and announced that Roger had decreed that operations should begin again. The idea was that the goons would be far less suspicious of any tunnel-making activity in the harsh Polish wintertime, when the ground was frozen. Roger wanted to blitz Harry, and complete it in a couple of months, but with snow on the ground, the problem of sand dispersal was even more difficult. And with the new American compound on the west side, the only real option was to go north. This time there wasn't to be even a hint of any sand to set the goon search-teams in motion. Roger asked the Committee to go away and see if they could come up with any ideas.

I believe it was Fanshawe whose inspired idea it was to use the theatre. The theatre had been built by kriegies; its walls went right down to the foundations, and without any trapdoors in the walls, the ferrets could not search the large space beneath the floor of the sloping auditorium. The theatrical crowd were less than happy with this solution; if the theatre were shut a great source of morale would be gone with it. But the SBO declared that escaping was the priority, and after making sure that the theatre was indeed suitable, he gave orders that it could be used.

It was now up to Fanshawe to make the plans for transporting the sand from Harry to the theatre, a distance of about 200 yards. There was also still a useful length of tunnel in Dick which could be filled up, but it was decided to use that as a standby only. Communication between the blocks was allowed up to 10 pm, when we were all locked into our respective blocks. During this time, as just before lockup it was after normal working hours, there was only one ferret on duty in the entire compound, so it seemed the best thing to use the long winter hours of darkness to transport the sand. It now became more important than ever that the officers detailed to look after the various ferrets on duty should divert them from the 'danger' areas, if possible, even to the length of entertaining them in their rooms. Any difficulties depended on which ferret it was.

The sand was to be carried under greatcoats in sacks slung around the neck, but much larger sacks than the ones used before down the trouser legs. We really were going for broke. Each sack weighed about thirty-five pounds. Fortunately, the entrance to Hut 104 could not actually be seen from the goon-boxes, which speeded things up considerably. The dispersal rate went up, too, whenever the tame ferret on duty was safely settled with his illicit coffee and fags in a room somewhere else. First thing each morning the route used by the penguins the night before was inspected for any traces of sand in the snow-covered ground. I believe that on the best nights we got rid of almost four tons of sand, which represented about thirteen foot of tunnel.

The theatre was a real godsend. Twelve kriegies in two shifts of six worked under its floor, one team run by Jimmy James, the other by Ian Cross. When the penguins arrived at the theatre, they would empty the sand from their sacks through the trap. The sand was then hauled in aluminium wash-basins with ropes attached along channels to an area where it would be packed down.

Harry itself had remained in pretty good order, as we saw when it was re-opened on 13 January. Crump Ker-Ramsay went down first to inspect, and apart from a small amount of sand which had seeped through, and a few twisted shoring boards which he replaced, everything was fine. Work could start immediately, and we were all keen for that to happen.

Three teams of experienced diggers, about ten in each team, were picked. Happily, Bren, Red and myself remained on Johnny's team. All our room were working in one or another capacity for the escape committee, four of us as diggers. It was on 14 January that I went down for the first time, accompanying Johnny to the face, about eighty feet in. We found the air down there quite good, considering the length of time the tunnel had been closed down; it turned out to be a good thing that the air intake valve had been left open all those months. In spite of the bitter cold outside, down in the tunnel it was warm. We moved forward about four feet that first time. It might have been more, except for a cave-in which meant I had to haul Johnny out by his feet, then we spent the rest of the time on the tiresome job of shoring and then packing in the loose sand around the shoring.

The next time we went down, the tunnel was about one hundred feet long, and the first so-called 'Halfway House', called 'Piccadilly', had been constructed. This was a part of the tunnel about seven foot long and about six inches wider than the tunnel itself. The first railway line finished here, and another started for the next stretch of tunnel. This railway was a necessary feature, since pulling the heavily-laden trolley all the increasingly long way from the face was becoming too much of a strain, both on the ropes and on the wrists doing the work. Eventually there were – somewhat confusingly – two Halfway Houses, the second one about 220 feet from the shaft, called 'Leicester Square'. Two people were kept in each Halfway House for transferring sand from one trolley to the other.

I found that as far as I was concerned the best place to be was at the face, either digging or as digger's mate. It could be a little unnerving when there was a sudden fall of sand and you were left in complete darkness until another fat lamp could be sent up, but generally you were kept far too busy to brood on any danger. If you were on Halfway House duties, though, you had a lot of spare time to consider your position. It could suddenly occur to you that you were actually in a two-foot square tunnel, twenty-five feet down under the Vorlager, and totally dependant for your survival there on basically only flimsy bedboards holding off the tons of earth above you. And as the goons above were not exactly in on the operation, it would have taken quite some time to organise a rescue. I don't think we were all that certain about our position, so digging down for someone trapped would be difficult, to say the least. There was one rather disturbing episode when Red and I were on Halfway House duty. We had just passed our fat lamp up to replace one at the face which had been covered in sand, and were waiting in the darkness for a replacement from the shaft, when there was a rumble; all around the earth shook and bits of sand trickled free. For a long, very bad moment we both thought the tunnel was about to collapse and bury us both right there, but after a few seconds it stopped, and all was silent again. My heart was pounding so hard I could barely speak, but after a moment of intense, damp silence I managed to croak to Red, 'Must have been a truck.' That was the first time we ever heard one underground.

The dispersal of the sand was working smoothly, interrupted only once for a week in early February, when the bright moon and clear skies made it too dangerous for the penguins to move back and forth. First, the penguins would be dispatched from a room opposite the room in Block 104 where the shaft of Harry went down. This room was manned by George Harsh, who was constantly in touch with his security boys monitoring the ferrets. Pat

Langford was in charge of the tunnel entrance itself, and could close down the trap in twenty seconds flat, if necessary. Unfortunately, the contact officer for Rudy, one of the tame ferrets, also lived in Block 104, and whenever Rudy came on duty he would make directly for his contact's room to talk, smoke and have a brew. It was arranged so that Rudy always occupied the chair farthest from the door, and then there were always two people between him and the door. Outside the door, George had stationed a stooge with a parcel. If Rudy decided to leave in a hurry, there would be a loud scraping of feet from the room and as he opened the door he would collide with the stooge 'bringing in the parcel', which gave Langford just enough time to close up the trap. We did our best night's work – four tons of sand – when Rudy was on duty, but Rudy wasn't on night duty all that often.

So, all was going smoothly, with only a few slight hiccups in our routine, like the time Langford dropped a bedboard thirty feet down the shaft, which landed on Cookie Long's head. Slightly bruised and looking green, Cookie retired hurt and shaking from that shift. A few days after that there was a panic shutdown, during which a large metal jug, loaded with sand, was dropped. Luckily it scored not what would have been a fatal direct hit but a glancing blow to Wally Floody's head, giving him a very nasty cut which needed bandaging for days after. He told Hauptmann Pieber he'd tripped on the ice.

By February 'Leicester Square' had been installed, and we were now under the outer wire with about eighty feet to go in order to emerge in the wood. I think Rubberneck suspected something. One morning in late February we came off Appell to find Block 104 surrounded by guards, with ferrets banging about inside. We waited outside and watched, spirits sinking, but there was nothing to be done about it. After about two hours of what must have been very determined searching Rubberneck emerged, looking fed up. He must not have noticed the huge collective sigh of relief. 'In the clear,' someone said. 'Not so!' Roger was sharp. 'Now everyone has got to be even more careful.'

It was the beginning of March when we got the news that Rubberneck was going off on a fortnight's leave. Harry was far too close to completion to allow any glitches now, so when Hauptmann Brioli, together with lots of extra guards appeared one morning at Appell, I can say that we were more than a little worried. Briskly he called out nineteen names, including those of Wally Floody, George Harsh, Fanshawe and Bob Tuck. They were searched, allowed to collect their kit, then brusquely marched off to a new compound some four miles away. How the nineteen were selected we never knew, but about a third were workers on the tunnel. It was a bitter blow for them and for us, since they would have been right at the top of Roger's list of escapers. Later I'm sure they thought differently.

After the nineteen had been sent off to Belaria, the goons decided to make the numbers up to fifty and called for volunteers. Gwyn decided it was time to leave off digging, as he put it, and go for a change of scenery, together with Willie Williams, Digger Carter and Kingsley Brown. 'It's up on a hill, at least. I've had enough of the all-enveloping pine forest with its grey-black floor.' I was sad to see him go. I could see his point of view, but at the same time, in spite of all we'd been through together there was no way I was going to abandon the tunnel now it was so nearly finished.

Crump now took over from Floody as chief tunnel engineer, and it was quickly settled to take advantage of Rubberneck's absence and finish Harry before he returned. Over about ten days a real effort was made, with over a hundred feet of tunnel having been dug, right up to its full length of three hundred and fifty feet, not including the shafts. During one session alone we moved forward thirteen feet, producing about three tons of sand, which were quickly dispersed, matching our best efforts.

The surveyors had estimated it to be three hundred and thirty feet from the shaft to the edge of the wood, and Crump thought it about twenty-five feet to the surface there. Digging up was both difficult and dangerous, as the sand kept tumbling down in your face. Travis had worked on sections for the shoring, using both bedposts and bedboards to make solid box framing. On 14 March, Crump and Johnny Bull, working together, came to some pine roots, which made them think that they must now be about two feet from the surface. They then roofed the shaft across, packing in sand to make it solid in case someone patrolling outside walked on it. That was the last shift. The tunnel, Harry, was now finished. We were ready for breakout. With some sense of occasion Pat Langford put down the trap for the penultimate time, and sealed up the entrance. The next time it opened would be for the real thing.

Looking back on it I am amazed at what we accomplished; it was on a vast scale. About thirty of us plus about six technicians and carpenters worked down Harry. I understand that 4,000 bedboards were used, 1,370 beading battens, ninety double-tier bunk beds, 600 feet of rope and nearly a thousand feet (thanks to Red Noble) of electric cable, besides various tables and chairs, and a large number of towels and bed-bolsters. I didn't actually count all this up, but somebody did. In all, about five hundred people were involved in the diverse departments of the undertaking.

The next day Rubberneck was back fresh from his hols and immediately moved in on Block 104 with his gang of ferrets. He cleared everyone out and searched for four hours. But even all his fresh energy was not enough, and he departed looking as miserable as ever, thank goodness. It was now all over to the X Committee and the SBO to fix a date and select the lucky ones who would be going out. At the time every one of us hoped we'd be 'lucky'.

CHAPTER NINETEEN

The Breakout

Kriegie 'If'

If you can quit the compound undetected,
And clear your tracks, nor leave the smallest trace,
And carry out the programme you've selected,
Nor lose your grasp of distance, time and place –

If you can walk at night by compass-bearing,
Or ride the railway in the light of day,
And temper your elusiveness with daring,
Trusting that bluff will sometimes find a way –

If you can swallow sudden, sour frustration,
And gaze unmoved at failure's ugly shape,
Remembering for further inspiration –
It was, and is, your duty to escape –

If you can keep the great Gestapo guessing,
With explanations only partly true,
And leave them in their heart of hearts confessing
They didn't get the whole truth out of you –

If you could use your 'cooler' fortnight clearly,
For planning methods wiser than before,
And treat your past miscalculations merely
As hints let fall by fate to teach you more –

If you scheme on with patience and precision –
It wasn't in a day they built Rome –
And make escape your single, sole ambition,
The next time you attempt it – you may get home!

Anon. (with apologies to R. Kipling)

On the days leading up to the breakout[1] the atmosphere in the camp was so charged it seemed astonishing that the goons didn't pick up on it immediately. Although we diggers had now finished our job, Tim Walenn and his 'Dean & Dawson' forgers, including racing driver Gordon Brettell and Henri Picard, were all working overtime on up-to-date travel documents and accurate identity cards. Tommy Guest's clothing department, Plunkett's map-makers and Al Hake's compass manufacturers were all beavering away every available minute of the day or night, too.

Our little group – myself, Red Noble, Johnny Bull, Clive Saxelby and Bren Hooper – were kept busy with the preparations we fervently hoped would be put to use. Apart from Johnny, who would be responsible for opening the exit, none of us knew for sure if we'd been given a place on the list of two hundred the X Organisation planned to get out that night, but for months everyone in the room had been saving up their chocolate to make escape rations. We had altered our tunics to look more like workmen's plain jackets, but for obvious reasons – namely, that we were still wearing them – had left the RAF buttons on them, and would leave any necessary final alterations until we heard for sure if our names were on the list.

Roger and his committee, after much intense and prolonged discussion, decided at last that the breakout would have to be as soon as possible. It had been pointed out by John Marshall that with the current weather – snow-covered ground and below freezing conditions – the hard arsers would stand very little chance of getting far. Even surviving would be a problem. But Roger insisted that after all the work over the last twelve months it would be disastrous to risk waiting any longer, especially as the goons were beginning to get suspicious again that we were tunnelling. He consulted the SBO and Wings Day, who both agreed that he should go ahead and fix the breakout for the first opportune moment. It must have been a difficult decision for the SBO, Group Captain Massey, as I understand that during one of his recent conversations with von Lindeiner, the Kommandant had strongly hinted that it would be very unwise to escape, since he had reason to believe that in the future the Gestapo intended to shoot escapees. All Massey could reply to that was to restate the position: it was the duty of every POW, as it was for every German POW, to try to escape.

The same day Harry was completed, 14 March 1944, Roger went straight into the final plans. It was agreed that he himself would pick the first thirty to go out the tunnel, and these would be the kriegies who had been essential workers and/or who spoke German, therefore having the best

---

[1] We didn't have a name for it then. 'The Great Escape' came later, from Paul Brickhill.

chances for making a 'home run'. These, too, were to be better equipped, and I think in all cases would be travelling by train, while only a few others would be. Everyone was in agreement with all this. Roger also anticipated another possible hiccup: that most of the people going through the tunnel had never actually been down one before. When I recalled my own initial anxieties, I could see how bad an experience it might prove for some, and so we needed experienced hands to help haul people smoothly through Piccadilly and Leicester Square. Another potential problem was a cave-in, so experienced diggers had to be on hand to repair any damage from falls. This was extremely advantageous for Red and myself, as we got an automatic place, albeit a bit down the line. We were to go down and take over from Cookie Long and Tony Bethell, who were sixty-five and sixty-six on the list, and after pulling through twenty people, we'd pull through our own replacements and with any luck, we thought, be off, out and on our way home. The thought that you had a chance, even a very slim one, to get out kept you going.

Now Roger had to go firm on the date, and once this was fixed there could be no turning back, since Tim Walenn and his team had to put dates on all the passes and travel documents. You might have postponed D-Day, but not this one. After a swift consultation with Hall, the met. man, it was confirmed that the nights of 23-25 March would be moonless. The night of 24 March it was to be.

Red and I now really got cracking with our tailoring work. We finished off our uniforms with civilian buttons, shaved off some of the nap and boiled them in a can of water with some black book-binding in it to dye them. The result was not exactly Gieves, but it would have to do. We rubbed margarine into our boots to get them waterproofed in time, and began to collect together the useful bits we would take with us, the ration bars, matches, compass, maps and so on. At one point I remember us both stopping all this frantic activity and simultaneously looking out the window at the snow-covered, frozen ground, then at each other, the same thoughts passing through our minds: would we be able to do it, to make it the sixty-odd miles to the Czech border, walking mostly by night, sheltering by day wherever we could find a hole? At best we might be able to grab an illicit ride on a goods train, or even liberate a bicycle. We were so confident then that none of this would prove any problem at all, I cannot think why. Our papers said that we were both Norwegian workers going on leave.

'We'd better not be stopped, that's all,' I said to Red. Two extremely scruffy individuals, a short, dark-haired Welshman and a six-foot Canadian redhead, posing as a couple of Norwegians, actually going in the opposite direction to Norway, well . . . it would be a hard one for most people to swallow, much less trained and suspicious officials. Our only money was a 1,000 Reichmark note, which I felt was not a lot of use. Still, we were confident. We had to be.

Of the others in our room, Johnny Bull would be one of the first to go out; he was travelling by train as a worker going on leave, complete with all the necessary papers. I can't remember who he was travelling with. Sax, like us, was to travel 'hard arse', with Joe Moul.

Two days before the scheduled breakout, details of the plans for the night were circulated, since it was necessary to move out the occupants of Block 104, and during the evening, slowly move in about two hundred escapees. David Torrens was to be organising the people arriving in the block, allocating them the rooms from which they could be called to the tunnel shaft. Pat Langford was in charge of the entrance trap, and Crump was to do the final check of the tunnel, then place some blankets right at the end to stop any light showing through in the exit shaft.

We were ready.

Our room had big-heartedly got together a farewell meal – nothing special, just a bit more than usual – for the four of us lucky enough to have our exit numbers: Johnny Bull would be leaving first, Sax was number seventy-nine, while Red and I were to follow soon after Sax. The weather outside was as grim as it could be – well below freezing with lots of snow – so I dressed accordingly: long-johns, long-sleeved vest, thick pullover from my parcel, greatcoat and cloth cap. Our pockets were stuffed with matches, escape rations, maps, a compass, a tin oil light and tin can hopeful for any hot drink. Gloves, spare socks and some toiletries completed the kit; we thought we looked bad enough without having to add a few days stubble to our convict-like appearance. The tension in the room was stomach-churning, almost worse than before any operation I could remember. We were bubbling over with excitement. It was a genuine adventure in the sense that no-one really knew what would happen, but the ultimate prize, of getting home and being free again was vivid in the minds of every one of us. This was a lottery and that winning ticket might be ours. Red, staring down at his feast, but like the rest of us almost unable to eat it, said, 'This should see us through the first couple of days. We won't need to touch any escape rations.'

There was a lot of good-humoured banter and leg-pulling about what to do when we got back home, then at 19:00 hours we shook hands and slipped out into the dark.

When Red and I entered Block 104 for a horrible moment I thought we'd had it: in the dim light the first thing I saw standing before me in the corridor was a German unteroffizier. Panic hit me and I nearly passed out, then from under the hat I made out the face of Tobolski, a Polish flying officer, going out with Wings Day. They were going to catch a train to Stettin, then try to stow away on a Swedish ship. Wings was resplendent in a very smart suit, while Tobolski's German uniform, even now I had the chance to see it up close, was a masterpiece, every swastika, badge and belt in the right place. Tommy Guest was a genius. There were about 200 of us spread evenly in the rooms throughout the hut. I can't honestly remember if we had been allocated rooms according to our escape numbers, but that was probably the case. Everyone was nervous, checking constantly papers, escape rations, appearance – all the small details your life might depend upon later.

Pat Langford had already opened up the entrance, and as planned, Crump and Conk Canton were down the tunnel. Apart from hanging blankets to block the light, they also fastened six-inch strips of blanket to the shaft ends of the railway lines to muffle any sound, and made sure that all the electric light bulbs were working. Yet again I sent up a prayer of thanks that Red had bagged that cable; electric light would make a big difference to those who had not yet been down the tunnel. At 8:45 pm, Crump and Conk emerged from the shaft and announced that everything was complete and ready to go.

The first group now went down the shaft to the tunnel led by the two hauliers for Piccadilly and Leicester Square, who then hauled the group through to open the tunnel exit. Johnny Bull and John Marshall were first, as they would be opening the exit, followed by Roger Bushell and his partner, the Frenchman Bernard Scheidhauer. These two were making for Paris, where Bernard knew people who might be able to put them in touch with the Resistance or underground. Then came Ernst Valenta (Marshall's escape partner), Rupert Stevens and Sydney Dowse, who would remain at the exit to pull up twenty more people from Leicester Square before being relieved so he could escape into the night himself. The organisation was smooth.

There were, however, a few factors outside anyone's control.

When Bull climbed the ladder at the exit shaft and tried to remove the boards placed across the top of the shaft to stop anyone falling in, he couldn't do it. The wood had swollen with damp and then frozen solid. It would not budge. Working in turns and trying to stay calm, Bull and Marshall slowly and gradually cleared the boards, and then Johnny himself carefully removed the last two feet of soil and grass. Slowly, with infinite caution, he put his head up to ground level, then his eyes. He was facing the compound, and there silhouetted against the night sky was the goon-box with a sentry inside it pacing up and down outside the wire. Turning his head slowly around, to his horror he saw that the wood was another fifteen feet away, the exit shaft was exposed in open ground. Somehow, the surveyors had miscalculated. Quickly he descended the ladder to break the bad news to Roger waiting below.

Lying more or less on top of each other in the cramped space, they began immediately to sort out a possible plan of action. Marshall suggested that they close down and dig the extra twenty feet to be inside the cover of the wood, but Roger vetoed this as the documents had all been painstakingly date-stamped; it had to be today. Roger's own idea was more dangerous and daring. Bull was to tie a rope to the top rung of the ladder, while Marshall crawled out the mouth of the shaft, across the open ground and into the wood, where he would tie the other end of the rope to a tree. From there he would have a perfect vantage-point. When Marshall saw the coast was clear, he would tug the rope and Bull would send the next escaper through. When eight had passed through in this way, the next two would take over and dispatch another eight, and so on. All this took up a lot of time. By the time the revised plan had been sent back and a rope sent up over an hour had gone by, with no-one yet out.

Eventually, with the rope tied to a tree well inside the wood, Marshall gave two tugs on it to let Bull know all was clear and they could proceed. But of course the whole process would be now much slower, with one at a time and then a pause before the next one. Back in Block 104 we were all wondering what the hold-up could be. Shortly after 10 pm we heard the lock-up goon walking around the hut, closing the shutters for the night. If anything he must have thought we were unusually quiet that night, because really, you could have heard a pin drop in that place, even with two hundred men there who didn't belong. At any rate, he moved on to the next block, and we heard the shutters being closed down the line. When we were free to breathe again I looked around me at the very odd collection crowded into the corridor: neat businessmen in suits with suitcases contrasting with the hard arsers in everything under the sun, some carrying blankets for warmth, while others padded up like the Michelin Man. I must have been in the latter category.

More things began to go wrong. First, someone carrying a suitcase caused a fall which took Cookie Long ages to repair. Then the RAF stepped in and really put things back. Without any consideration of their former colleagues they had decided to raid Berlin tonight, approaching the city from the south, which brought them virtually over Stalag Luft III. We could hear a distant familiar roar, which pleased us a lot, but unfortunately the goons suddenly put out all the lights, causing mayhem down in the tunnel. Escapers who had never been down it before abruptly and without explanation found themselves in total darkness trapped in a claustrophobic hole. Everything stopped until some oil lights were lit and passed down the tunnel.

A few more escapers got stuck, causing more delays, and by now, with only about two hours of darkness remaining it was realised that we would be lucky to get a hundred out. Hard arsers with blanket-rolls seemed to be the main trouble so these were banned, much to the annoyance of their owners. At last Red and I went down the tunnel to take up our places, Red at Piccadilly, while I went on to relieve Tony Bethell at Leicester Square. Tony shook my hand. 'See you in the Regent Palace,' he said, and off he went.

Tony was number sixty-five out of the tunnel. I was supposed to pull out twenty escapees, pull up my own relief, then go off myself. This was not to be. After I'd hauled through about fifteen, at about 4:45 am, Crump and Torrens decided that it would soon be light and we'd have to call a halt. The word was passed along, and as I pulled Clive Saxelby up he said, 'That's it. That's all. You follow me out, all right?'

Crump had sent down Michael Ormond, Tim Newman and Muckle Muir, who would try to close up the tunnel against discovery as they got out. I pulled up Red and set off for the exit shaft at last, heart pounding with excitement. We'd nearly got to the shaft when I heard a shot. Everything stopped.

At the time I did not know what had gone wrong. I understand now that a patrolling guard had decided he needed a pee and had wandered idly towards the woods, only to stumble upon a big hole in the ground with a kriegie lying across it and Len Trent just crawling away into the woods. A shot rang out. Len leapt to his feet, yelling, 'Nicht shiessen, nicht shiessen!' (Although according to Reavell Carter, right beside him, what he actually shouted was, 'Nicht sheissen!' God knows what the sentry thought.)[2]

Heart in my throat, fear battling with complete frustration, I went backwards to Leicester Square. As I got there, Joe Moul and Clive Saxelby shot past me, if this is the right word for the accelerated caterpillar movement we were stuck with. I called to Sax, telling him to take it easy or he'd bring the damned thing down. He was over six foot tall, crawling with great difficulty in a kind of kangaroo hop, backside up and hitting the roof, and I thought the tunnel might collapse at any moment. It had also occurred to me that a guard might go down the tunnel and shoot experimentally up it, and all I would need was to be stuck in a cave-in with a bullet up my backside. With this in mind I kept trying to kick out shoring-boards as I went along, but sod's law, they just would not shift. I cannot describe the sheer and intense relief I felt climbing up that ladder and into the room. I was the last man up. They shut the trap behind me.

Meanwhile throughout Block 104 all hell was breaking out. One escaper tried to jump out the window to get back to his own block, but a

---

[2] 'Shiessen' means 'shoot', while 'sheissen' means 'shit'. Perhaps he did know what he was saying.

shot from the goon-box stopped that. Torrens was yelling, 'Everybody, destroy your papers, your maps, everything!' Whilst burning our papers, we all stuffed our faces with escape rations; we knew that everything we had would be confiscated. Any punishment we'd had up to now would be as nothing to what was about to hit the fan. It must have been only a few minutes of such frantic activity before we could hear at last the bar on the door being lifted, and in walked the Hund Führer and his dog. There was a pause. He seemed uncertain as to what the procedure should be, so simply told everyone to get to their rooms. Meanwhile the dog was pretty happy, since every hand he turned to was trying to feed him nice little snacks. But then things really started to hop: guards poured into camp, armed to the teeth with machine guns and all. Too much, too late, crossed my mind. There was the thump of booted feet: von Lindeiner, wearing a face like thunder, entered the block and we were all ordered out into the freezing morning.

As we all lined up outside the hut, breathing and stamping with the cold, Rubberneck spotted Red and myself, his *bête noire*, and his face went deep purple with frustrated rage. He already loathed us beyond reason, and now he had every excuse. He barked at both of us to strip off, so slowly, insolently slowly, Red and I began to take off our coats, button by button. This was too much for him. Furious, he yelled at a couple of the guards to tear the coats off our backs. By this time, though, I was feeling pretty fed-up with being pushed around myself; I wrenched myself free of the guard and gave him a defiant shove. Then froze. Rubberneck had got out his revolver and was aiming the barrel straight into my face. Staring into that barrel, two feet from my nose, I thought, 'God, this is it.'

A crisp order from the door, though, saved me. Von Lindeiner had just emerged from the hut and barked at Rubberneck, who reluctantly lowered his revolver, his eyes still on me. Von Lindeiner was himself red with controlled anger as he ordered us to strip, which we did in peace but rather more quickly.

By the time we had got down to our vests and long-johns it was actually snowing, and Red and I were marched off, hands high, through snow-covered ground to the Cooler, two guards holding automatics in the small of our backs. I can still feel the cold hard little circle of that gun in my back. 'That was close,' I whispered at Red. 'It could have been the mortuary, not the Cooler.'

'Not you two again.' The NCO in charge of the Cooler was resigned when he saw us, not angry, and heaving a great sigh, put us in our cells. Once the cell door had shut I flung myself on the cot, suddenly overwhelmed with cold, completely exhausted in mind and body. The adrenalin that had kept me going those long hours of waiting all night had run out. I was shaking, nearly weeping with frustration at the thought of all that work gone to waste. I'd been within minutes of getting out of that bloody tunnel and off into the woods and freedom, even a few minutes of such freedom would have been worth it all. Instead, here I was again, stuck in this tiny cell, cold and miserable and lucky not to have been shot. At the time, of course, I did not realise just how lucky I was. With my track record I would have been on that list with the Fifty.

Despite the cold right down into one's bones, I came to when they brought the watery soup and a couple of potatoes for lunch. Revived, I spent the afternoon shouting and calling into the other cells as I passed them on the way to the toilet. From these bits and pieces I could work out that four others had been caught at the exit: Reavell Carter, Len Trent[3], Langlois and Bob McBride. Mike Shand and Ogilvy had been with them but managed to dash for it in the confusion.

This was my worst ever spell in the Cooler, a full fortnight. The cold was unrelenting and the rations poor – just Reich bread, soup barely removed from water and a few potatoes. Since all food parcels for the entire compound had been cancelled there were no kriegies passing the window on their way to the parcel store, so no cigarettes or anything kindly thrown in through the window. All I could do was sit there on the bed and feel extremely sorry for myself. Hours and days dragged by before the first of the escapers to be picked up joined us: Marshall, Ogilvy, Royle and McDonald. They were astonished to be the first back into camp, since they had all been detained in a gaol with a group of about twenty other captured escapees, who had all left before them. It was several days more when we all found out the reason for this, shouted to us from outside: forty-one of the escaped men had been shot.

I cannot begin to describe the collective shock at this news. In wartime you are, if not actually ever used to death on a daily basis, at least prepared for it. You take your chances against the enemy, and on the whole, you know what you're up against. But this was murder.

After about two weeks, another thirteen escapers arrived for the Cooler, which was getting rather crowded by now. Red and I had served our time and cold, hungry and angry, but also I cannot deny, relieved, we returned to our room.

---

[3] After the war he was to receive the VC for 'suicidal determination' when he was shot down.

CHAPTER TWENTY

The Aftermath

But each one, man for man, has won imperishable praise, each has gained a glorious grave – not that sepulchre of earth wherein they lie, but the living tomb of everlasting remembrance wherein their glory is enshrined. For the whole earth is the sepulchre of heroes, monuments may rise and tablets be set up to them in their own land, that no pen or chisel has traced: it is craven, not on stone or brass, but on the living heart of humanity. Take these men as your example. Like them remember that posterity can be only for the free: that freedom is the sure possession of those alone who have the courage to defend it.

Funeral oration of Pericles

Red and I arrived back in our room to hear confirmation of the terrible news. The Kommandant, von Lindeiner, had already been arrested, taken away and replaced by Oberst Braune. While I was still in the Cooler, Group Captain Massey, together with his interpreter, Squadron Leader Wank Murray (even though Braune spoke good English), had been called to the new Kommandant's office.

Braune did not beat about the bush. 'Forty-one of your officers have been shot whilst trying to evade capture.'

'What?' Massey could not believe he had heard correctly. 'How many were wounded?'

'None. I am afraid I cannot give you any more information.'

The entire compound was horrified at this news. Those Germans who were Luftwaffe shared the horror and tried to distance themselves from what they saw as nothing less than an act of murder. For days the Luftwaffe guards would say to any of us, 'You must not blame the Luftwaffe. All of this was in the hands of the Gestapo.'

A few days later the list of the dead was posted, only now it contained forty-seven names, then to these were added a further three names, bringing the total murdered now up to fifty. At the top I saw Johnny Bull's name. Team-leader, roommate, friend. We all wept for Johnny. We had spent hours pounding the circuit. I'd told him all about Mary and our future plans, while he'd told me about his wife and the infant son he had never seen. It all seemed so cruel, so unreal. I sat there on the edge of my bunk and stared across the room at his empty top bunk. For some stupid reason I felt guilty. But for a guard wanting a pee, I would have been with him on the list, and back in England Mary would have been reading about me.

Gradually, we learned what had happened while we were stuck in the Cooler. On the day of the breakout, von Lindeiner and his staff had immediately been busy checking the records of every officer missing, and a Kriegsfahndung, a manhunt involving the army, had been declared. Once the true picture emerged of exactly how many men had escaped, there is no other way to express it, the shit truly hit the fan. Hitler was hopping mad, and a Grossfahndung (a national alert) ordered, which meant troops, police, Gestapo, Landwacht (Home Guard) and Hitler Youth were all brought in to the hunt. At first Hitler ordered that everyone captured should be shot, but his generals managed to convince him that such an act could not be concealed and might encourage reprisals with the thousands of German POWs in British hands. Eventually Hitler calmed down, but still insisted that an example be made: fifty were to be shot and cremated. He took the matter out of the hands of the military and gave it to Himmler and his Gestapo. General Nebe, head of the Kripo, the Kriminalpolizei, would select the fifty to be shot.

It will never be known exactly how Nebe decided who was to die, but singly, or in small parties of two or three they were driven to quiet locations and shot. All the official reports stated that the prisoners were shot as they dashed for freedom while their guards allowed them to relieve themselves. Despite this end, they had more than achieved Roger's aim to disrupt the war effort and divert it. I think he would have been pleased to know the breakout had succeeded to that extent; he'd known that realistically very few of us had much chance of making a home run, while the real mayhem caused in Germany was always a main object. Although he had baldly said he himself expected to be shot if captured, I think what happened would have horrified him. The price was too terrible.

As life in the compound slowly settled down, the camp authorities allowed us to build a memorial. It wasn't simple kindness on their part, more a pragmatic gesture to allow the festering bad feelings an outlet. The memorial was designed by Squadron Leader Hartnell-Beavis, a former architect, and a working party under parole with an armed escort built it in the local cemetery. The urns containing the ashes of the fifty were buried there. After the war, the urns were taken to the Old Garrison Cemetery at Poznan.

CHAPTER TWENTY-ONE

Life Returns to Normal

I hope that I will never eat
When Jerry's dust is off my feet
Another tin of Morton's stew
Or drink another Kriegie brew

I hope that I will be immune
From all the Kultur of the Goon
From nicht, verboten, aus and nein
And from the Deutsche Allgemein

I hope that I will never see
When final victory sets me free
Another Goon Box, fence or wire
Or so much dirt and mud and mire

I hope my cup will overflow
With all the joys I used to know
With wine and women to be kissed
To make up for the things I've missed.

Joe 'Red' Noble

Life, even such life as there was in a place like this, must go on, and slowly we all found some kind of status quo, not to return to, rather a way to keep going. I say 'all', because everyone in camp had been affected by the escape, goons and kriegies alike. For the majority of us kriegies, and certainly for me, most of what we did over the last year had been focused on that major escape attempt, so for a while everything post-escape was relatively dull, peppered only with the unwelcome attentions of the Gestapo. In the weeks following the escape and murders we had more frequent searches, one of these conducted by the Gestapo. The goons were themselves terrified of the Gestapo – with good reason – and so could barely conceal their delight when two Gestapo lost their gloves and a hat whilst searching our hut. Someone had lifted these while we were all being turned out, and had quickly buried them in the sand. The Gestapo, who look as thuggish in real life as they appeared in films, simply could not believe that anyone would dare to humiliate them in such a way, and kept us outside for a full two hours while they conducted a fruitless search. We didn't mind a bit.

It was May 1944, and after one of the worst winters of the century the weather was picking up, and the news from all fronts was exciting. In May we heard that Stalingrad had fallen, and the Eastern Front seemed in complete disarray; the main topic of conversation all that month was when the second front would start. I was standing one day in June in line at the cookhouse to get our water when the news came over the German tannoy system that the Allies had landed on the French coast. Instantly, every German speaker in the compound was out there translating for the benefit of the excited crowds gathering to hear what had happened. It was wonderful, the atmosphere, and it was the best news I'd heard since being made prisoner. Of course everyone ignored the inevitable propaganda rider: 'We are containing the Allies and pushing them back to the sea . . .'. 'Home' was on everyone's lips, but when? The most optimistic reckoned we'd be home in a few months; most of us hoped for Christmas. My unfinished honeymoon was all I could think of!

But through all the good news there were still practical problems to be considered. The SBO thought that in view of the likely Allied victory it would be a good idea for us to be organised and ready in case the Germans attempted to use us as hostages to obtain better terms of surrender for themselves. So bands of commandos were formed, called for security reasons 'Klim Clubs'. I teamed up with Red, and we organised groups all ready to go into action, armed with softball bats, iron bars, anything that could hit back hard. One particularly nasty device involved knocking nails into the bottom half of softball bats, entirely lethal and medieval. I am glad we were never called upon to use them.

In between such planning we all took up sport again: a little cricket and much more softball. I discovered a real enjoyment of softball, and I always liked being actively involved, either in the field or screaming abuse at the opposition whilst waiting my turn at bat. At the end of May I also started boxing again, got myself into training, and on 22 June, a competition was staged for the benefit of the rest of the camp, with several bouts on the bill. The referee was Squadron Leader Fielden, the judges, Flight Lieutenant Bjelke-Peterson RAAF and Flight Lieutenant Stamp. My opponent was Flight Lieutenant Ginger Jones, and because we both wanted it to be a classy affair, both of us spent hours at our technical training. In the event, though, all the science went to the wall, and we simply stood there and slugged it out, toe to toe, the spectators baying for blood, until the last round, by which time I could barely keep on my feet, seeing Ginger also gasping for breath and swaying. I suppose we must have hit each other the same number of times, because the fight was declared a draw. Everyone said it was the most entertaining bout of the evening.

To add to the quality of life Red and I continued with our illicit distilling activities. Late into the night after we had been locked in, we sat up making hooch for our own room and, for a small percentage of the goods to 'cover our labour costs', for some of the others as well. On one memorable occasion, instead of our labour costs we accepted an invitation to the party being thrown in Block 103, right at the other end of the compound. But 103's parties were legendary, so we felt it worth the risk. It was. I must say that nothing really happened at such parties; the success was often measured by the amount taken on board, since the more of the stuff you drank the better it got. At about midnight, in spite of protests from the other revellers, but fully primed with Dutch courage, Red and I decided to make the perilous dash back to our own block. Some care in this operation was necessary; only weeks earlier a squadron leader doing much the same thing had been shot in the thigh. I really don't know how we managed it; the night world was wobbling as in between searchlight sweeps from the goon-boxes we scrambled into the shadowy cover of the huts. On our final dash we only just managed to scrabble through the window as the Hund Führer came round the corner with his keenly sniffing dog.

Oh, the war seemed to move so painfully slowly! By October it was obvious even to the most optimistic that we would not be home for Christmas, so yet once more I began saving scraps from our parcels for what I was certain would be our final, last, absolutely last Christmas lunch in captivity. My Christmas cake recipe had improved at least.

Rees's Improved Christmas Cake
3 Klim tins of biscuits, $1/2$ Klim tin of barley, $1/4$ Klim tin of sugar,
$1/4$ tin of Klim milk, $3/4$ lb margarine, 2lbs raisins,
1 tin egg powder, few odds and ends like breadcrumbs for bulk.

Get George Smith, Deputy Cook, to grind biscuits, barley, stale bread in washbasin (this also helps to clean the basin). Add margarine and work it in until you have a granular mixture. Mix in raisins. Mix egg powder with water, until you have a paste, then add to mixture. Add the milk powder. Mix the lot until you have a thick, sticky mess, adding water if necessary. Put in baking tin lined with greaseproof paper (NB: any paper covered with marg will do). Place some greaseproof paper on top and bake in hot oven for about 3-4 hours, (or until starting to smoke) and nothing sticks to a knife put into the cake.

If the knife will not go into the cake it is definitely done.

On the other hand you may wish to stick with Delia Smith.

At the end of the summer a Sports Day was organised by the sports officer, Wing Commander 'Hetty' Hyde, with lots of willing helpers, and Digger Larkin organising the side-shows. All the usual events were keenly fought. For once I had a day off, while two unusual events – Digger's ideas – 'Throwing the Cricket Ball' and 'Throwing an American Football' were won by the Canadians. Winners got cigarettes. The stalls consisted of 'Rolling the Pennies' (i.e. Deutschsmarks), a coconut shy and one wonderful stall which charged a cigarette to go in and watch a 'fire-walker'. Like everyone else I went into the tent to discover the fire-walker to be a kriegie walking on bona fide glowing coals, with one foot in the coals. I have to add that he did have a wooden leg, which by the end of the day was pretty charred.

We had also started up the rugby again before the ground got too frozen. The Big Match that October was North Compound v. East Compound, East Compound being allowed to come to our compound on parole. I have to say that this was one of the hardest games of rugby I have ever played, which we won, but only just. Towards the end of the match I was taken off the field with a dislocated elbow. It hurt like hell, but was useful, since it got me a few days in the camp hospital where the food was much better.

That autumn the new escape committee decided to start up another tunnel from under the theatre. Red Noble and myself were asked to form two teams of diggers, and our teams were drawn mostly from our room. We only needed a few to disperse the sand, since it would all be done under the auditorium, where we'd finished off dispersing sand from Harry. There was still plenty of room there. Unfortunately before we could really get going, the Germans had left a notice in everyone's rooms one day while we were all out on Appell. 'To all Prisoners of War! The escape from prison camps is no longer a sport! . . . In plain English: Stay in the camp where you will be safe! Breaking out of it is now a damned dangerous act . . .' and so on. What was made clear was that now we could be shot if caught even trying to escape. This notice together with the good news coming in from all fronts made it difficult to get together an enthusiastic team. The old keenness to escape was gone, and there did not seem to be a lot of sense in risking getting yourself shot with the end of the war in sight, or at least, in the not too distant future. Still, three members of my team from my room, George Smith, Larry Somers and Joe Lorree, proved enthusiastic enough. But another friend who joined us, Charles Hobgen, came down the tunnel as my number two one day, only to be overcome with the most dreadful attack of claustrophobia which left him a sweating, quivering wreck. He said he'd never been so frightened in his life before. After that, he volunteered instead to work the air-pump or haul the sand back from the face.

I don't think that the real object of digging this tunnel was so much for escape – although that was always a possibility – but rather for security purposes, as a backup for the Klim Clubs. At least we might be able to get some people out of camp to find some more weapons should we need them. But as it turned out, although we were under the wire by Christmas, events overtook us and the tunnel was never used. It had been a lot of hard work, but it had passed the time and given us a sense of purpose again. I suspect Red the mad sod never lost his real desire to escape, and he would have had me there with him, willy-nilly.

The December weather was now bitterly cold, the ground covered in snow. The Red Cross parcels were still coming through, thank goodness, and we were still given our small rations of goon coal. We were determined to make this – surely our last – Christmas as kriegies a memorable one. Christmas Day began with a good lunch saved up from food parcels and supplemented by the Red Cross, then as a *digestif* we started on the hooch, complemented by a tiny amount of very weak and tasteless beer supplied by the goons. By late afternoon it had been decided somehow that room-visiting was in order. I can remember laughing a lot, especially at Bren Hooper who had got himself in the middle of the home-made ice rink and could not get up, his feet going up to the sky, a real cow on ice. After several futile drunken attempts to rescue him, a more sober kriegie finally took pity on him and hauled him by his feet off the ice. The goons were being fairly tolerant, even when a very inebriated Canadian climbed over the warning rail, then over the wire. A guard at the wire asked him where he thought he was going.

'I'm fed up with this bloody place and I'm pissing off back to Canada. That's where!'

It took several of them to pick him gingerly off the barbed wire. It was a torn and bloody kriegie, recovering from a major hangover, who had ten days in the Cooler to recover and reflect on just how lucky he had been.

In January the weather was very severe, but the news was good: the Russians were getting closer and closer, and we all wondered what the Germans would do with us. The general feeling, including that of the SBO, was that we would be moved, probably east, so a few of us, myself included, began making some preparations like converting kit bags into backpacks and manufacturing our primitive weapons. On 25 January the Russians had reached the Oder River, about forty-six miles away; the entire camp listened in tense silence to the distant rumble of the guns coming our way. Red's newest idea was to construct a sledge using two ice-hockey sticks.

On 27 January, at about 9 pm, we were entertaining Group Captain Wray RCAF with coffee, when John Nunn burst into the room.

'Get packed up,' he said. 'We're off in an hour.'

After a moment's stunned silence there was frantic activity. No-one could believe it. What a time to be on the move, in deepest winter, the weather as foul as it could be. Red and I hastily finished off our sledge using bedboards and wood torn from the walls, besides the wooden box the block had used to collect the daily potato ration. I felt quite proud of our sledge, but there was no time to stand around and admire it. Apart from the clothes we stood up in we managed to grab a change of underwear, extra socks (you always need extra socks) and as many cigarettes as we could lay our hands on for any future bartering. What food remained in the room was shared out. Then there was nothing more to do but wait for the order to move. The last thing I carefully packed away was my log book, which I'd kept all the years I'd been there. It was my most precious possession, full of photographs, drawings and cartoons, all done by various friends, and all the bits and pieces of camp life. I looked at it hard before stowing it safely away. Already it was a part of my past.

I remember staring around at that room while we were forced to wait. It was icy cold, the winter wind howling outside. I would never as long as I lived forget that cold, those two harsh winters with no heat but the nine other bodies in the room, having night after night to crawl into bed wearing every stitch you owned, and having to break the ice before you could wash. Even so, some felt the need to open a window from time to time, when the stench of our common humanity got worse than the cold. No, there was no regret. I would leave without a backward glance.

CHAPTER TWENTY-TWO

The Long March

The March

It's easy to be nice, boys, when everything's okay,
It's easy to be cheerful when you're having things your way,
But can you hold your head up and take it on the chin
When your heart is nearly breaking and you'd like giving in?

It was easy back in England, amongst the friends and folks,
But now you miss the friendly hand, the songs, the joys, the jokes.
The road ahead is snowy, and unless you're strong in mind
You'll find it isn't long before you're lagging far behind.

You know there is a saying that 'Sunshine follows rain',
And sure enough, you'll realise that joy follows pain.
Let courage be your password, make fortitude your guide
And then instead of grousing, just remember those who died.

Anon

Nothing was happening.

Only an hour before I had been listening to Group Captain Wray's opinion that the Germans would not move us, although they would most likely move the senior officers. Well, he was wrong. With a blizzard raging outside and the snow already more than six inches deep we had been under starter's orders for hours now, but nothing further had happened. Red and I kept making little changes and adjustments to the load already on the sledge, adding a blanket each and even more cigarettes, and destroyed everything else rather than let the goons have anything. At 21:30 we could hear the Americans leaving the South Compound; two hours after that the West Compound was evacuated. It wasn't until 01:30 that they started to move the North Compound, but being at the far end of the compound we weren't moved until about 03:00. As we left the compound we collected some more Red Cross parcels piled up, free for all now; some could only manage one, but with our sledge running smoothly we decided to take two. As Group Captain D.E.L. Wilson SBO says in his book *The March from*

Luft III: 'At least 23,000 Red Cross parcels were left behind intact. Prisoners' belongings worth an estimated £250,000 were abandoned.'

The lines had formed up inside the compound, and because the dark and the heavy snowfall made visibility almost nil, the 1,500 in our compound simply followed the people ahead, the different compounds joining up until there were about 10,000 of us on the march. Even what should have been a glorious moment, when we finally passed through the gates of Stalag Luft III, came and went, everyone too busy concentrating on simply keeping going through the cold, cold wind and snow. Though we were mostly young and reasonably fit we weren't used to walking long distances, and it was hard going but simply too cold to stop. We hadn't gone very far before the ground became littered with discarded items: blankets, books and clothing – all things the over-ambitious had tried to carry but found they couldn't. They must have been desperate; our clothing was inadequate anyway, and many were wearing only improvised hats and gloves.

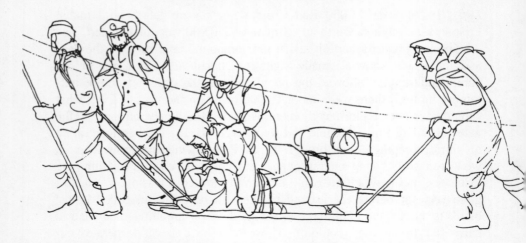

Below zero – noon 29/1/45. Taken from Tony Bethell's log book.

For some seventeen kilometres we marched in this white-out with only the briefest of halts, until we reached Halbau at about 07:00. Whilst we were kept waiting around, stamping feet and waving arms in a vain attempt to keep from freezing, the goon officers accompanying us tried to find some accommodation, but to no avail. They ordered us on to Freiwaldau, some fourteen kilometres further up the road. It was almost a relief to keep moving in the cold.

Along the way more and more items were being cast aside and left in the snow, as prisoners got exhausted and the hastily home-made sledges started packing up. Even precious food parcels and cartons of cigarettes were now being discarded. Unfortunately for me pulling our already overloaded sledge, Red kept cheerfully picking things up and piling them on top. During the few short stops we managed to eat a few biscuits, but snow makes you thirsty and we badly needed a drink. People in the villages along the way were actually quite friendly, and if part of the column was lucky enough to stop in one of these they would be provided with hot water to make some precious, much-needed coffee. At no point did any of us have any idea where we were headed.

After eight hours marching in cold wind and snow, a few could carry on no longer and fell behind to the back of the column, where they were picked up by an open cart and simply piled in. I felt that on balance we were better off walking; at least we could keep reasonably warm if we moved, but when you stopped, your sweat immediately began to freeze on your back. It was around 12:00 when at last we reached Freiwaldau. The snow had stopped, but it was still very cold, the collective breath of 10,000 cold men frozen in the air. We had now covered thirty kilometres, with very little to eat or drink, and must have been quite a sight for the citizens of this modest-sized town as thousands of wet, cold and tired kriegies trudged into the the town square, filling it, shivering in the bitter wind. We weren't the only ones passing through: the town was full of other refugees, running from the advancing Russian Army, women and children and old men. Still, the good people of Freiwaldau did what they could, handing out hot water and friendly smiles at our plight.

Although we'd been told that Freiwaldau was to be our billet for the night, it became clear from the sheer mass of humanity around, refugees, soldiers and thousands of POWs, that this simply would not work out. A few of us decided to try to find our own accommodation, using our cigarettes as barter. I managed to sell a few cigarettes for Reichmarks to buy some beer and maybe warm myself at a nice pub fire, but once inside the pub we found the soldiers there took exception to our intrusion and we were smartly bundled back to the cold outside. In fact the local miltary were objecting to our presence there altogether, so Major Rostek decided that it would be better to march on to Lieppa, about six kilometres further on, where they hoped to billet us in barns.

This final six kilometres was the worst yet. Standing around in the cold wind in Freiwaldau, we had all frozen up. We'd had no sleep, barely any food and the wind was if anything getting worse. The march was painfully slow now, too, with more people falling back to be picked up by the carts. Arriving at Lieppa at about 17:30, we found that the barn could only hold 600 men. Eventually 700 were packed in there, while the rest of us – Red and I included – were forced to stand stamping our feet and shaking our hands in the cold wind until more barns were located. We had now been on the road for sixteen hours, covering thirty-six kilometres, but that wait, for four hours, in the dark with the temperature now at minus twenty, was horrible. You've gone numb long since, and lack the energy even to worry about freezing to death. Your clothes and boots have been saturated, the slush turned to ice; our only food apart from a few crumbly biscuits had frozen solid. But at last they rounded up 400 of us and packed us into a not terribly big hay barn. Hay is at least warm, and sweetly-scented; we certainly were not either. I can still smell the stench of the sodden wool of our clothes. Red had found a pitchfork and, standing up, yelled into the general darkness: 'Anyone lights a cigarette here I will *personally* stick them with this pitchfork!'

We were wedged into the hay so tightly that the necessities of life had to be performed without moving. At least like this it was a bit warmer; the night outside was the coldest of that winter. My own feet were completely numb with cold. I've no idea how many of us already had frostbite and the vomiting that comes with exposure, and when I managed to wrest my boots off, they came off socks and all, the socks frozen to the soles. I shoved my cold feet under some bloke's bottom, and some tingling feeling was just creeping back into them by the time I drifted off into exhausted sleep, punctuated by the coughs and snores of 400 other cold and tired men. I had recently read Shackleton's *The Worst Journey in the World*. Well, this was mine.

After an ineffectual attempt by the Germans to count us, the march resumed at 08:00 next morning. The fact that apart from the sick all were present was entirely due to the organisation of the prisoners themselves, by the simple expedient of asking one person in charge to check his own party. It was still freezing outside, the road hard. By midday we had reached Priebus, where we stopped for 'lunch'. Once again, we mananged to eat a few biscuits only, while some water was supplied by friendly locals. At 18:00 we reached Muskau, where at last the authorities appeared to be a bit more organised. Some 300 of us were billeted in a cinema, some in a riding-school, about 150 in a stable, while the rest were shared out between a laundry, a pottery and a French POW camp. I was in the last group, who were marched a further two kilometres to a glass factory on a hill outside town, where we were given some of the usual Reich sawdust bread. Herr Sallmann, the owner of the glass factory, was more generous than many. Our party took over his manager's office, complete with fire. I cannot describe the sheer bliss of that glowing warmth. In no time we had made ourselves completely at home, drying clothes, thawing out our tins of Red Cross food and boiling hot water for reviving drinks. I only discovered later the next day how lucky we had been: hundreds billeted in conditions far less sanitary had come down with dysentery. We were allowed to linger there in our little paradise all the next day, moving out the following morning.

The weather, meanwhile, had taken a sudden warm turn, everything frozen now a messy slush, which meant that our sledge would be out of action. Swings and roundabouts. We now had to decide what to carry with us and what had to be abandoned. Two food parcels each and as many cigarettes as possible were deemed essential. Some cord was found, and soon both Red and I each had a Red Cross parcel and packs of cigarettes dangling along each side. It was dark on Thursday, 1 February, when we finally set off for Spremberg.

It was colder at night, the reformed ice crunching under hundreds of pairs of boots, while some men had frostbite so severe they were forced to walk in their socks. The combined effects of the earlier march, the darkness and hilly country, besides the total inability of the Germans to exercise normal marching discipline, with set times for the columns to stop and start up, made this the worst part of the journey to date. Imagine an endless column of weary men spread out by now into smaller groups, miserable with cold and hunger and some fear of what was going to happen to them, with very little noise apart from the coughing, plodding through the night and the icy slush. Before we had set out a quarter of a loaf of bread had been given to each man, who would take a few desultory bites of it at every halt; with nearly 2,000 prisoners in our long, straggling column there were plenty of halts. I don't think I can remember actually saying anything during that march. There was nothing, really, one could say. I suppose it must have been the same for everyone.

At about 14:00 hours on 2 February we came into Spremberg, where we were accommodated at the 8th Panzer Division's reserve depot and issued with some soup and hot water. My twenty-fourth birthday, and we weren't even being allowed to stop here. Two hours later we formed up again to march to a train station about four kilometres further on, where finally we were told that our destination was to be Milag-Malag Nord, a Royal Navy POW camp about thirty kilometres from Bremen. By this time our numbers had diminished. At Muskau and also at Spremberg many of the Americans and some of the RAF men were taken away from the main column and sent to other camps: some to Nuremberg, some to Moosbure, with the Belaria contingent being sent off in another direction entirely, to Luckenwalde.

As soon as we arrived at the train station we were surrounded by guards who herded us into cattle-trucks. The absolute capacity of each truck should have been forty, but since there were obviously too few trucks, forty-five was closer to the norm. Inside the trucks were filthy; there had not been enough time to clear away much of the ordure, human and bovine, which filled it. But by the time we were under way the walls of our truck were festooned with all our kit, and to start with, Red, myself, George Smith, Bren Hooper and Sax stood up so that the sick could have more room. But as we bounced along in the darkness, exhaustion took over, and before long everyone had slumped to the filthy floor, all wedged in. In this cramped, stinking, heaving box, everyone slept.

In the morning things really became chaotic. People were vomiting, one or two obviously had dysentery, and the atmosphere was soon completely foul. Several of us managed to enlarge a crack in the floor for people to relieve themselves, but given the conditions their aim was not always good. There was supposed to be a field kitchen waiting for us at Halle, but we got there late that night to find that all supplies had been co-opted by a hospital train in from the Eastern Front, so on we went, unfed. The train reached the outskirts of Hannover early on 4 February, and Major Rostek, appreciating the state most people were in, allowed everyone out of the foul trucks to pick up some water from neighbouring houses. It was the first water we'd had since leaving Spremberg thirty-six hours before. God only knows what the good people of Hannover thought when they saw us coming, dressed in rags sodden with dirt and damp and excrement, filthy and ill.

The train drew into Tarmstedt station at about 17:30 hours that evening. I don't think I was ever so pleased to leave a train. Inside, the stench and conditions had gone well beyond unbearable; I for one was nauseated by the reek of vomit and shit. The suffering of some was terrible to see, but there was little one could do. Getting out of it would make the biggest difference. We formed up in a ragged, shuffling column to march the remaining four kilometres into camp. The head of the column reached the camp gates at 19:00, and a personal search of each prisoner began, which took ages. By now it was raining, the track filled with pools of water, and we were forced to stand there in the wet and wait to be searched individually, and for what? Apart from exhaustion, many were now obviously suffering from frostbite, dysentery and vomiting; several collapsed and had to be taken to hospital. Those of us at the back of the column eventually were allowed to enter the camp at about 02:00 hours.

Ten of us stood looking into what was a familiar sight, a room with bunk beds, straw for the palliasses in a heap in the middle of the room. It was dark inside and out, and we were all too worn out to mess around with bed-making, so just spread the straw along the walls, pulled our dirty blankets up over us and collapsed. Someone told me later that rats had run over us during the night, but I didn't notice a thing.

CHAPTER TWENTY-THREE

The Long Road Home

For the first week or so we were there there was little movement within the compound for a simple, horrible reason: about 70% of us were suffering from exhaustion, while many were also suffering from either gastritis, frostbite, dysentery, colds, influenza or other various illnesses. I was lucky, as all I had was aching muscles and exhaustion, but it was distressing to witness such rapid and pervasive deterioration in fit young men. The compound had been a POW camp for merchant seamen but was now officially condemned, and they had long since been moved out. It was damp, smelly and rat-infested, but after the last ten days felt luxurious to us, and now we had the time we set about making the rooms less grotty and a bit more comfortable for those of us who were ill.

Otherwise, it was almost like being in any other camp, except that now we had actually been told not to try to escape, since the Allies were rapidly approaching the Rhine. News was all-important, and soon after we'd arrived, Fanshawe asked me to help dig a chamber in the cookhouse so that they could keep the radio going more or less twenty-four hours a day. I took Charles Hobgen as my number two, and the trap was, once again, under the stove in a small room at the end of the cookhouse, and as the German security was pretty lax these days, we completed it quickly. This, I vowed, was to be absolutely the last of my underground activities. I must say that on my return to the UK I never felt the smallest desire to have anything to do with the National Coal Board.

The latrine in camp I am sure would have warranted an entry in the Guinness Book of Records. It must have been the biggest working bog in Europe, basically a vast hole with a rail over it to sit upon, and another rail for back support (and so you didn't fall in). Shortly after we had arrived in the compound, Charles Hobgen and Barnes, a South African, were taking a constitutional around the compound, and as they passed the latrine a plaintive cry could be heard coming from somewhere inside. 'Help!' it said. It was dark, and the latrine was without any lights, so Barnes lit some matches (possibly not the most prudent thing to do) and they followed the cries: 'I'm in the shit!' Finally they found of all people, the RC padre. While he had been having a quiet session, the back rail which was rotted through had snapped, landing the poor man in it. Hobgen and Barnes couldn't get him out on their own, so they ran to our room and found the only help available, Red and me. Grabbing a broom for him to hang on to, as good Christians we immediately rushed to the rescue. With some group effort and a lot of very restrained language we managed to heave him out from the vast ocean of excrement. He, poor soul, was all set to rush off back to his own room, but Red pointed out quite reasonably that he might not be very welcome in his present state, so we threw buckets of water over him. Not enough, so he stripped off for further cleansing. It took quite a while. 'Sweet Christ,' he kept saying, shivering there in the cold night air as yet another bucket of icy water hit him, 'it's cold!' I felt his boss must have been off-duty that night. As at last he rushed off to his room, the security lights reflecting off his little white bum, I'm afraid we just gave in and collapsed with laughter.

Given the acute shortage of fuel for our stoves, the goons allowed small parties under parole to leave the camp with a guard to forage for wood. Our turn came, and about a dozen of us left the camp and came out into the nearby fields and woods. This, the first real sniff of freedom, exhilarated us all. Apart from the terrible long march this was the first time most of us had been outside without a goon-box or barbed wire in sight, and we all of us spent as much of it as we could just smelling the fresh countryside scents, feeling the hot spring sun. We fed the guard cigarettes to prolong the outing.

It was now the middle of April, and everyone knew from our illicit radio news that soon the Germans were going to have to move us quickly if we were not to be liberated by the forces rapidly advancing from the west. What they might actually do with us formed the subject of most discussions these days. It was felt that on balance rather than leave us behind to be liberated by one or other army, the Germans would be far more likely to keep us with them for any potential bargaining with the Allies, so preparations were made in anticipation of another march. Rod Ball, an ex-Mountie from the RCMP, showed us all how to construct a solid, sizeable back-frame out of wood to strap on enough worldly possessions to see us through this time: essentials such as as much food as we could lay our hands on, as well as cigarettes, coffee, chocolate and soap. Everyone knew from recent bitter experience that you needed not only enough for yourself, but also enough to trade with.

On Monday 9 April, the orders came through to evacuate the compound at 18:00 hours. After one false start at 20:00, only a little way from the compound, the order was rescinded and we were all marched back inside. The next day, Tuesday, we set off again, at 11:00. Group Captain Wray had appointed Red as his adjutant and, I suspect, minder; this was the first time I'd ever been separated from Red during my entire term as a POW. I think that by this time the Kommandant and all the Germans marching with us realised the war was fast approaching its conclusion, so Wray, with the tacit agreement of the Kommandant, made sure that the march proceeded at a much more easy pace. There was after all nothing to run away from, really.

The weather was reasonably warm, and the march began in a damp fog which by lunchtime had cleared into a fine day. You could almost enjoy it. We kept to a leisurely crawl, about one mile per hour, reaching Zeven at 18:00 hours, and after a short rest there, pressing on to Hesslingen, where we bedded down in a damp open field. The only incident which marred this trip was that two officers were shot in the legs by an over-zealous guard. Wray was furious, and it is a measure of how things were by this stage that at his insistence the Kommandant put the guard in the local jail, while his replacements were older and far less trigger-happy.

We left Hesslingen at midday, still at the same slow pace. That afternoon the rear of the column was strafed by an RAF fighter; three Royal Navy officers were killed and four wounded. 'Friendly fire' they call it these days. In any event it is inexcusable. All squadrons had been warned to watch out for columns of POWs on the march, and certainly our ragged column in no way resembled a military target. After that, whenever an RAF or American aircraft was spotted, everyone dived into the nearest ditch. I never did find out who was responsible. I would have had a few things I wanted to share with him.

After seeing to the wounded and dead, eventually we arrived at Bokel at about 18:00 hours. By this time most of us had been busy doing a little trading (or in some cases stealing), swapping our precious coffee, soap or chocolate for a *kleinerwagen*, prams or indeed anything with wheels to transport kit and any parcels we still had about us. Already there were terrible food shortages throughout Germany, and goods such as coffee or chocolate were now real luxury items. It became commonplace to see a kriegie approaching a Frau with a pram, and after a few goodies had changed hands, the baby would be lifted out and the pram would join the column. One enterprising room group – I'm pretty sure it was Foo McHardie's – managed to obtain, heaven knows how, a light Governess trap, but no horse. They loaded all their own kit into it, while three of them took it in turns to pull it along, and when the going was easier, took it in turns to ride. Accommodation, as usual, was in a field.

We had a bit of a break the next day, Thursday 12 April. After a long stop for lunch, we camped about two kilometres outside Harsefelt, where a twenty-four hour rest break was declared, and the leisure time was put to good use. The guards were far more relaxed about such things, and because the weather continued to be fine, spirits generally were high. Fortified with a ration of goon meat and bread, some wandered around the pleasant woods collecting up fuel for fires, while others did a bit of trading. Quite a few local wheelbarrows went missing and could be seen later the next day piled high with kit off on the road to Cranz, on the River Elbe, not far from Hamburg itself. After spending a cold and misty night camped beside the river, next day we crossed by ferry to Blankensee, then on to Sulldorf. It was here that a party of New Zealanders caught and killed a lamb: the first lamb chops they had enjoyed in years.

It was around this time that I teamed up with Doug McKenzie, a New Zealander who had joined the RAF on a short-service commission before the war and had been shot down in 1940. He spoke reasonable German, so armed with a few goodies, we eased away from the column and wandered off along some side roads, calling in at isolated farms and trading our bits for eggs, German sausage or indeed anything else in the way of food. The locals were amazed to see us, but were mostly friendly. We told everyone we met that the war was indeed nearly over, and suggested that they hang white sheets from their upstairs windows. The particularly nice ones we left with a chit to that effect to give to any advancing army. At the end of the day we caught up with the rest of the column and shared out the spoils with our mess. I undertook some omelettes for supper, but as I had never before made one this involved some improvisation. Unfortunately I didn't realise that you don't put flour in an omelette, and the results were rather solid, but enjoyed by all – or so they averred.

Each day as we pushed on towards Lübeck the distant sounds of war became clearer: lots of cannon-fire, with aircraft constantly going overhead. By now we really were a sorry sight, a tatterdemalion lot, kriegies and guards alike. It was almost amusing to see a POW pushing along a pram or dog-cart, with a guard slouching alongside, his kit and rifle in the cart. By this time I think the guards were all resigned to the fact that the end was near and actually felt safer if they stayed with us.

On Saturday 28th, we arrived at Wulmenau, a few miles from Lübeck, where part of our column was billeted in a large barn alongside a farmhouse. Once we had settled in, Barnes and I took some chocolate and coffee up to the house to see if we could persuade the inhabitants to let us listen to their radio. When we knocked on the door it was opened by two females, who expressed only polite blankness to see a pair of really rough-looking men standing in their doorway smiling at them. The way I looked then I think I would have been frightened of me. We asked them in our kriegie German for some hot water to make coffee, then invited them to have some coffee with us, which was gladly accepted. It must have been some time since they had been able to have real coffee. Barnes spoke

Afrikaans, not so far removed from German, so between that, their bits of English and my kriegie German, and some willing give-and-take, we got by. In the stilted conversation over coffee we found out that they were living there alone, and when pressed confessed that they were frightened about what might happen to them, even if the war was drawing to a close. We tried to reassure them that it would be the British, not the Russians, in this area, which seemed to relieve them, and they were quite happy for us to use their radio. They, too, wanted to know how things were really going.

On the Sunday morning, armed with more coffee, we returned to listen again to the radio. We passed the news on to the ladies of the house, then on our return, to the guards back in camp. Perhaps it was on the strength of this, I don't know, but to our surprise the ladies asked us back to the house for a meal that same night. We arrived at seven that evening, as cleaned-up as we could make ourselves under the circumstances, arms full of cigarettes and a bar of soap. Wartime changes everyone's notions of etiquette; certainly both our presents and our grimy selves were made most welcome.

When we were shown into the dining-room there were already three goons sitting there at the beautifully-laid table, eating bread and sausage. I think our mutual reactions were the same, but to my amusement it was the goons who were asked to remove themselves to a back room. The women, whose names I cannot remember, gave us some schnapps they must have made themselves, which tasted not unlike my kriegie hooch. There wasn't much actual food to go on the lovely dishes they had put out for us, since they were severely rationed, but the two bottles of wine (also homemade, I assume) and the generous spirit with which it was offered to us made it a real banquet. After the meal they insisted on walking us back to our barn, and to our complete surprise (and I must add the envy of all the other kriegies watching us silhouetted in the moonlight), they kissed us goodnight, a truly generous gesture. But perhaps it was after all simple prudence, only to make sure that we wrote them the note we had promised them, to be handed to any advancing troops, telling them how kind and helpful the bearers had been to some RAF POWs.

The very next day we were moved on again, this time to a rather grand estate at Trenthorst, certainly an improvement on anything we had had so far. True or not, we had been told that the German owner of the estate had himself been a POW in Britain, now repatriated. He had been treated well, and this, I suppose, was his response. We were late getting there, and as all the buildings were already occupied and the weather was fine, our mess decided to construct our own wood-and-straw lean-to in a field. Several others followed suit, and we all wound up eating off a large communal table, almost a party. That night everyone was woken up by a tremendous barrage we were told was the crossing of the Elbe. Rumours began to fly, the end must surely be near. Lots of retreating goons could be seen throwing away their equipment and being suddenly very friendly. Tuesday we made up the biggest warning signs we could: 'RAF/POW' in large straw letters.

At about midday on Wednesday 2 May, a small armoured car drove into camp. Out stepped a Lieutenant Radcliffe, one of ours, and the cheers went up. I cannot remember what it was he actually said, but it didn't matter, I think he was a bit taken aback by the warm reception and the cheering. We were liberated. I can't begin to describe what complete fools we made of ourselves, but honestly, we were overcome. Ted Wardley, Clive Saxelby, George Smith and others – we all danced around, crazy free men, hugging each other, tears streaming down our cheeks. The liberation was also a liberation from all those years of having to keep a lid on your feelings, and we really let rip. I borrowed a horse and rode it bareback, whooping like a savage, off to the other camp about a quarter of a mile away. I could do that now. I was free.

This new-found freedom went swiftly to our heads. As soon as I'd got back into camp and returned the horse, puffing and blowing, I met up with Doug MacKenzie, who suggested that we commandeer a couple of bicycles and make for Lübeck. Amazing the sudden energy one can find with freedom. We'd only gone a few miles when a roadblock appeared and we were stopped by soldiers in green berets and asked who we were and where we were going. When we told them we were RAF POWs heading for the bright lights of Lübeck I don't think they believed it, staring at our tatty, filthy, barely-recognisable uniforms. Still, they hustled us into the house they had occupied and plied us with white bread and jam and some wine they had found in the cellar.

'The wine's a bit dry,' said the sergeant, 'you'll find it's better if you put a spoonful of sugar in it.'

I really don't think he noticed our ecstatic faces as we drank that nectar neat and rapturously, languorously, ate the bread. After two and a half years of goon bread made of sawdust, this plain white bread was the sweetest thing on earth. We grinned. When we got outside they'd organised a car for us to go into Lübeck.

On the way we passed an airfield, and Doug suggested we pull in and have a look to see if there were any aircraft there we might commandeer and fly to England right now. I stared at him, but he was being serious. But fortunately the airfield was completely deserted; I wasn't going to have to spell it out for him the sheer idiocy of flying back to Blighty at this late stage only to be shot down by the RAF. But as we stood there, idly gazing across the airfield, thinking about the real possibility of getting home at last, a light aircraft appeared, landed and taxied over to us – I suppose because we were the only people there. The pilot, in Army uniform, climbed down first, came over and asked who we were. While we were telling him, my eye was caught by the other occupant climbing out who also joined us, the one with the mass of stripes and medals on his battle dress. My God, I thought, an air marshal, and I stared at him, suddenly all too aware of my own appearance. For his part he didn't show the least surprise at finding two extremely scruffy officers as his greeting party. Doug at least still had the shreds of his flight lieutenant's stripes on one shoulder, while I had nothing at all.

'Can you tell me,' he said politely, 'which is your camp and who is your senior British officer?'

We told him.

'Ah. Please give him my regards.'

'Of course, sir,' Doug said. 'But who are you, sir?'

He blinked. 'Broadhurst.' And stalked off, rather hurt, it seemed to me.

Returning to the car Doug and I pressed on to Lübeck. I think I must somehow have simply reverted to my old pre-kriegie style, because in no time at all we had met up with two Army officers who took us back with them to the house where they were billeted and there we gorged on lovely food and drink, falling asleep at last on some beds provided. I was happy. We returned next day to Trenthorst, almost immediately to be trucked to Lüneburg and billeted there in empty German barracks. My lot, true to form, quickly took over what must have been a married officer's flat, large and very well-furnished, and that night we were all entertained by the male and female nurses of the 74th Brigade General Hospital, who produced some small medical miracles, bottles of whisky and Benedictine. The next morning, 6 May 1945, we flew home.

Our Lancasters landed at RAF Wing, Hertfordshire. I was still in a complete daze from the effects of the night before on top of the previous three years. I can remember watching out for the white cliffs of Dover, staring down at them, not quite believing where I was.

Our actual arrival I must say was rather undignified. First thing, everyone was marched into a hangar where a mass of medical orderlies had us peel down then squirted clouds of white delousing powder all over us. By one of those peculiar quirks of fate the orderly who attacked me had been at school with me. He said he'd ring my parents to tell them I was safe and sound. And deloused. But still I had no idea where Mary was. I had been out of touch with her since the long march from Sagan. We were moved to RAF Cosford for de-briefing, then kitted out with new battle dress, underwear and shoes, and given a medical test. I asked them what chance there might be of my getting a flying refresher and a posting out to the Far East. I meant it; I was desperate to get back on the job I loved.

'Sorry,' they said, 'not a hope. The RAF is awash with pilots waiting for a posting.'

At least, I thought, I'll be home for VE Day. But when the squadron leader came round with our leave passes there was not one for me.

'Why not, sir?' I asked him.

'Well, your X-ray isn't what it should be. You're to report to sick quarters tomorrow for another X-ray.'

'I'm not,' I said, 'sir. Sorry.'

"You will, lad. Orders are orders. So hop to it.'

'Look, sir. There are no goon-boxes out there guarding the perimeter now. I don't see how you can stop me, really. With respect.'

I suppose there must have been some steely determination written all over my face, because after only a token gesture he backed down, gave in, and after getting my firm promise to report back in a couple of weeks, actually issued me with my railway warrant.

I arrived at Ruabon station to be met by my entire family, apart from my sister, young Helaine, still at school, and my brother Neville, posted to India as a lieutenant in the South Wales Borderers. And to my intense disappointment, no Mary. She was, my sisters told me, at her cousin's farm near Swanton Moreley, but was now well on her way and due to arrive in the small hours. Poor girl, she'd have to cross London to Paddington on VE night. I could wait. There was noise enough and fuss and catching up with family right now to keep me occupied. We celebrated VE night at a huge party in the Commando mess at Wrexham Barracks, getting home only well after midnight. At about 4:30 am I met the London train with Mary on it. She was laughing and hugging and kissing me all at once, when suddenly she stopped and smiled at me in a way that made my heart stop altogether.

'For you the war is over,' she said.

'Fourth day of our honeymoon,' I said. 'It only took us a few years.'

CHAPTER TWENTY-FOUR

An Afterword

The story of course does not finish when the war did.

When I returned home I could not settle. I think this was true for a lot of us ex-kriegies. I felt that we had missed the best part of the war just when we were winning it, and that strong sense of frustration remained with me in spite of the real joy at being home again. Probably the best thing that could have happened would have been if I could have got straight back into flying. I did try. My request to go back onto operations and join the conflict against Japan was turned down; at that time there were simply too many spare pilots around, and it was not worth retraining so many of us. So reluctantly I decided to leave the RAF.

I tried farming, and for a while we lived back at my old home, Gardden Hall. I tried selling meal. I played a lot of rugby. But all the time I was restless, and there was no way then to talk about it as any kind of problem to be solved. For some time after the war ended you simply did not talk about it. People were far more interested in rebuilding their lives and looking to the future. These were the days before counselling. It wasn't until November 1945 when I went to Bren Hooper's (one of my Stalag Luft III roommates) wedding and met up with all my ex-kriegie friends that I realised what I was missing.

The very next morning I went to see Wings Day, now an air commodore in the Air Ministry, who arranged for me to rejoin the RAF in my old rank of flight lieutenant. It felt right for me, although Mary was not too keen. The thought of having to move around the country with our first-born just about to arrive did not appeal to her, and she always said how much of an outsider she felt at RAF functions. While I went off on my various courses to catch up on all I'd missed, Mary stayed in our house on Marford Hill near Wrexham, where our son Martyn was born on 14 February, 1946.

After a flying refresher course on Oxfords and Harvards I was posted to the Central Flying School at Little Rissington to train as a flying instructor, then posted to Ternhill instructing on Harvards. This time around I found I loved instructing, not least because there was leisure time to spend on the finer points of flying, and I enjoyed passing on everything I knew to pupils. All in all I was now more happy than I had been in years. I was stationed only twenty miles from home in Marford; we now had a daughter, Suzanne, I was back in the company of people I liked, and I could play a lot of rugby.

It felt good to get back to first-class rugby. In 1947 I joined Birkenhead Park Rugby Club, and played wing forward for Cheshire from 1948-1951, the year they won the County Championship. The following season – 1948 – I managed to get into the RAF XV and the Combined Services XV, playing the French B XV. In 1950 I was taken off the French tour to play before the Welsh selectors. But I had a poor game, mostly I think owing to the small matter of a dislocated thumb from a bruising match against Leicester the day before, and blew thereby my chances of a cap. I wish I had gone on the French tour. It's odd, but playing rugby at Stalag Luft III had helped my game, in spite of the circumstances and the light diet: playing with international standard players hones your skills whatever the surroundings.

Later in 1950 I was posted to Cambridge University Air Squadron, at the same time playing for London Welsh, which I had the honour of captaining in 1953. I had an enjoyable career in the RAF. In 1952 I was promoted to squadron leader, moving all around the country with many interesting postings, learning to fly many different kinds of piston and jet aircraft. But even so I seem to have had a nose for trouble. My two staff postings are cases in point: first in 1954 I was sent to HQ Middle East Air Force, Cyprus, during the Eoka troubles, when the Greek Cypriots struggling for independence were hostile to everyone, and we had to keep our revolvers handy. Then came the Suez Crisis and the Mau-Mau troubles in Kenya. In 1964, I was posted to HQ Far East Air Force in Singapore, at the time of the confrontation with Indonesia. In between these postings, in May 1957, I was made a wing commander, and in 1961, took over 148 Squadron on Valiants, a 'V' bomber squadron. We found ourselves on quick readiness alert during the Cuban missile crisis. After commanding RAF Gan, a small island in the middle of the Indian Ocean with no crisis at all, I retired from the RAF in 1968, aged forty-nine, much to Mary's relief. She had had enough of moving around the world.

When we came back we had nowhere to live, so we bought a Post Office Store in Bangor-on-Dee, which we ran for five years before moving on to Anglesey, where we bought a Private Members Club – The Sandymount – in Rhosneigr, and live to this day in happy retirement. Mary plays a lot of bridge, and although golf is now out for me, owing to one hip and two knee replacements, I continue to keep up with my ex-kriegie friends scattered all over the world.

I had caught up with Gwyn soon after repatriation, at Cosford, and we remained close friends until his death in 2001. He had been evacuated with the rest of Belaria and also went with the rest of us on that long, hard march. But at Spremberg he and his companions were put onto a train and taken to Luckenwalde near Berlin, where they were liberated by the Ukrainians. Typically, he and a few others managed to acquire some bicycles and cycled over to the nearest American army attachment, from which he was flown home. He left the RAF and went to Cardiff University. He played rugby for Cardiff at the same time I was playing for London Welsh, so there was much opportunity for meeting up on or off the pitch.

Since just after the war there have been regular kriegie reunions, which have always been an important factor in my life, increasingly so in the last thirty years. For some time immediately after the war we former kriegies found it difficult to speak about being POWs. But public interest in POWs and Stalag Luft III was gradually being sparked off, first in 1947 when Paul Brickhill's first, much shorter book about 'The Great Escape' was published, and later, in 1952 with the success of *The Wooden Horse* as well as the subsequent film. In 1957 *The Great Escape* was first serialised in the *Daily Express*, then published in its lengthened form. But it was the film of that book, a fictitious but fairly accurate (apart from Steve MacQueen and his motorbike) view of events, which seems to have excited the interest of the new generations. In 1992 our ceremony for the Fifty back at the site of Stalag Luft III was filmed for television, the first of several excellent programmes about POWs. In 1994, for the fiftieth anniversary of the breakout, a very moving Service of Remembrance was given at St Clement Danes, the RAF church in London. People do not want to forget what was done for them. I am glad of that.

APPENDIX I

The Fifty Murdered

(NB: Polish officers have their RAF ranks quoted.)

J5233 F/L **Henry J Birkland**, Canadian, born 16/08/17, 72 Sqdn, (shot down 07/11/41, Spitfire Vb, W3367), recaptured near Sagan, last seen alive 31/03/44, murdered by Lux and Scharpwinkel, cremated at Liegnitz.

61053 F/L **Gordon Brettell** DFC, British, born 19/03/15, 133 (Eagle) Sqdn (shot down 26/09/42, Spitfire IX), recaptured Scheidemuhl, murdered by Bruchardt 29/03/44, cremated at Danzig.

43932 F/L **Lester G Bull** DFC, British, born 07/11/16, 109 Sqdn (shot down 05-6/11/41, Wellington IC, T2565), recaptured near Reichenburg, murdered 29/03/44 by unknown Gestapo, cremated at Brux.

90120 S/L **Roger J Bushell**, British, born 07/11/10, 92 Sqdn (shot down 23/05/40, Spitfire I, N3194), recaptured at Saarbrucken, murdered 29/03/44 by Schulz, cremated at Saarbrucken.

39024 F/L **Michael J Casey**, British, born 19/02/18, 57 Sqdn (shot down 16/10/39, Blenheim I, L1141), recaptured near Gorlitz, murdered 31/03/44 by Lux and Scharpwinkel, cremated at Gorlitz.

400364 S/L **James Catanach** DFC, Australian, born 28/11/21, 455 Sqdn (crash-landed in Norway, 6/09/42, Hampden I AT109), recaptured at Flensburg, murdered 29/03/44 by Post, cremated at Kiel.

413380 F/L **Arnold G Christiansen**, New Zealander, born 08/04/21, 26 Sqdn, POW 20/08/42, recaptured at Flensburg, murdered 29/03/44 by Post, cremated at Kiel.

122441 F/O **Dennis H Cochran**, British, born 13/08/21, 10 OTU, POW 09/11/42, recaptured at Lorrach, murdered 31/03/44 by Priess and Herberg, cremated at Natzweiler Concentration Camp.

39305 S/L **Ian K P Cross** DFC, British, born 04/04/18, 103 Sqdn (shot down 12/02/42, Wellington IC, Z8714 PM:N), recaptured near Gorlitz, murdered 31/03/44 by Lux and Scharpwinkel, cremated at Gorlitz.

378 Lt **Halldor Espelid**, Norwegian, born 06/10/20, 33 Sqdn, POW 27/08/42, recaptured at Flensburg, murdered 29/03/44 by Post, cremated at Kiel.

42745 F/L **Brian H Evans**, British, born 14/02/20, 49 Sqdn (shot down 06/12/40, Hampden I, P4404 EA:R), recaptured at Halbau, last seen alive 31/03/44, murdered by Lux and Scharpwinkel, cremated at Liegnitz.

742 Lt **Nils Fugelsang**, Norwegian, 339 Sqdn, POW 02/05/43, recaptured at Flensburg, murdered 29/03/44 by Post, cremated at Kiel.

103275 Lt **Johannes S Gouws**, South African, born 13/08/19, 40 Sqdn SAAF, POW 09/04/42, recaptured at Lindau, murdered 29/03/44 by Schneider, cremated at Munich.

45148 F/L **William J Grisman**, British, born 30/08/14, 109 Sqdn (believed shot down 05-6/11/41, Wellington IC, T2565), recaptured near Gorlitz, last seen alive 06/04/44, murdered by Lux, cremated at Breslau.

60340 F/L **Alastair D M Gunn**, British, born 27/09/19, 1 PRU, POW 05/03/42, recaptured near Gorlitz, murdered 30/03/44 by unknown Gestapo, cremated at Breslau.

403281 F/L **Albert H Hake**, Australian, born 30/06/16, 72 Sqdn, POW 28/12/41, recaptured near Gorlitz, murdered 31/03/44 by Lux and Scharpwinkel, cremated at Gorlitz.

50896 F/L **Charles P Hall**, British, born 25/07/18, 1 PRU, POW 28/12/41, recaptured near Sagan, murdered 31/03/44 by Lux and Scharpwinkel, cremated at Liegnitz.

42124 F/L **Anthony R H Hayter**, British, born 20/05/20, 148 Sqdn, POW 24/04/42, recaptured near Mulhouse, murdered 06/04/44 by Schimmel, cremated at Natzweiler.

44177 F/L **Edgar S Humphreys**, British, born 05/12/14, 107 Sqdn (shot down 19/12/40, Blenheim IV, T1860), recaptured near Sagan, last seen alive 31/03/44, murdered by Lux and Scharpwinkel, cremated at Liegnitz.

J10177 F/L **Gordon A Kidder**, Canadian, born 09/12/14, 156 Sqdn (shot down 13-14/10/42, Wellington III, BJ775), recaptured near Zlin, murdered 29/03/44 by Zacharias and Knippelberg, assisted by their drivers Kiowsky and Schwartzer, cremated at Mahrisch Ostrau.

402364 F/L **Reginald V Kierath**, Australian, born 20/02/15, 450 Sqdn, POW 23/04/43, recaptured near Reichenburg, murdered 29/03/44 by unknown Gestapo, cremated at Brux.

P0109 Maj **Antoni Kiewnarski**, Polish, born 26/01/1899, 305 Sqdn (shot down 28/08/42, Wellington X, Z1245), recaptured at Hirschberg, murdered there 31/03/44 by Lux, place of cremation unknown.

39103 S/L **Thomas G Kirby-Green**, British, born 28/02/18, 40 Sqdn (shot down 16-17/10/41, Wellington IV, Z1277 BL:B), recaptured near Zlin, murdered 29/03/44 by Zacharias and Knippelberg, assisted by their drivers Kiowsky and Schwartzer, cremated at Mahrisch Ostrau.

P0243 F/O **Wlodzimierz Kolanowski**, Polish, born 22/03/13, 301 Sqdn (shot down 08/11/42, Wellington IV, Z1277 GR:Z), recaptured near Sagan, murdered at Liegnitz 31/03/44 by Lux and Scharpwinkel, cremated at Liegnitz.

PO237 F/O **Stanislaw Z Krol**, Polish, born 22/03/16, 74 Sqdn (shot down 02/07/41, Spitfire Vb, W3262), recaptured at Oels, shot at Breslau 14/04/44, probably by Lux, cremated at Breslau.

J1631 **Patrick W Langford**, Canadian, born 04/11/19, 16 OTU (shot down 28-9/07/42, Wellington IC, R1450), recaptured near Gorlitz, last seen alive 31/03/44, murdered by Lux and Scharpwinkel, cremated at Liegnitz.

46462 F/L **Thomas B Leigh**, Australian in RAF, born 11/02/19, 76 Sqdn (shot down 05-6/08/41, Halifax I, L9516), recaptured near Sagan, last seen alive 12/04/44, murdered by Lux and Scharpwinkel, cremated at Breslau.

89375 F/L **James L R Long**, British, born 21/02/15, 9 Sqdn (shot down 27/03/41, Wellington IA, R1335 WS:K), recaptured near Sagan, last seen alive 12/04/44, murdered by Lux and Scharpwinkel, cremated at Breslau.

95691 2/Lt **Clement A N McGarr**, South African, born 24/11/17, 2 Sqdn SAAF, POW 06/10/41, recaptured near Sagan, last seen alive 06/04/44, murdered by Lux, cremated at Breslau.

J5312 F/L **George E McGill**, Canadian, born 14/04/18, 103 Sqdn (shot down over Germany, 10-11/04/42, Wellington R1142), recaptured in Sagan area, last seen alive 31/03/44, murdered by Lux and Scharpwinkel, cremated at Liegnitz.

89580 F/L **Romas Marcinkus**, Lithuanian, born 22/07/10, 1 Sqdn (shot down 12/02/42, Hurricane IIc BD949 'J'), recaptured at Scheidemuhl, murdered 29/03/44 by Bruchardt, cremated at Danzig.

103586 F/L **Harold J Milford**, British, born 16/08/14, 226 Sqdn, POW 22/09/42, recaptured near Sagan, last seen alive 06/04/44, murdered by Lux, cremated at Breslau.

PO913 F/O **Jerzy Tomasc Mondschein**, Polish, born 18/03/09, 304 Sqdn (shot down 08/11/41, Wellington IC, R1215), recaptured in Reichenberg area, murdered 29/03/44 in Brux area by unknown Gestapo, cremated at Brux.

PO740 F/O **Kazimierz Pawluk**, Polish, born 01/07/06, 305 Sqdn (shot down 29/03/42, Wellington II, W5567 SM:M), recaptured at Hirschberg, shot there by Lux, on 31/03/44, place of cremation unknown.

87693 F/L **Henri Picard** Croix de Guerre, Belgian, born 17/04/16, 350 Sqdn, POW 02/09/42, recaptured at Scheidemuhl, murdered 29/03/44 by Bruchardt, cremated at Danzig.

402894 F/O **John P P Pohe** (also known by his Maori name, Porokoru Patapu), New Zealander, born 10/12/21, 51 Sqdn (shot down 22-23/07/41, Halifax II, JN 901), recaptured near Gorlitz, murdered 29/03/44 by Lux and Scharpwinkel, cremated at Gorlitz.

30649 Sous-Lt **Bernard W M Scheidhauer**, French, born 28/08/21, 131 Sqdn, POW 18/11/42, recaptured at Saarbrucken, murdered 29/03/44 by Spann, cremated at Saarbrucken.

213 P/O **Sotiris Skanzikas**, Greek, born 06/08/21, 336 Sqdn, POW 23/07/43, recaptured at Hirschberg, murdered 30/03/44 by Lux, place of cremation unknown.

47341 **Rupert J Stevens**, South African, born 21/02/19, 12 Sqdn SAAF, POW 14/11/41, recaptured at Rosenheim, murdered 29/03/44 by Schneider, cremated at Munich.

130452 F/O **Robert C Stewart**, British, born 07/07/11, 77 Sqdn (shot down 26-7/04/43, Halifax II, DT796), recaptured near Sagan, last seen alive 31/03/44, murdered by Lux and Scharpwinkel, cremated at Liegnitz.

107520 F/L **John Stower**, British, born 15/09/16, 142 Sqdn (shot down 16-17/11/42, Wellington III, BK278, QT:C), recaptured near Reichenberg, murdered 31/03/44 by unknown Gestapo, place of cremation unknown.

123026 F/L **Denys O Street**, British, born 01/04/22, 207 Sqdn (shot down 29-30/03/43, Lancaster I, EM:O), recaptured near Sagan, last seen alive 06/04/44, murdered by Lux, cremated at Breslau.

37658 F/L **Cyril D Swain**, British, born 15/12/11, 105 Sqdn (shot down 28/22/40, Blenheim IV, T1893), recaptured near Gorlitz, last seen alive 31/03/44, murdered by Lux and Scharpwinkel, cremated at Liegnitz.

PO375 F/O **Pawel W Tobolski**, Polish, born 21/03/06, 301 Sqdn (shot down 25-6/06/42, Wellington Iv, GR:A), recaptured at Stettin, shot at Breslau 02/04/44, probably by Lux, cremated at Breslau.

82532 F/L **Ernst Valenta**, Czech, born 25/10/12, 311 Sqdn (shot down 06/02/41, Wellington IC, L7842 KX:T), recaptured near Gorlitz, last seen alive 31/03/44, murdered by Lux and Scharpwinkel, cremated at Liegnitz.

73022 F/L **Gilbert W Walenn**, British, born 24/02/16, 25 OTU, POW 11/09/41, recaptured at Scheidemuhl, murdered 29/03/44 by Bruchardt, cremated at Danzig.

J6144 F/L **James C Wernham**, Canadian, born 15/01/17, 405 Sqdn (shot down 08-9/06/42, Halifax II, W7708 LQ:H), recaptured at Hirschberg, murdered 31/03/44 by Lux, cremated at Brux.

J7234 F/L **George W Wiley**, Canadian, born 24/01/22, 112 Squadron, (shot down 12/03/43, shot 30/03/42 by unknown Gestapo, cremated at Breslau.

J7234 F/L **John E A Williams** DFC, Australian, born 06/05/19, 450 Sqdn,

POW 31/10/42, recaptured near Gorlitz, murdered 31/03/44 by Lux and Scharpwinkel, cremated at Gorlitz.

106173 **John F William**s, British, born 07/07/17, 107 Sqdn (shot down 27/04/42, Boston III), recaptured near Reichenberg, last seen alive 06/04/44, murdered by unknown Gestapo, cremated at Breslau.

APPENDIX II

The Survivors

Evaded recapture and returned to England:

F/L **Peter Bergsland** (aka 'Rocky Rockland'), 332 Sqdn (shot down 19/08/42, Spitfire Vb AB 269) and F/L **Jens Muller**, 331 Sqdn, both Norwegian, reached England in March 1944 via Stettin and Sweden.

F/L **Bram ('Bob') van der Stok**, Dutch, 41 Sqdn (shot down 12/04/42, Spitfire Vb BL595), reached England in July via Spain.

Recaptured and returned to Sagan:

109946 F/L **Albert Armstrong**, 268 Sqdn.

120413 F/L **R Anthony Bethell**, 268 Sqdn (shot down near Alkmaar, 07/12/42, Mustang AP212 'V').

122363 F/L **L C J Brodrick**, 106 Sqdn (shot down 14-15/04/43, Lancaster ED752 ZN:H).

J6487 F/O **William J Cameron**, RCAF.

41255 F/L **Richard S A Churchill**, 144 Sqdn.

76904 F/L **Bernard 'Pop' Green.**

Lamond Carter (details unknown).

F/L **Roy Brouard Langlois** 12 Sqdn (shot down 05/08/41, Wellington II, W5421 PH:G).

36103 F/L **Henry Cuthbert 'Johnny' Marshall** (by then a wing commander), gave evidence at the trial of the accused murderers.

F/L **Robert McBride** (details unknown).

115320 F/L **Alistair T McDonald.**

Lt **Alexander Desmond Neely**, 825 Sqdn Fleet Air Arm.

70811 F/L **Thomas Robert Nelson**, 37 Sqdn.

42872 F/L **Alfred Keith Ogilvie** DFC, Canadian, 609 Sqdn.

Lt **Douglas Arthur Poynter**, Fleet Air Arm.

F/L **Laurence Reavell-Carter**, 49 Sqdn.

42152 F/L **Paul Royle**, 53 Sqdn RAAF.

NZ/391368 F/L **Michael Moray Shand**, 485 Sqdn RNZAF.

39585 F/L **Alfred Burke Thompson.**

S/L **Leonard Henry Trent** VC, 487 Sqdn (shot down 03/05/43, Ventura II AJ209 EG:G).

Recaptured and taken to Sonderlager 'A' Sachsenhausen, later returned to Stalag Luft III, Sagan:

78847 F/L **Desmond Lancelot Plunkett**, Zimbabwean, 218 Sqdn (shot down Emden 20-21/07/42, Stirling I W7530 HA:Q).

30268 F/L **Ray van Wymeersch**, 174 Sqdn Free French Air Force (shot down 19/08/42, Hurricane IIc BP299'U'), sent first to Buchenwald Concentration Camp.

Recaptured and sent to Oflag IVC, Colditz Castle:

82542 F/L **Bedrich Dvorak**, Czech.

83232 F/L **Ivor B Tonder**, Czech.

Recaptured and sent to Sachsenhausen, later escaped 24/09/44:

5175 W/C **Harry Melville Arbuthnot ('Wings') Day** DSO OBE.

Major **Johnnie Dodge** DSO DSC MC. Dodge, related to Winston Churchill, was released by the Germans into Switzerland in an unsuccessful effort to sue for peace.

86685 F/L **Sydney Henstings Dowse** MC.

42232 F/L **Bertram Arthur ('Jimmy') James** MC, 9 Sqdn (shot down Duisberg 05-6/06/40, Wellington IA P9232 WS:M).

APPENDIX III

The Investigators

W/C **Wilfred ('Freddie') Bowes**, F/L (later S/L) **Francis McKenna**, F/L (later S/L) **'Dickie' Lyon**, F/L **Stephen Courtney**, F/L **Harold Harrison** and W/O **H J Williams**, all of the RAF Special Investigation Branch, spent months travelling around Europe, piecing together enough evidence to identify the murderers. Lt Col **A P Scotland**, an Army intelligence expert, interrogated many of the suspects in the London Cage. Bowes, McKenna and Scotland were all later awarded the OBE for their efforts in bringing the culprits to justice.

The trials were presided over by Major General **H L Longden**; the Judge Advocate was Mr **C L Stirling**. A panel of six senior military officers – three Army colonels, two RAF wing commanders and an RAF air commodore – formed the rest of the prosecution. Ten German lawyers formed the defence. The Court pronounced its verdict on 3 September 1947, and in early February 1948, thirteen of the murderers were hanged at Hamelin Gaol, Hamburg. A short while after this a second trial was held for three more of the accused.

For further information on the trials of the killers of the Fifty see Paul Brickhill's *The Great Escape*, and Oliver Clutton-Brock's *Footprints on the Sands of Time*.

APPENDIX IV

Prisoner of War Poster

To all Prisoners of War!

The escape from prison camps is no longer a sport!

Germany has always kept to the Hague Convention and only punished recaptured prisoners of war with minor disciplinary punishment.

Germany will still maintain these principles of international law.

But England has besides fighting at the front in an honest manner instituted an illegal warfare in non combat zones in the form of gangster commandos, terror bundits and sabotage troops even up to the frontiers of Germany.

They say in a captured secret and confidential English military pamphlet,

THE HANDBOOK
OF MODERN IRREGULAR
WARFARE:

". . . the days when we could practise the rules of sportsmanship are over. For the time being, every soldier must be a potential gangster and must be prepared to adopt their methods whenever necessary."

"The sphere of operations should always include the enemy's own country, any occupied territory, and in certain circumstances, such neutral countries as he is using as a source of supply."

England has with these instructions opened up a non military form of gangster war!

Germany is determined to safeguard her homeland, and especially her war industry and provisional centres for the fighting fronts. Therefore it has become necessary to create strictly forbidden zones, called death zones, in which all unauthorised trespassers will be immediately shot on sight.

Escaping prisoners of war, entering such death zones, will certainly lose their lives. They are therefore in constant danger of being mistaken for enemy agents or sabotage groups.

Urgent warning is given against making future escapes!

In plain English: Stay in the camp where you will be safe! Breaking out of it is now a damned dangerous act.

The chances of preserving your life are almost nil!

All police and military guards have been given the most strict orders to shoot on sight all suspected persons.

Escaping from prison camps has ceased to be a sport!

Index